TOWARDS A JUST SOCIETY

The Personal Journeys of Human Rights Educators

Edited by
**Abraham Magendzo K., Claudia Dueñas,
Nancy Flowers, and Natela Jordan**

English Translation by
Humberto Schettino and Nela Navarro

Published by the University of Minnesota Human Rights Resource Center
and the Academy of Christian Humanism University, Santiago, Chile

Copyright © 2015 University of Minnesota Human Rights Resource Center.

All rights reserved. No part of this book may be reproduced, stored, or transmitted by any means—whether auditory, graphic, mechanical, or electronic—without written permission of both publisher and authors, except in the case of brief excerpts used in critical articles and reviews. Unauthorized reproduction of any part of this work is illegal and is punishable by law.

Towards a Just Society: The Personal Journeys of Human Rights Educators may be reproduced without permission for educational purposes only. Adapted material from this publication must include full citation of the source. To reproduce for any other purposes, including the reproduction of images, a written request must be submitted to the Human Rights Resource Center, University of Minnesota. Permission is granted for nongovernmental organizations and non-profit groups to translate into other languages. The only conditions for other language versions are 1) that the language of the United Nations bodies appears in its entirety, 2) that no human rights are deleted, and 3) that the Human Rights Resource Center receive a) notification of intention to translate, b) a hard copy of the translation, and c) an electronic version of the translation and permission to make it available on its website.

University of Minnesota Human Rights Resource Center
229 19th Avenue South
Minneapolis, MN 55455
1-888-HREDUC8 humanrts@umn.edu
www.hrusa.org

ISBN: 978-0-9964-5830-6 (sc)
ISBN: 978-0-9675-3349-0 (e)

Library of Congress Control Number: 2015915728

Because of the dynamic nature of the Internet, any web addresses or links contained in this book may have changed since publication and may no longer be valid. The views expressed in this work are solely those of the authors and do not necessarily reflect the views of the publisher, and the publisher hereby disclaims any responsibility for them.

Cover image provided by Shutterstock.com.

Lulu Publishing Services rev. date: 1/13/2016

About the Human Rights Education Series

The Human Rights Education Series is published by the University of Minnesota Human Rights Resource Center. Edited by Nancy Flowers, the Series provides resources for the ever-growing body of educators and activists working to build a culture of human rights in the United States and throughout the world. Other publications in the series include:

Human Rights Here and Now: Celebrating the Universal Declaration of Human Rights
Edited by Nancy Flowers

Topic Book #1: *Economic and Social Justice: A Human Rights Perspective*
by David Shiman

Topic Book #2: *Raising Children with Roots, Rights and Responsibilities: Celebrating the UN Convention on the Rights of the Child*
by Lori DuPont, Joanne Foley, and Annette Gagliardi

Topic Book #3: *Lesbian, Gay, Bisexual, and Transgender Rights: A Human Rights Perspective*
by David M. Donahue

Topic Book #4: *The Human Rights Education Handbook: Effective Practices for Learning, Action, and Change*
by Nancy Flowers, Marcia Bernbaum, Kristi Rudelius-Palmer, and Joel Tolman

Topic Book #5: *Lifting the Spirit: Human Rights and Freedom of Religion or Belief*
by the Tandem Project and the Human Rights Resource Center

Topic Book #6: *Human Rights. Yes! Action and Advocacy on the Rights of Persons with Disabilities* (2nd **Ed.**)
by Janet Lord, Joelle Balfe, Allison deFranco, Katherine Guernsey, and Valerie Karr

Topic Book #7: *Acting for Indigenous Rights: Theatre to Change the World*
by Mariana Leal Ferreira

Topic Book #8: *Towards a Just Society: The Personal Journeys of Human Rights Educators*
Edited by Abraham Magendzo K., Claudia Dueñas, Nancy Flowers, and Natela Jordan

Towards a Just Society: The Personal Journeys of Human Rights Educators
is dedicated to the memory of Edward O'Brien,
a pioneer and inspiration for human rights education
in the USA and many other parts of the world.
His vision and commitment to social justice touched many lives.

Table of Contents

Acknowledgments i

Using *Towards a Just Society* for Learning and Reflection ... iii

Introduction: Why Are We Human Rights Educators? 1
Abraham Magendzo K.

Utopia Makes the Journey Possible 3
Rosa María Mujica Barreda (Peru)

**Experiences, Quests, and Conquests:
Building a Commitment to Human Rights Education** 13
Vera Maria Candau (Brazil)

**Entanglements and Efforts: Towards a Commitment to
Human Rights Education** 20
Nélida Céspedes (Peru)

**All the Women I Have Been: The History of an
Educator's Training and Program of Action** 27
Silvia Conde (Mexico)

Education for Peace: Signs along the Road 38
Enver Djuliman (Bosnia, Norway)

**In My Own Voice: Stories and Musings to Reflect on
Human Rights Education** 45
Mónica Fernández (Argentina)

**The Road Less Traveled: Odyssey of a Human Rights
Educator** 55
William R. Fernekes (USA)

The Integrative Power of Human Rights Education 61
Nancy Flowers (USA)

Closing the Gap of Dignity 65
Shulamith Koenig (Israel, USA)

Why Did I Become a Human Rights Educator? 80
Elena Ippoliti (Italy, Switzerland)

Empowerment! A Dialogue on Why We Are Involved in Human Rights Education 83
Judy Gummich and Claudia Lohrenscheit (Germany)

Human Rights Educators: Subjects of Their Own History 99
Abraham Magendzo K. (Chile)

Why I Am a Human Rights Educator? 111
Edward O'Brien (USA)

Widening Educational Horizons: Critical Plans for Education for Peace and Human Rights 113
Greta Papadimitriou (Mexico)

Engaging People through Human Rights Education 121
Jefferson R. Plantilla (Philippines, Japan)

Education: Justice, Freedom, Non-violence, Pastries, and Boleros 133
Aura Helena Ramos (Brazil)

Letters to Abraham: My Roots as a Human Rights Educator 142
Kristi Rudelius-Palmer (USA)

A Multicolored Fabric: My Life in Human Rights Education 153
Susana Sacavino (Argentina, Brazil)

Teaching against Forgetting 159
Cosette Thompson (France, USA)

Shadow **165**
Felisa Tibbitts (USA)

Personal Narrative in Three Acts **167**
José Tuvilla Rayo (Spain)

Appreciating Paolo Freire, Antonio Gramsci, and this So-called Life: A Human Rights Educator's Story of Journeying out of Hegemony and Awakening the Conscious Self **181**
Feliece I. Yeban (Philippines)

Life as an Educator for Human Rights and Peace: A History of Conjunctions and Possibilities **194**
Anita Yudkin (Puerto Rico)

Subjectivity and Truth in Memory **207**
Manuel Restrepo Yustin (Colombia)

Publication Partners **231**

List of Organization Websites **232**

About the Book **240**

Acknowledgments

First and foremost, we would like to acknowledge and thank the twenty-five authors, who shared their personal narratives in *Towards a Just Society: The Personal Journeys of Human Rights Educators*. Their contributions to the field of human rights education and willingness to share their stories is what makes this publication unique. On behalf of all of the authors and project partners, we would like to celebrate and recognize our families, friends, and colleagues, who support us as human rights educators and allow our energy to flow toward our lifelong commitments and community.

We are saddened by the loss of Edward O'Brien, a dear friend and colleague, who passed away suddenly as this book was about to be published. We dedicate *Towards a Just Society* to Ed and his lifetime of social justice work, and hope it will inspire a new generation of human rights educators and learners.

We cannot express enough gratitude and appreciation to Abraham Magendzo for his vision, leadership, inspiration, and coordination of this publication. We are truly grateful to partner with Abraham and Universidad Academia de Humanismo Cristiano in order to have this publication available in both Spanish and English.

A project of this scope can only be envisioned and achieved when participants commit to working as a strong, cohesive team. Certain individuals and institutions made unique contributions to this publication, without which it could not have been realized. Dr. Richard De Lisi, Dean of the Rutgers Graduate School of Education, provided funding for the translations of fifteen Spanish language chapters, responding to a request by Dr. Mary Curran, Associate Dean of Local-Global Partnerships, and Bill Fernekes, Part-time Lecturer in the Educational Theory, Administration and Policy Department. Once the funding was obtained, Nela Navarro, Associate Director of the Rutgers Center for the Study of Genocide and Human Rights (CGHR), organized a team to complete the translations, with support from CGHR's Director Alexander Hinton. We want to highlight the significant contribution of Nela Navarro in designing and overseeing the translation project and team. Special thanks go to Dr. Humberto Schettino, a visiting scholar at the CGHR, for his thorough work on translating the chapters from Spanish into English.

Nancy Flowers has played a substantial role as chief editor and reviewer of the English chapters and chapters translated from Spanish. She volunteered her time, skills, and insights to make *Towards a Just Society: The Personal Journeys of Human Rights Educators* a reality in both its Spanish and English editions. Bill Fernekes provided essential assistance in reviewing and editing the book while sharing his expertise to move this project forward. This book would not have been possible without their unwavering commitment. We are very thankful for their generosity.

We would also like to acknowledge Natela Jordan who served as the English edition co-editor and project manager. She was instrumental in drafting and finalizing the publishing agreements and copyright permissions as well as reviewing and preparing the manuscript for publication. Jolena Zabel and Grace Corry were also integral to the project in respectively coordinating copyright approvals and assisting in proofreading and editing.

All in all, *Towards a Just Society: The Personal Journeys of Human Rights Educators* took a village of committed human rights educators across the globe to support Abraham's vision. We truly hope that both the Spanish and English editions will encourage all human rights educators to share their stories and foster cultures that promote and protect human rights throughout the world.

Your Forever Partner in Human Rights Education,

Kristi Rudelius-Palmer
Human Rights Education Series Publisher
University of Minnesota Human Rights Resource Center

Using *Towards a Just Society* for Learning and Reflection

The personal narratives of these human rights educators make for engaging and inspiring reading. Their voices and stories are richly diverse, but share a common trajectory. All authors speak of the people and experiences that shaped their journeys to make human rights education (HRE) a life's work.

However, these personal narratives also provide valuable opportunities for learning and reflection. Below are some sample ways to use *Towards a Just Society* as a resource:

History

- Many narratives depict major human rights crises of recent decades through the eyes of individuals deeply engaged in those struggles. Research a crisis described in this book, both then and now. Has human rights played a role in improving people's lives?
- Historically what human rights crises have been experienced in your own country or region? How were they dealt with? How were they resolved? Did human rights activism play a role?
- Use the experiences of the authors as models to determine if people in your own region, country, or area are undertaking similar or comparable actions.

Human Rights

- Consider current world crises. Does the human rights framework offer an effective way to address them? Why or why not?
- The human rights system is sometimes criticized as being "Western" or "Christian" and therefore inappropriate for some cultures. Do any narratives in this collection offer evidence for or against these views? Are human rights truly universal?
- How can human rights principles stand up against armed violence, tyranny, or systematic discrimination?
- Why is it important for people to know their human rights?

Education

- Are the problems of discrimination, racism, sexism, and other violations of human rights described by these authors evident in your own school, town, region, or country? How do you know? What examples can you cite?

- What principles for human rights education (HRE) can you derive from the goals and methods described by these educators?
- What does it mean to have what one author describes as a "political commitment to education"?
- HRE aims at creating a "culture of human rights," which means instilling the values of human rights. Can education really change people's values? If so, how?
- Many authors mention the influence of Brazilian educator Paolo Friere. Read about Friere and his books, *Pedagogy of the Oppressed* and *Pedagogy of Hope*. How do you see his thinking reflected in the descriptions of HRE in this collection?
- Match the desired outcomes in the *UN Declaration on Human Rights Education and Training* with the activities of the authors in the narratives. How well do the real-life experiences of the authors reflect the goals of the Declaration? Where do you see significant gaps between the aspiration of the Declaration and present realities?
- How have governments and other state-sponsored entities attempted to support or hinder human rights education in specific countries? What patterns of response do we find from nongovernmental organizations (NGOs) and other civil society organizations, as well as government, to such challenges?

Activism

- One goal of HRE is to empower people to stand up for their rights and the rights of others. Is education for action appropriate for young people in schools? Can a state educational system really teach skills that might criticize or oppose state policy and action? Is HRE more effective or appropriate in informal education? Among adults?
- Many narratives trace the personal development of social conscience, dedication to social change, and commitment to building a culture of human rights through education. What are the principal factors that motivated and inspired these activists? What motivates and inspires you?
- What are some of the common personal attributes and experiences of the authors in this book?
- Why do you think the authors turned to human rights rather than some other means of bringing about social change? Why did they believe HRE could bring about social change? What audiences were they trying to reach through HRE and why?
- Why do you think so much of the activism portrayed in these narratives is done by elements of civil society, especially NGOs?

Reflection

- What are the principle human rights issues in your own community? How could you address them? In what way could HRE help to improve conditions in your community? Consider adapting to your own context the learning activity "Taking the Human Rights Temperature": www1.umn.edu/humanrts/edumat/hreduseries/hrhandbook/activities/18.htm.

- What has been your own personal response to injustice, discrimination, and human rights violations? Consider the learning activity "Perpetrator/Victim/Bystander/Healer": www1.umn.edu/humanrts/edumat/hreduseries/hrhandbook/activities/17.htm.
- Tell your own story!

Introduction: Why Are We Human Rights Educators?

Abraham Magendzo K.

This book is composed of several human rights educators' answers to a question we posed some time ago: "What are the personal motives that made you commit to human rights education?" Through this question we invited them to reconstruct their own stories and explore the profound reasons that made them choose this particular path.

Some might question why we made this invitation. They could even ask: Isn't this a futile academic exercise? Isn't human rights education an obvious task that does not require any explanation? What is the purpose of delving into our personal stories? What do we gain as educators?

In my opinion, there are several different reasons to justify why we human rights educators should explore our personal histories and stories to identify the factors that made us commit to this field.

1. First, I think about the intellectual and emotional effort to identify the reasons that we became human rights educators. Articulating and sharing those reasons will make our arguments more compelling to both our students and others with whom we might interact. They will come to understand that we do this work because it involves our entire humanity, our total being, and our sense of existence.
2. Second, in the progression of our stories, histories, and experiences, we have been building, both implicitly and explicitly, an understanding of human rights. Consciously and sometimes unconsciously, we have allied ourselves with particular frames of reference and doctrines. We have not been neutral or indifferent. We have taken some positions. We have accepted or refuted certain conceptions. To a great extent these positions have conditioned the content, the pedagogy, and the methodology of our educational practice in human rights. In my opinion, going deeper into this history marks us as critical educators, distances us from complacent routine, and above all stops us from falling into blind and dogmatic ideological generalizations.
3. I believe it is necessary to delve into our concept of human rights within the frameworks of reference mentioned above. We should do this to guide our educational practice. Without a doubt this practice will differ in its objectives, contents, and methodology, depending on our frames of reference. For example:

- Whether one's main motivation is a commitment to education in human rights that is linked primarily to legal and normative aspects, a moral or religious doctrine, or ethics grounded in rational a priori principles;
- Whether one argues that human rights come from the exercise of Kantian reason or from an ethical-emotive vision of humanity;
- Whether one regards human rights as universally valid, or if one believes that they are social and historically conditioned to certain cultural settings and therefore that their legitimacy is valid only for those cultures and societies that gave rise to them;
- Whether one thinks that the knowledge of human rights rise basically from a "normative model" or from a "constructivist model." In the former, knowledge emerges and is validated by an external authority that holds a "legitimated truth" that is transmitted by exposition. In the latter, the knowledge of human rights is built from contact with daily life and from the personal and collective experience of the students; this implies an exploratory, critical, and problematic pedagogy.

4. I believe excavating our personal histories and the reasons that made us commit to human rights education and sharing them with our colleagues and students will foster dialogue and communication among human rights educators. There is no better way to build networks of human rights educators than to immerse ourselves in the mutual understanding of each other's stories and histories. This allows us to know each other better. It also confirms that in spite of the fact that we have very different approaches to human rights, we form a community of interests and common destiny, linked to sensibilities that transcend us.
5. Finally, I believe that an interesting collection of narratives by human rights researchers and educators from diverse settings can provide valuable educational material for training and promote debates about human rights education.

Clearly, no single reason explains why people get involved in human rights education. Those who have taken on this task probably have had many different motivations ranging from the rational, the emotional, the practical, the legal, and even the accidental. Their commitment will appear as the result of many different factors, contexts, and situations that each has experienced in different places and time. Nevertheless, I don't think I'm mistaken in saying that in spite of the multiplicity of factors, there is always a central factor, a reason that articulates other reasons, a motivation that structures many other motivations, a set of ideas and experiences that have impacted us, touched us, and left very profound marks on us. We have constituted ourselves as human rights educators as part of a personal and collective history that has woven the process of our existence out of many components. There exist, however, a few aspects that have marked us, that have produced a fracture, and that have expanded our outlook.

We have invited twenty-five educators who come from very different settings and who have worked in diverse locations on earth to think and write about their human rights education experiences. Each one had absolute freedom to write. We now invite the reader to encounter these stories that both converge and diverge. At the same time, we invite the readers to delve into their own stories, the stories that made them human rights educators.

Utopia Makes the Journey Possible

Rosa María Mujica Barreda (Peru)

Rosa María Mujica Barreda has a bachelor's degree in education with a minor in philosophy from the Pontifical Catholic University in Peru. She has a long trajectory in the fields of education and human rights, developed mostly at the Instituto Peruano en Educación en Derechos Humanos y la Paz (Peruvian Institute of Education on Human Rights and Peace; IPEDEHP), an institution she helped establish. Between 2011 and 2014, she was director of rural education at the Peruvian Ministry of Education.

Life in a Large Family

I was born in Lima to a well-to-do family that belonged to the old city aristocracy, a strict family with clear-cut values and rules. My father was a lawyer and notary public, an honest, simple, warm man who was always willing to help those in need. My mother was a resilient woman who made everyone welcome to our house: sons and daughters, friends, neighbors, and later, grandchildren who filled her life with laughter and joy. She was the root in my family and my father the trunk. We had everything we needed at home, but we never squandered money or lived in excess. My parents taught us to respect all individuals and told us that the poorer a person was, the better we should behave toward him or her. And never, for any reason, should we accept injustice or the mistreatment of anyone.

I am the fourth of eight children: four brothers and four sisters. We were a big and noisy family, with diverse ways of seeing the problems and solutions of the world. Debate and discussion were main ingredients at our Saturday lunches. One Saturday afternoon after lunch, a friend who had participated in one of our weekly discussions said, quite wide-eyed, "I am amazed by the freedom in your home. Only in an atmosphere of freedom can the diversity that I have seen here today bloom." At that moment, I became aware of the truth of what he was saying. Each one of us found our own way forward, and our parents respected all of us, even though in some cases they did not agree with our decisions.

Values were an important part of our upbringing, and family unity was one of them. Collective activities, excursions, parties, and dinners with friends were always encouraged. Our parents' last wish before they died was for us to remain close.

Literacy or the Beginning of Commitment

From a very early age, and undoubtedly because of my family's influence, I chose to work with the less fortunate. My parents were both practicing Catholics who constantly tried to help those in need. My mother worked as a volunteer with poor women in what at the time were called the *barriadas* (slums) in Lima, so that they could improve their income. She taught them to knit baby robes that she would later clean and sell so that they could have some additional income to allow them to meet their basic daily needs.

She used to say that she had blind faith. She believed in God, and that was that, so she had to live a good life and help those in need. My father, a notary public in Lima, was well known for working for free on behalf of the needy. As an anecdote, a few days after he died, I gave a talk in Villa El Salvador, and one of the organizers asked me if I was related to "Don Elías." When she learned he was my father, she made a moving public tribute. She recalled that every time she went to his office, "I was treated like a queen." It was the only place where she did not feel poor or displaced. Her testimony was the best homage he could ever have received.

I studied in a school run by nuns of the Sacred Heart, where my mother and grandmother had also studied. From very early on, we learned the real meaning of solidarity, commitment, and responsibility. We learned that being a Christian meant helping others, especially those who were poorer and weaker. This meant working in the slums in the Chorrillos district close to our school. Every Saturday, we gave literacy and early-development lessons to boys and girls who gathered in the parish. It was then that we began visiting the women of the Chorrillos penitentiary and helping in its nursery. "Duty before all, duty forever" was one of the maxims we followed, which influenced our upbringing and left a deep impression in our minds.

In high school, I was invited by a group of students from the Catholic University to work in another slum. The government had decided to change the name *barriadas* (shantytown) to *pueblos jóvenes* (young towns). The one I visited was called Comuco and stood at the heart of one of the wealthiest districts of Lima, Miraflores. Every Saturday we had training, literacy, and early-development sessions with both children and adults from the area. This new experience made me question many issues, for it allowed me to see and feel the contradiction between those who lived outside the slum walls and the extreme poverty inside the walls of Comuco.

It was there that I met the man who would become my husband. He was in charge of a group of young dreamers, all convinced that we could promote justice and change our country. He taught me to understand my work with the poor sectors of society and encouraged me to take my commitment further, to make it a way of life.

When I left high school, I enrolled in general literature studies at the Pontifical Catholic University. It was there that this commitment, which had been more an emotion than a conscious or well-reasoned decision, compelled me to work for popular literacy and help strengthen peasant organizations in the north of Lima. The Ministry of Education, which was in charge of this work, was in the midst of a very interesting process of reform that encouraged the students' commitment to popular education. The reform was headed by a group of brilliant educators coordinated by Augusto Salazar Bondy. Readings and debates were the order of the day, from Herman Hesse to José María Arguedas, Erich Fromm to Margaret Mead. Paulo Freire's work made us feel enthusiastic. Gustavo Gutiérrez and liberation theology confirmed our intuitions and directed our objectives.

A Few Months in a School in the Amazon Rainforest Opens the Door to Education

I did not find it easy to choose a career after two years of basic studies. I was not sure whether to study social sciences or education. I chose education because it would enable me to take courses in psychology and social science. Fieldwork later reinforced and strengthened my vocation in education.

A small group of students from the Catholic University decided to do our professional practicum in a community called Concepción in Puerto Maldonado, Madre de Dios, in the Amazon rainforest of southern Peru. The town where we stayed was located four hours down the river from the nearest city. We reached the town by means of a small boat called *"peque-peque"* because of the particular noise it made as it sailed down the river.

The community in which we stayed did not have electricity. We bathed in the river, and it was the stars that lit the nights. Those were hard times, not only because of the rainforest and its environment, but also because we had to learn to work with children from different towns — and they sometimes had to walk four or five hours just to reach the school. We learned about the beauty of the rural world, but also about injustices and inequalities. It was a time of personal development and of lessons that would follow us for the rest of our lives and influence our decisions.

Political Life in the University

When we got back from the rainforest, we, along with a group of fellow students, proposed that we be nominated to direct the Federated Student Center. The mid-seventies, the last years of the Velasco government, saw fierce confrontations between the military and university students. We wanted to restore democracy and respect for university autonomy. Our experience in the Centro Federado made us live out our commitment to the country and to Peruvian politics. It made us believe that in spite of our youth, we could change history and future events. We had a great deal of naïveté but also much enthusiasm and commitment.

A long, important teachers' strike began when we were still in college, and from the start, we were deeply committed to it. Most of the union meetings took place in our school, without the university authorities being aware, of course. On one occasion, we had to hide union leaders in our university rooms from political and military persecution. Our university's president, the well-remembered Father Felipe MacGregor, privately acknowledged and supported our decision, though not publicly. From that moment, he became my unconditional ally. He would sign all press releases in defense of human rights, thus helping us with his national and international reputation. During those years of violence, whenever I called him, he would ask, "What do you want me to sign today?" He was always willing to uphold any cause related to people in need, regardless of our differences.

The Transformation of a Private School

Once I graduated and came back from the United States, where my husband obtained his master's degree, I wrote my bachelor's degree thesis. I began to work at a private school run by nuns. There I met a group of teachers dedicated to the idea of developing an alternative educational model that differed from the traditional one. We wished to instill in our students (all of them girls) freedom, analytic and critical skills, and solidarity with those in need, as well as a commitment to Peru and its future. One entire generation of women, who are now upstanding citizens and qualified professionals, prove that it was worth the effort.

I learned a great deal from those girls, though I was not much older than they. The most important lesson had to do with being a teacher, thus strengthening my calling and commitment.

With the creation by law of the Escuela Superior de Educación Profesional (Superior School of Professional Education: ESEPS), I agreed to head an educational training program within the academic concentration of education for art. For four years, I was part of the students' theoretical and practical training to become art teachers. This experience was possible thanks to a group of first-rate German and Peruvian professionals who had created an educational opportunity for students from sixteen years of age. This was an opportunity that put into practice the whole idea of education "in freedom and for freedom." It was a period of innovation and creativity. The department heads agreed with our ideas, though with certain misgivings. However, we managed to convince them of the need for innovative educational experiences for the students and were allowed to impart rural education lessons in the field. We traveled with groups of students to places like Tarica, in the northern mountain range, or Oxapampa, in the central rainforest. For fifteen days the students were in charge of teaching music, painting, drama, and body language to the children of these rural areas. During the evenings we clarified our understanding and tried to make sense of this experience. It was a much better learning experience than if they had simply attended more hours of theoretical lessons in a class.

The Challenge of Training Teachers in Peru

When the Belaúnde government decided to close all ESEPs, in that eternal practice of undoing everything done by the previous government with no consideration of its benefits, it signaled the end of what I considered an interesting opportunity for young people who did not have a university degree as their main objective but who wished to train for a career requiring mid-level educational training. Nevertheless, and this is how things go, I found a new opportunity working in the National Education Institute of Monterrico, one of the most important public institutions in Peru for training teachers.

Those years strengthened my belief in the importance of the task: if we could only train good teachers, we could then dream of creating a new school, a school different from the ones we had that would enable the creation of a just and more democratic country and that could support economic development. This continues to be an on-going challenge.

From Amnesty International to the Creation of IPEDEHP

Around that time, along with our work at the Education Institute, we organized volunteer work for Amnesty International-Peru. We were a group of professionals invited to do the educational work that Amnesty International (AI) required. This was the beginning of Instituto Peruano de Educación en Derechos Humanos y la Paz (The Peruvian Institute of Education for Human Rights and Peace: IPEDEHP). We lived in times of great political violence, bombs, assaults, deaths, and disappearances. However, as a way to protect its volunteers, Amnesty did not allow them to work on their own countries' cases. For this reason we decided to create a distinct, autonomous institution that would enable us to work in Peru and address the problems of our country. The issue of human rights education became, then and forever, our banner both in life and work.

In 1985, working as a group linked to AI, we decided to create IPEDEHP. We felt that violence and human rights violations worsened every day. We noted that it seemed that each time we were reporting worse cases, and that although necessary, simply presenting these complaints was not enough. We needed to work against violence, to develop opportunities for peace, and to accept that education was an important element in this purpose.

We began as a group of volunteers, and so we remained during the first years. During the first months, we worked on establishing a theoretical framework for our team and a proposal for an intervention in education. It was then that we decided to work mainly with teachers, for they can be found all over the country, have a key role in their communities, and are in charge of developing consciousness and awareness. The teaching profession also had become one of the places where those who defended a violent solution to the problems of Peru confronted those who stood for human rights.

Our local meetings still took place at AI, and there we created our first educational materials and planned the first workshops in different places around the country. We applied everything we had learned previously. Our analysis indicated that the Peruvian school was the ideal place to foment notions of authoritarianism because it was a school that educated for dictatorship, which taught children to accept authority and submit to it. It did not educate for critical thinking or for the critical analysis of facts. It created passive individuals, used to obeying whoever was in power. Even then our aim was to work against the current and encourage teachers to rethink their work and develop a different attitude. From there they could question their attitudes, thoughts, and feelings and would willingly introduce the necessary changes to become teachers educating in human rights for democracy, justice, and peace.

Weaving Networks

The Peruvian Network for Education on Human Rights and Peace

A year after the creation of the IPEDEHP, we decided to bring together all those individuals who worked around the country in human rights education and shared our views and objectives. We had to be united in order to strengthen ourselves, learn from each other, and make quicker progress. We announced the first national meeting of what would later become La Red Peruana de Educación en Derechos Humanos y la Paz (The Peruvian Network for Education on Human Rights and Peace), which brought together people and institutions related to human rights: teachers, social leaders, women, youth, police, military, legislative sectors, and many more. This network has now been in existence for twenty-five years. It is organized by regions, and each has its own agenda and work plan. IPEDEHP always encouraged working within the network.

The Latin American Network for Peace and Human Rights of the Adult Education Council in Latin America: CEAAL

After the creation of the IPEDEHP, we were invited to become part of Consejo de Educación de Adultos para América Latina (The Latin American Network for Peace and Human Rights of the Adult Education Council in Latin America, or CEAAL). This network included people and institutions from all over the continent that worked on education for peace, democracy, and the defense of human rights in both the political and educational spheres of our countries. We met every three years in the country that was serving as the coordinating unit. For a time, IPEDEHP coordinated CEAAL in Peru.

The Network of Teacher Advocates

Another network we have encouraged is La Red de Maestros Promotores (The Network of Teacher Advocates), teachers all over the country who promote and advocate for human rights. We have worked with them in the classrooms with the idea of human rights as a cross-curricular issue through all levels and areas of the educational system. We meet to share experiences and to assess progress on the construction of a democratic school, both as a theoretical proposal and as a practical experience. We also concentrate on the difficulties we find along the way so that we can have democratic schools that can encourage other teachers who are looking for new models to transform the schools.

Reasons for Hope: The Creation of the Movement for Peruvian Life and Peace

During the mid-eighties, the worst years of the terror, fear paralyzed most of the population. The Sendero Luminoso (Shining Path) made its presence felt with blackouts, bombs, and assassinations; and the Armed Forces replied with the same violence and terror, creating in the population a feeling of insecurity, of being caught in the crossfire, and a sense that life was worthless. At this moment, two of us got together and decided to create Movimiento Perú Vida y Paz (Movement for Peruvian Life and Peace). We wished to unite all Peruvians opposed to violence and death, regardless of their origin. The slogan we created for our movement was "If we join our efforts, if we join our wills, if we act now, we have reasons for hope." It quickly spread across the country, moving people to say, "Enough! We want peace. We want respect for human rights. We believe in life."

The Movement turned into a network which organized thousands of peaceful resistance activities, like painting peace slogans on walls, demonstrating for peace, opposing forced work stoppages enforced by the Shining Path, marching down the streets with white flags, and organizing festivals for peace, among many other activities. Peruvian Life and Peace meant breaking away from the fear, the possibility of hope for many, and a public space where all citizens of good will could gather together, certain that they could do something because it was an all-inclusive movement with no ideologies or partisan convictions, open to all religions, to all parties, to all ages, and to all proposals. It was one of the most extraordinary experiences of peaceful resistance that I have known, and even today it is used as a model in many parts of the country.

The National Human Rights Coordinating Committee Experience

At the end of 1992, I was asked to take the post of Executive Secretary of the National Human Rights Coordinating Committee, replacing my dear and much-admired friend Pilar Coll. Though I felt some apprehension, I undertook this task convinced of its importance and fully aware of the responsibility. During those years I was able to get to know the best and worst of human beings. The most gratifying experience was the solidarity, especially among the victims. It was equally gratifying to experience the unconditional support of people who made many tasks easier, the courage of many defenders of life, and the strength of those who had witnessed severe human rights violations. At the same time, I witnessed violence and destruction, the capacity of human beings to harm other human beings without any compassion whatsoever, hate, fanaticism, the most brutal racism, and also indifference.

This position afforded me a task that I would never have chosen because it brought me face to face with politicians and politics. The government at that time accused us of being "fools useful to terror." The military considered us enemies and promoters of terrorists. We lived under the constant threats of the Shining Path, who accused us of being "OAS and UN agents" or "wolves in sheep's clothing." Those were years of living in the midst of wars, certain that we were defending the innocent, that we gave voice to those who could not be heard, and that we represented the only hope for thousands of people who wanted justice. My time at the Coordinating Committee deserves a book describing what we experienced there and its significance.

During my years at the Coordinating Committee, I became aware of the need for psychological support for the families of the victims, for the victims themselves, and for the workers of the Coordinating Committee, who each day had to hear terrible stories and did not have emotional tools to face these facts without hurting themselves. Because of the demand for help, we decided to organize a group of psychologists who, thanks to their commitment and solidarity with the victims, volunteered psychological assistance, physiotherapy, and medical help to victims of political violence without considering whether or not they were members of the military or civilians.

At the beginning I called upon a few psychologists I knew and explained our need. Their generosity made possible the immediate creation of a volunteer support group. It was not easy because they had to be trained in new issues and situations ignored by most. They also had to build much-needed trusting relationships, while at the same time assisting victims of different types, ages, cultures, and backgrounds. I worked with this group first as Executive Secretary and later as part of my work in the IPEDEHP. This group has produced many publications and testimonies that have helped us to better understand violence and to propose mental health policies for the victims of direct or indirect violence.

Weaving Friendship, Confidence, and Commitment: The Creation of the Network of Social Leaders and Promoters of Human Rights

When my tenure as Executive Secretary of the Coordinating Committee was over, I returned to my work in the education sector. With my recent experience, I felt the need to widen the work undertaken by the IPEDEHP in order to include social leaders and the general population. Having realized how little people knew about human rights, having faced the feeling of many who thought they had "no worth" and "no rights," having heard many times "This is how it is; it is normal for people to abuse," made us decide to take our work to a wider sphere that included more than teachers. We began to nurture and develop social leaders and advocates of democracy and human rights.

We trained more than 2,500 leaders, men and women, youths and adults, peasants, and city dwellers, illiterate and literate, speakers of Quechua, Aymara, Spanish, Aguaruna, and Ashaninka. They are authorities or social leaders, who today continue to work actively promoting respect for the dignity of all peoples and the defense of rights and who demand that their communities fulfill their duties and responsibilities. Many of them now hold political and public posts: they are mayors, regional education directors, judges, governors, etc. The training they received made a deep impression in their lives, and they still work in favor of human rights education.

Girls Are Important: The Right to Equality and Quality in Rural Education

Recently, the importance of a preferential option for the education of boys and girls has become significant. We believe that equality in Peru Peru is still a work in progress and of great importance for the viability of human rights and for creating a truly democratic society.

Those of us who work in the field of human rights in general, or in human rights education more specifically, believe that our work has to aim first at the acknowledgment of people's dignity as a basic value for human coexistence. Because this acknowledgment of individual dignity, independent of any specific features or conditions, still does not exist in our country, we are encouraged to develop proposals that will address this problem from an educational basis and transform the current situation.

The rural schools are where we find the worst indicators of school performance and the lowest levels of learning; this is also where we find the lowest retention rates, total or partial absenteeism, and the highest rates of drop-outs, as well as students who are much older that the regular age for each school grade. The lack of attention and commitment, especially to the quality of the teaching for children and teens in rural areas, weakens the practice of citizenship and of democracy as a way of social coexistence. These problems are worse in the case of rural girls, who do not have the same opportunities as boys. From the standpoint of justice, working for girls' education is a necessity.

In a very few years the educational gap in areas where we have worked has been closed. Girls have won the right to education. They have more possibilities to build a different life. They are active agents for their rights, which they defend not only in education, but also in the way they are treated. They know they have the right to a life without violence, to share their opinions, to satisfy their need for food or clothing, and to be educated in their own language, among other rights. These girls and boys are the reason for our hope.

From Rural Schools to the Head of Rural Education in the Ministry of Education of Peru

I had some doubts when I was asked to take over as Head of Rural Education. I had never worked inside the government, and I had always been critical of a bureaucracy and a public sector that had done little or nothing to advance equality, justice, and democracy in Peru. But those same arguments also convinced me that I had to accept this responsibility and use my years of experience in public service to work on these issues. This is where I am now, learning to move among these structures, pressing for long-awaited changes, and fighting for the rights of our children to receive quality education. I am still convinced that one teacher can make a big difference.

I will stay here as long as I believe it is possible to make change. The moment I stop believing it, I will resign and go back to my work in rural areas, which is what moves me and is what I am committed to.

What is it all for?

The search for happiness, the need to fill those gaps in the soul which searches for "something more," the dissatisfaction with a comfortable and easy life, the indignation at injustices, the need to help the needy or those who suffer: those are all reasons that explain much (or almost all) of the road I have chosen and the work I have undertaken.

Nevertheless, I have to say that the warmth I have received, the appreciation I have heard, the gratitude and affection of the people I work with today as well as those with whom I have worked in the past, have more than made up for what I might have contributed. What I have received can in no way be compared to the little I have given.

I have always had the feeling, and it grows when I look back on my life, that I have not been the one to choose the roads or the most difficult decisions taken during my life. I can easily say that many times I have tried to say no to certain choices because I knew what I would have to face. But there has always been an internal force, a kind of voice that comes from the bottom of the soul that has made me say yes and has led me to take on challenges I had not looked for. Every attempt to flee, and there were many, was to no avail. Suddenly and almost without knowing how, I saw myself in the midst of a thousand adventures that have defined me as I am and that are part of my history.

I believe that my choice for human rights and human rights education is validated every day. I think that it is more than a job; it gives purpose to my life. It has been a privilege and a gift to work in something I feel passionate about.

Experiences, Quests, and Conquests: Building a Commitment to Human Rights Education

Vera Maria Candau (Brazil)

> **Vera Maria Ferrão Candau** has a bachelor's degree in pedagogy from the Pontifical Catholic University of Rio de Janeiro (Brazil). She attended graduate school at the Catholic University of Leuven (Belgium), and received her Ph.D. and did her post-doctoral work in the Education Department at the Complutense University Madrid (Spain). She is currently Professor at the Department of Education of the Pontifical Catholic University of Rio de Janeiro. She is a member of the coordinating team for the non-governmental organization Novamerica. She is also a member of the National Commission on Human Rights Education of Brazil, as well as a consultant for various organizations dedicated to the promotion of research in education. She sits on several editorial boards focused on education. Her research areas include teacher training and development, education, human rights education, and intercultural education, and she has published many essays on these subjects. She coordinates the Continental Commission on the Education Proposal for Educating in Challenging Times.
>
>

The invitation to recall my life in human rights education is an encouragement to evoke many memories, even some with no apparent relation to the subject, that have awakened a sensibility, a special focus, to a greater consciousness of certain issues and experiences on a personal and social level.

I will begin by mentioning the origin of my interest in human rights education, experiences that today have a new meaning, all belonging to circumstances where this issue was neither explicit nor the subject of reflection. I will then mention my explicit commitment and militancy in human rights education that started in the 1990s.

What Does It Mean to Be Different?

I will refer to three personal experiences. My middle-class family consisted of my parents, my brother, and myself. During my first school years, I did everything with my left hand. My mother, who worked in a state research center on education, took me for "talks" with several specialists who worked there. After I underwent many tests, they told my mother I was left-handed and that I would be able to do all normal activities with my left hand. So it was, and I did not face any issues until I was twelve. In Brazil some traditional celebrations called the *festas juninas* take place in June, where fireworks are one of the main attractions. When I tried to light one, the firework bounced back, burning my left hand severely. It was quite painful and my hand was immobilized. June was also the month for mid-term exams, which were quite important in those days. The school would not allow me to take the exams orally. Their only concession was to give me more time to write them. I practiced calligraphy with my right hand for hours in order to write the tests. It was very painful, and I now consider it an example of the homogenization of school culture and its inability to identify and face differences, even in cases that were self-evident. Although simple, this episode from the mid-1950s made me see my left-handedness as a negative difference, as something undesirable.

A second experience, which took place mainly during my teen years, had to do with my name, specifically my surname, *Candau*. A frequent question whenever I introduced myself to a group was and still is, "How do you pronounce your name: 'Candó' or 'Candal'?" This question made me explain, "Candó, because it is of French origin." I said it with pride, and this statement created a positive and admiring response. In those days European heritage was highly valued, especially if it was French. Nevertheless, it meant being silent about the other origin of my family, that of my mother, who had African roots. Brazilian society placed great value on all that was European and tended to disown what was Indigenous and African, which were not considered positive references for the construction of our identity. We wanted to be European, especially French. Affirming this European distinction and ignoring others gave me (gave us) a superior status. Of course, in those times – the end of the 1950s – I was not aware of how this social issue related to power, but it unconsciously had a hold on me.

Once I received my bachelor's degree in pedagogy, I went in 1962 to study at the University of Leuven in Belgium with a scholarship bestowed by the university. This was a dream for many students: studying in Europe. I was twenty-three years old and faced this challenge with enthusiasm. However, after the first impressions when everything was new and interesting, daily life in a different culture turned out to be hard, and what I had understood as "natural" made a noticeable contrast with the style, habits, and ways of being among the locals. It was in this context that I understood intimately what "being Brazilian" or "being Latin-American" meant to Belgian students. Stereotypes began to appear. If there were fights or loud demonstrations at night, next day the police would go to where Latin Americans and Africans lived. They were considered violent. The so-called "Third World" was thought to be uneducated, aggressive, and undisciplined, with little academic training; in other words, "uncivilized." Acknowledging this conception of myself was a new and extremely difficult experience for me. One feature was especially challenging: demonstrating my academic skills. I managed it, and it was of great importance as an actual demonstration of the fact that we were "different" but not incapable of meeting European academic requirements. This fact changed my relationship with the Belgian students, and we grew closer and more respectful of different points of views and behaviors. This experience helped me think about my cultural identity and the stereotypes that we create in reference to "others" whom we considered different.

These experiences, diverse and small, were part of my daily life and broadened my ability to look at others in a different way, making me more critical of my own assumptions, stereotypes, and ethnocentrism.

Commitment to Social Transformation: a Horizon of Meaning

Another element I consider essential on my road to human rights education was the development of a social and political commitment, as well as an understanding of the relationship between education and social transformation.

I received my bachelor's degree from a very well regarded Brazilian teacher's college in the second half of the 1950s. When I finished my studies, I entered the public system as an elementary school teacher in a rural area of the Río de Janeiro district. My training was in pedagogy linked to what were then called "new schools,"[1] and I was eager to put into practice all I had learned. The school I was assigned to was housed in an adapted home, with small rooms and many students in each, almost forty per room. My first students – I can still remember them today – were between the ages of nine and twelve and attended the third grade in elementary school. A significant number worked from six in the morning selling fruits and vegetables in a farmers market on the street, and by the time they got to school at one in the afternoon, they were tired and hungry. The school offered them lunch before starting activities, and they literally went to sleep during class. Learning to face this situation, getting close to the reality lived by those children, and talking to their families allowed me to learn about the life of the working class and to discover, in practical terms – I had studied the topic in theory – the relationship between education and social conditions. The pedagogic challenge was great; I both succeeded and failed, but it was undoubtedly the most important teaching experience of my life.

While still in this school, by the end of the 1950s and the beginning of the 1960s, I began graduate studies in pedagogy and education at the Pontificia Universidad Católica de Río de Janeiro (PUC-Rio). It took around two hours to get to the University from my house. Those were times of intense

---

[1] The term *"escuela nueva"* ("new school") refers to the progressive ideas that arose during the nineteenth century and developed during the twentieth century as an alternative to traditional teaching, which was considered authoritarian both towards the subjects (focused on the teacher and teaching), as well as in regards to knowledge (the transmittal of content with no consideration for the student's context, and with the principal focus on memorization). With these ideas in mind, a didactic model was proposed that has children as the main focus of the teaching and learning process, with more attention on their process of education, their interests, and their needs. (Translator's note).

social unrest and student demonstrations, and I participated actively in student centers. Together with other comrades we created the Movimiento Solidario Universitario (University Solidary Movement), inspired by the ideas of Father Lebret and his *Manifiesto por una Civilización Solidaria* (*Manifesto for a Civilization of Solidarity*). We read a lot, organized seminars on Brazilian reality and popular education, initiated demonstrations, discussed the Cuban Revolution, and much more. At this time students in pedagogy and education put pressure on the president of the University to establish a day nursery for children of a *favela* located near the campus.

Those were times of passionate experiences during which I strengthened my social and political commitment in different spheres, as well as my conviction that education had an important role to play in social transformation processes. Those were also times of debates; of a plurality of social actors, sometimes opposed; of renovation and search; of risks and generosity; and of dreams of a different society, fair and democratic. Unfortunately, a tough and tragic dictatorship interrupted this process.

Dictatorship: Amid Silence, Fears, and Commitments

The civilian-military Brazilian dictatorship began in 1964. A few years later in 1966, I left Brazil to work on a Ph.D. in education in Spain. When I arrived in Madrid to enroll in the Universidad Complutense (Complutense University), I found myself in a country under a dictatorship. Franco governed with a firm hand. The university was full of the so-called *grises* or "grays" (police in Franco's Spain wore grey-colored uniforms), policemen who watched the students. They could be found in the halls of the Philosophy and Literature Department and inside classes, and on several occasions they gave the order to "abandon" the university. I lived in a student residence on the university campus. When several students participated in resistance movements against the Franco regime, I supported and joined them in demonstrations. However, some friends took me aside and told me that if I wanted to finish my Ph.D., I should be more prudent because if the police detained me in a demonstration, as a foreigner I would be sent back to Brazil. During those years in Spain, I experienced for the first time what it was like to live in constant tension and to be unable to demonstrate, and I understood what the denial of freedom of expression, of thought, of movement, and of association meant: to have your civil and political rights denied.

I returned to Brazil at the end of the sixties. The Brazilian dictatorship was firmly established and showed its ruthlessness and cruelty: torture, murders, denial of freedom, censorship, resignations by professionals from public institutions – including universities – and exile. Any kind of criticism of the regime was considered subversive, and its authors were labeled as communists and enemies of the nation. *"Brasil: ame-o ou deixe-o"* ("Brazil, love it or leave it") was the predominant slogan, with the explicit threat of exile. I taught education at the university and had to watch out for those in my classes, since representatives of the police had infiltrated the classrooms. Many professors were questioned at the National Information Service because of statements they had supposedly made in class; they were denounced without ever knowing who the informer was. Helicopters frequently flew over the university. We had to be careful about what we said, about the readings we assigned to our students, and about whom we talked to. A mood of fear, suspicion, self-censorship, and a constant feeling of being watched, of being invaded, was always with me.

During those days PUC-Rio played an important part in the resistance and defense of its workers, faculty, and students. In a homage by the university in 2013 to many of those who took part in the resistance, one of the University chancellors stated that PUC-Rio had been an "island of freedom," a "refuge" for many intellectuals who had been the subject of threats.

This experience forced me – forced us – to stress even more the importance of human dignity and human rights in the construction of fair and democratic societies. A culture of fear and cruelty must be faced with the development of a culture of human rights, freedom, solidarity, acknowledgment, and equality. By the end of the eighties we could envision the opening of a difficult process. The struggle for amnesty,[2] which brought together many social movements and civil associations, gained strength from the middle of the seventies; by 1979 an Amnesty Law was passed that, in spite of its limitations, meant a step forward in the democratization of the country. I vividly recall an event at the beginning of the eighties at a reception for Paulo Freire, who had just returned to Brazil after many years in exile. The event was marked by a show of emotion, joy, and a renewed commitment to democracy. We all left convinced that we were building a new epoch. Hope was reborn.

In Times of Democracy: Emergence and Reaffirmation of Human Rights Education

The eighties were a time of democratic transition. Social movements appeared on the public scene. Opportunities for debates, inquiries, and proposals multiplied. Hope for better times was reborn. We fought for a constitutional convention. Once this convention was established, its president, Ulysses Guimaraes, stated in the opening session:

> This is a parliament that turns its back on the past, that opens today to decide the constitutional destiny of the country. Many new social groups play an important part in it, thus conferring a new legitimacy on the representation of the Brazilian people. These months have proved that there is no place in Brazil for the historical limitations that the exploiters, whom we know well, want to impose. Our people have grown, accepted their destiny, and joined in the multitudes demanding the restoration of democracy, of justice, and of the dignity of our state.

The new Brazilian Constitution approved in 1988 was called the "Constitution of the Citizens" because of its inclusion of human rights for future generations. It was the beginning of a new stage in national life, marked by the enthusiasm and generosity of many people who insisted – we insisted – on building a new social fabric. Conscious that the democratization process implied a

---

[2] The struggle for amnesty in Brazil worked for a liberalization that would lead to the democratization of the country. The concept of amnesty is understood in this context as freedom and reparation. Although it fell short of including all the objectives that many demanded, the 1979 Amnesty Law brought with it many signs of political liberalization, such as the return of many political exiles. (Translator's Note).

change in mentality, behavior, and practices, human rights activists started promoting education projects in addition to protesting. The idea was that education should be directed toward an active and participatory citizenry, with the aim of asserting a culture of human rights in all social spheres. The first experiences in the eighties took place in those provinces with governors that came from the left. The preeminent political actors were organizations from civil society.

By the beginning of the nineties, small groups of professionals, social scientists, and educators joined together with the goal of promoting a non-governmental organization (NGO) whose main focus would be human rights education not only from a national point of view, but also on Latin American terms. It was thus that the NGO Novamerica was established in 1991 with the following main objectives:

- To analyze and debate in depth Latin American reality in a multidisciplinary, multiethnic, and multicultural context;
- To strengthen democracy as a way of life and organizing principle for diverse civil society actors, with a primary commitment to popular movements and organizations;
- To create educators as social agents and cultural multipliers, promoters of human rights, committed to the construction of a just, compassionate, and democratic society.

This was a seed thrown to the wind without any of us knowing what the outcome would be. We met in order to reflect on human rights education and to create a document that would serve as a guide to our views on human rights and the pedagogic ideals we believed in. We placed greater value on pedagogic workshops as a training strategy, organizing workshops on human rights education oriented toward both formal and informal education; we contacted diverse groups and began implementing our proposal. Those were years of full-time work and dedication. Little by little, the task of Novamerica widened, obtaining important social recognition around the country and expanding its influence to different areas of Latin America. In 2003 it received the National Prize for Human Rights Education from the Department of Human Rights, a department linked to the presidency of the Republic.

During its twenty years of existence, Novamerica has undertaken constant, systematic work on human rights education, creating multiple agents and debates, as well as producing an important number of publications. Part of our task has been building a network of human rights educators linked to the movement "Educating in Challenging Times," with representatives from twelve countries of the South American continent. We recently held a seminar on this movement with the topic "Educating in Challenging Times: School, Memory, and Citizenship," with special emphasis on the importance of the Commission on Memory and Truth, established in my country in 2011.

Along with my work with Novamerica and closely linked with it as a professor in the Education Department at PUC-Rio, I am responsible for courses on human rights education at both the graduate and postgraduate levels – Masters and Ph.D. – in addition to doing research work, tutoring graduates, and promoting extension activities on this topic. These academic activities are extremely gratifying. I find great joy in seeing how knowledge of this topic widens students' horizons and gives them sociopolitical, ethical, and cultural perspectives on issues related to education. I work on the relationships between multicultural and inter-cultural human rights and education. I am especially interested in the articulation between equality and difference.

Responding to the Vienna Conference on Human Rights (1993), in the mid-nineties the Brazilian government began systematically to formulate more and more far-reaching policies related to human rights. In 1996, it published the first National Human Rights Program – revised and updated in 2002, and later in 2009 – which was the subject of many debates in different social spheres and in the mass media. Several specific policies were formulated in relation to the assertion of the rights of ethnic and racial groups; of women, children, and youths; of the elderly; of people with special needs; and LGBT (lesbian, gays, bisexuals, and transgender people) groups, among others. Today the country has a broad legal framework and policies that have the explicit purpose of strengthening human rights in society. Nevertheless, violations are still clearly present, as is the awareness that laws and policies, important as they might be, are not enough. During this process, in 2003 the government created the National Council on Human Rights, and I was appointed a member of this Council. Our first task was to create a National Plan for Human Rights Education. After this plan was widely discussed in the provinces of the country, a second version was put forward in 2006. I am still a member of this Council, and we make every effort to analyze proposals and to choose actions that will broaden human rights education initiatives, with special interest in the creation of multipliers. UNESCO has significantly supported this interest.

I still work in these three spheres: in the NGO Novamerica, in PUC-Rio, and in the National Council on Education on Human Rights. I am aware that much has been done, but there is still more to accomplish. As I have mentioned, human rights education has to do with changes in points of view, behaviors, and practices. This will enable a culture of human rights to expand into all social spheres, from family life to public policies. It is a long and difficult process. I still feel the sense of always beginning again. Is this an impossible task? I ask myself this question every day. Nevertheless, I can feel a fountain of energy that emerges from inside me, which helps me renew my commitment and which gives me a sense of hope that each step we take in our daily lives generates numerous possibilities that enable us to move forward.

Entanglements and Efforts: Towards a Commitment to Human Rights Education

Nélida Céspedes (Peru)

> **Nélida Céspedes Rossel** is a teacher with thirty-eight years of experience. She heads the project Education and Rights of Children and Children Affected by Political Violence developed by Tarea, a non-governmental organization in Lima, Ayacucho, Cerro de Pasco, and Huancayo, Peru. She is also consultant for the Instituto Interamericano de Derechos Humanos (Inter-American Institute of Human Rights) to develop their human rights education curricula in El Salvador and Guatemala and the author of educational materials on human rights and citizenship. She is a member of the following institutions: Comité de Seguimiento a los Derechos sobre la Infancia (member), Grupo de Iniciativa por los Derechos de Infancia (Vice-President), Consejo de Educación Popular de América Latina (Secretary General and specialist in young peoples'and adults' right to education from a popular education perspective), and Consejo Internacional de Adultos (Vice-president for Latin America). She is a member of the editorial boards of *DVV Internacional, Deciso,* and *La Piragua*, publications of Consejo de educación popular de América Latina y el Caríbe (Council for Popular Education in Latin American and the Carribean, or CEAAL).

It is not easy to answer the questions posed by my friend Abraham Magendzo, a persistent and loving educator in the fight for human rights. I will attempt an answer based on my different life experiences working for human rights education, but as the song says, I will do it "my way."

Thinking of these efforts and how, without any preconceived plan, I became a human rights educator, I recall a song by Silvio Rodríguez called *Solo el amor* that expresses a great deal about my experience as an educator. "You ought to love these attempts," the lyrics go, and then continue "only love can illuminate the dead." Love is what led me to take this road.[1]

---

[1] *Sólo. El Amor* by Silvio Rodríguez (lines 8 and 12):
Debes amar el tiempo de los intentos, ... (8)
Solo el amor consigue encender lo muerto. (12)

Commitments That Have Given Meaning to Efforts

The seventies were full of turning points in my personal life, a time of rupture. It was a time of confusion among religious options, of understanding education as a fundamental human right, of political militancy in a leftist party that aimed to help build a new society, and of a handful of unforgettable, subversive women friends. Those were challenging times in terms of personal definitions: facing fears and deconstructing imaginary worlds, visions, and ways of understanding myself, others, my country, and the world. Latin America was undergoing the complex development of the political left and at the same time a period of painful tyranny. There was also a call for solidarity, disobedience, and urgent change.

In my country of Peru, workers, peasants, and a growing number of migrants to the city created a great popular struggle against a government that had forgotten them. Teachers, church activists, artists, intellectuals, women – we were all enriched by this complex movement. Our yearning for a new future inspired us: a social, political, economic, and cultural change that would humanize both peoples and towns.

Another important influence was Liberation Theology. It led me to the conviction that the dispossessed and excluded of this world also deserve a place and a paradise here on earth. I recall a beautiful song that expressed this idea: "…look at the earth, tell everyone that in man they can find the Lord." I interpreted this as a message to speak less about God and to show his presence through his works, for those works are the measures of what is true. It was not enough to pray to heaven; one had to live looking around at the earth. This relationship between politics and faith was a powerful interconnection.

As teacher and trade unionist, I was deeply influenced by class theories, human rights, and the profound teaching of popular educators like Paulo Freire and other Peruvian critical educators. Popular education had a political, ethical, and pedagogical meaning that enabled education to influence the popular movement. It also developed individuals in their awareness and their abilities to express themselves, understand the world, live in it critically, and transform it. Parties on the left were founded on the need for both cultural and educational change, essential components of any kind of social or political transformation. Lastly, the activities of non-governmental organizations (NGOs) were considered an important contribution to the struggles of the people. These are some of the most important facts of those times of confusion and commitments.

End of the Eighties and the Human Rights of the Child

In the eighties when I was a teacher in the state school Túpac Amaru, I had an unforgettable educational experience. The topic was identity, and I proposed to the students that they bring a big mirror to class. The task was to look into the mirror's image of what we were at that moment and one by one to name the features of the group we saw there. There was laughter in some and shame in others as they identified themselves as "mulattos," "somewhat white," "of Andean origin,"

"Chinese like," "pug-nosed," "aquiline," and so forth. Then we began to talk about ourselves. We discussed our right to be different, to equal opportunities for all, and to respect and value who you and others are. This discussion helped us learn to face discrimination.

None of this is easy, not even pointing it out to others, especially when racism is a fact of our societies and of that miniature world that is the school. It is even harder when those discriminating images are deeply rooted. But it is important to do so, and the taste of trying may spark a light in the children to recognize their own value and that of others. The attempt shows that without an "I," the "us" is impossible. Encouraging and building an "us" is a difficult, complex, and challenging task for educators, who must be remaking themselves in the process. Clearly, the life of a teacher provides many experiences that enable us to model and experience human rights.

Some historic periods are especially favorable for the promotion of human rights education. I am referring to the Convention on the Rights of the Child, a universal pact that includes the youngest individuals, children, and adolescents as holders of rights. On November 20, 1989, the adoption of the Convention by the UN General Assembly signaled a milestone for humanity by establishing a new type of relationship between adults and minors. The Convention is the human rights treaty most universally recognized in history and has been ratified by all countries except for the United States.

I apologize for my rambling, but today, September 19, 2012, a debate is taking place in Peru regarding military incursions against drug trafficking in the VRAEM area (Valleys of the Río Apurímac, Ene, and Mantaro Rivers). These incursions have led to a significant accident: the death of a young girl found in a thicket. A journalist narrating this painful event writes at the end of his article: "This is still a country where, if you are a woman, a girl, and come from the mountains, your life has no value."[2] This sentence hurts me, but it also encourages me to insist on my work as a human rights educator. Feeling pain and indignation and being part of a movement of educators are and will always be a constant factor of human rights education.

As an educator one doesn't only work with political, economic, and social factors that oppose human right education: the barrier of cultural imagination is also very powerful. We can establish and memorize rules, but it is not easy to deconstruct ideas about childhood only from an adult point of view, seeing children as all alike. Such a limited view prevents us from recognizing children as subjects of rights, as valuable people with the same rights as adults.

Such a change of perspective about children is not an easy task because it questions the very foundation on which adults stand, the lords and owners of truth and of childhood. To overcome this adult-centrist vision, we have adopted theories of childhood from sociology, anthropology, and education, all of which originated from the nineteen-forties. However, — and always with respect to all cultures — we have learned that many of those theories do not include childhood as a category.

---

[2] Marco Sifuentes. *La criatura ya está muerta*. Diario La República, September 19, 2012.

In our case, this heterogeneity challenges our efforts to communicate with the Andean world. These are the challenges I have faced in my life as a human rights educator.

Education and Political Violence in Ayacucho: Remember So It Will Not Happen Again!

In the nineties, Peru was going through one of the most painful stages in its history. During the guerilla war waged by the Shining Path, the Ayachucho region was one of the hardest hit by terrorism.[3] Tarea,[4] an NGO working on educational development, and its partners heard the call of Ayacucho children, who were living in an intolerable situation that resulted both from political violence and displacement and the almost non-existent response by the state in general and by the educational sector in particular. As a result, in 1992, in coordination with Save the Children Canada, we decided to help in our humble way to address this serious situation. We joined with the schoolteachers of Ayacucho to deal with the problem of violence and its effects on the lives of the children, as well as their own lives.

I remember the atmosphere of fear in those times. Nothing else could be expected: the *Plaza de Armas*, the main square of the regional capital of Huamanga, was surrounded by tanks; the authorities, for security reasons, were living in a hotel; and by six in the afternoon the city was empty except for the air of fear. The Coordinadora de Trabajo por los Derechos del Niño (Work Coordinator for the Rights of the Child), which was affiliated with the Grupo de Iniciativa Nacional por los Derechos del Niño (National Initiative for the Rights of the Child Group, or GIN) played an important part in the defense of the children. The same was true of the Casa del Niño Ayacuchano (House of the Ayachuan Child), which housed displaced children who had been torn from their families, towns, and culture by political violence.

Afterward in 1994, in order to reestablish communications and social links that had been broken by this violence, UNICEF promoted the establishment of summer schools that encouraged respect and trust between teachers and students, as well as the participation of parents and community leaders. These experiences created the project Educar para reconstruir la vida (Educating to Reconstruct Life), coordinated by the Dirección Regional de Educación, UNICEF, and Tarea. This happened during the last wave of political violence, times when more than once I felt great fear.

The main objectives of the project Educar para reconstruir la vida were:

- Creation by the Regional Directorate of Education of general methods for teaching self-esteem and identity as a part of the formal educational system in the region, and in doing so contributing to the design of specific policies for helping children in situations of violence;

---

[3] See the report of Peru's Truth and Reconciliation Commission, available at www.cverdad.org.pe.
[4] *Tarea Asociación de Publicaciones Educativas*: An NGO for the development of education. A teaching and critical thinking community working for the democratic transformation of educational policies and practices from the perspective of the equal and intercultural development of society. It consists of local, regional, national, and Latin-American groups working for a fair and democratic society. It is a part of the *Consejo de Educación Popular de América Latina y el Caribe* (CEAAL).

- Design of a strategy for training educators;
- Creation of a monitoring plan for the project;
- Creation of educational modules and materials;
- Coordination and incorporation of social and community institutions as a way of creating a sustainable project.

How Did Displacement Affect Children?

It is important to remember that the violence in Ayacucho resulted in the deaths of an estimated 25,000 people, the displacement of more than 120,000 families, and the forced eviction from their homes of ninety percent of the Quechua speakers in rural areas. Instigated by fear, terror, and insecurity, this kind of displacement was really a search for some place to stay alive; nevertheless, the main victims were children because when the family is so immersed in difficulties, the foundations of the child's whole development are weakened. The result was instability: all agricultural and grazing activities, socialization with other children, and school attendance were abruptly interrupted. On the other hand, even when displaced families found themselves in reception centers, they experienced exclusion and hostility, which further contributed to their insecurity, fear, and loneliness.

What about the School Factor?

The children of Ayacucho who managed to attend school suffered the effects of an institution that was dedicated to teaching in Spanish with no interest in their Indigenous mother tongue or culture, that failed to take into consideration either the psychological or social problems the children faced, and that therefore only succeeded in strengthening their exclusion: a school that turned its back on reality.

Such unfettered violence had a devastating effect on an education system that was already in a state of crisis, reflecting the general Peruvian economic, social, and political crisis. As Juan Ansión states: "… the extreme deterioration both in material and pedagogical terms and political violence are two fundamental conditions that have put into question the survival of the educational myth as a myth of mobilization" (Ansión et al., 1993).

Two other issues demonstrate state responsibility for the heightened violence and educational debacle. First, the government neglected public education in the midst of a conflict in which the educational system was an important issue of both ideological and symbolic debate. Second, the state assaulted and stigmatized whole communities of public university teachers and students, especially in the provinces, and colluded in serious violations of students' and teachers' human rights.

The report of the Comisión de la Verdad y Reconciliación (The Truth and Reconciliation Committee, or CVR) established that different governments had systematically abandoned the areas of education, childhood, teachers, and any educational focus, all of which led to the situation of injustice that created violent factions.

What Was Done in This Situation?

The best lessons from this experience come from the inhabitants and teachers who exhibited great resilience, accepting the challenge of rebuilding themselves and their communities instead of giving into despair. Hope is a powerful healing agent, as is the long struggle of our peoples during such periods of crisis. (But let's not be naïve: without comprehensive policies, education will be maimed).

The Regional Directorate of Education in the Ayacucho region made several proposals to help those in charge understand the significance of the political problem and undertake changes in education. The resulting discussions revealed the authorities' lack of awareness, as well as their inabilities to face the situation. Change was only accomplished by establishing relations with the communities and creating spaces for debate and proposals for educational policies.

We have continued our efforts, learning and sometimes marching for and against. We have gained strength from the struggle of so many Peruvians. We have also gained strength from the final report of the CVR, which I consider to be a milestone in our national history. César Rodríguez Rabanal once stated that it was important to read this report in order to learn the truth, as an open and unfinished task, thus indicating that an ongoing debate was required in all spheres of national life.

The truth is that we zigzag. There was some progress, as exemplified by the agreement signed by CVR with the Ministry of Education, to allow the discussion of peace and reconciliation as part of the curricula (Thanks to this agreement, materials based on the CVR were produced). However, a former American Popular Revolutionary Alliance (APRA)[5] minister initiated an inconceivable polemic, denouncing the textbooks for fifth grade as an apology for terrorism. In such circumstances, the Consejo Nacional de Educación (National Council of Education) and several historians, including the State Prosecutor, declared that the only conclusions promoted were those of the CVR. Another important factor in the agreement was the priority given to rural areas, specifically those who spoke Quechua, because the violence had begun in those areas. These are powerful reasons for understanding that human rights education is essential when related to the circumstances and lives of people, especially those forgotten by the system.

And so, we have kept on working and trying. It has been possible only due to the commitment of a group of educators in the Ayacucho region: Alicia, Ana María, Hugo, José, César, Julio, Derly, Héctor, Cristina, Abilio, unforgettable and dearly loved faces. In human rights education, people are important. They all worked for intercultural and bilingual education, both in urban and rural areas. This focus on the development of an intercultural citizenship is based on continuing education for teachers, as well as establishing relations with the family, community, and diverse institutions and social groups. We are certain that we deserve a just society, peaceful, democratic, and intercultural. A society that combines bread and beauty, solidarity and love, truth and transparency, along with

---

[5] Spanish initials of the Peruvian center-left political party Alianza Popular Revolucionara Americana (American Popular Revolutionary Alliance).

constructive criticism. A society that abolishes poverty in every possible sense. A society where everyone, citizens and authorities alike, accepts responsibility for building the society that we deserve as Peruvians.

CEAAL: Entanglements and Efforts at a New Possible World

I consider it a privilege to be a part of Consejo de Educación de Adultos para América Latina (The Latin American Network for Peace and Human Rights of the Latin America Council of Adult Education, or CEAAL) because it has allowed me to be a part of the dreams and quests of educators who believe that our Latin America and the Caribbean, our *Abya Yala* (In the Indigenous Kuna language, *Abya Yala* means "the land in its full maturity") should be fair, humane, and part of a committed and participatory democracy, creating a unity of human beings and nature: a worthy life for all.

This dream is possible through the popular education movement. My simple contribution to this collective effort is to insist to everyone that popular education is relevant, not just as a concept, but also as a political and pedagogic response to real-life situations. This view of popular education is essential for understanding how diverse practices and points of view can merge.

These changes continue to make us question reality and strengthen our commitment. We have had to redefine our understanding of who are the main actors of social change. We used to identify them as popular sectors, understood as a general class, but our work with women and native populations has encouraged us to further develop our social, cultural, and scientific thought. Categories like genre, ethnic group, and generation are now included, allowing for a wider reference for understanding and transforming reality. This is why the possibility of working for human rights, intercultural education, and respect for our environment contribute significantly to popular education.

We aim for a relationship between politics and education that promotes solidarity, cooperation, and caring for everyone; for an education that makes us human beings; for a fundamentally ethical and political education through pedagogy that empowers individual creativity. I am certain that we have to continue working to create a political, social, economic, and cultural humanitarian education respectful of human rights, inclusion, justice, peace, and democracy.

This is my work, a dream shared with young people, CEAAL, and other sister networks.

FOR HUMAN RIGHTS AND POPULAR EDUCATION THAT WILL MAKE THIS DREAM POSSIBLE, NOW!

BIBLIOGRAPHY

ANSIÓN, Juan, Daniel Del Castillo, Manuel Piqueras, Isaura Zegarra (1993). *La Escuela en Tiempos de Guerra*. Chapter I, pp. 29–52. Lima: Tarea.

All the Women I Have Been: The History of an Educator's Training and Program of Action

Silvia Conde (Mexico)

Silvia Conde holds a master's degree in education science. She is the General Coordinator of the Colectivo para el Desarrollo Educativo (Collective for Educational Development), Albanta, S.C. She has also written textbooks for courses on civic education and ethics at the elementary and high school levels.

I have short legs and a generous heart, and I am more fragile than it seems. I was born in Mexico City, but I am a *norteña* (northerner) by conviction. In October 1968 my family moved north when my father decided to retire from the army. I grew up in the city of Torreón, surrounded by honest and simple people, on the side of the Cerro de las Noas, under the desert heat and customary dust clouds. I learned to call things by their proper names, to speak plainly, and to enjoy the practical side of life.

Like many girls my age, I played in the rain (whenever it rained) and liked to spin with my arms open looking up at the shining sky, only to fall on the scorching pavement and feel the world moving. I liked the sky of the Lagunera region, not just because I could see the sun and the constantly changing clouds on the horizon, but because at sunset flocks of birds would return from their chores and paint it black. I loved their synchronized flight, which was methodical though it seemed erratic.

Childhood is destiny. I am what I am mainly due to those evenings of amazing colors and to my certainty that everything is in constant movement. Like the clouds, I find it difficult to stay still, to always do the same thing. I love the act of creation, to face a blank page, a brand new project, to give birth to ideas, and to feed them until they become real. Maybe this is why I deliriously dig into the first stages of processes and pull my colleagues along in a frenzy that for many is just another sign of my madness. I call it passion.

I consider myself a gentle woman, though in another world I was untamed and fierce. I believed I was a feminist; I enjoyed being a liberal and even a poet. I am easily angered. I cry and suffer for someone else's pain, but I am tough with my own. Passionate and energetic, I have twice been married and divorced. The first time I married, I was deeply in love with a man of words. I was seduced by *el compañero* (the partner) and was his shadow, running after his footsteps, pouring forth ideologies and dreams. With him I also got to know the hell of alcoholism and violence. I did not leave him when he beat me until I passed out. I left when I stopped feeling. I feared the silence that had taken over my conscience, as happens to many of us who have had our dignity shattered. The women around me – my sister, and Adriana, my almost-sister best friend – helped me to wake up.

Since yesterday I've torn up letters and memories. My face and hope hurt. My heart ticks irregularly. Since yesterday I am not the same.

From my second marriage I have a marvelous son: a free being with different ideas, a convinced democrat with a great capacity for amazement. One of my greatest pleasures is talking to him, feeling him throb, knowing he is also unable to stay still.

I reflect on the history of my life from the woman that I now am. I am convinced that all the women I have ever been were possible due to the people who accompanied me on this journey, whose stories are a necessary part of my own.

Professional Birth

I cannot think about my life only in professional terms, for all the most important decisions have resulted from of my values, beliefs, feelings, and pace of life.

Education is my passion. As a teenager I wanted to be a teacher, but my father asked me to go to college, so I worked as a tutor to pay for my studies, and I graduated with a degree in education from the Northeast Autonomous University. I learned a little from my teachers but much from books and much more from my students.

My professional birth happened the first time I made a decision that was inspired by indignation. I was a high school vice principal, and on one occasion the authoritarian principal rejected one of my questions with the phrase: "Chickens on the lower roost never crap on those on the upper roost." I quit, and with my cheeks still red from indignation, I bumped into Alberto Álvarez, a researcher from the Educational Studies Center. He was organizing a group of assistant researchers for the project *Atención global al rezago escolar en escuelas rurales de Chihuahua, Coahuila y Durango* (Focused Attention on Students Who Fall Behind in Rural Schools of the States of Chihuahua, Coahuila, and Durango). The first important decision in my professional life was taking part in this process.

The day I was born professionally was a Thursday when an earthquake shook most of the country. That day was September 19, 1985. I was also shaking inside because it was my first day of "real work." I learned of the earthquake by radio as I was traveling with Alberto from Torreón to Ciudad Jiménez, Chihuahua, to begin our fieldwork. During the three hours of the trip, I felt pain because of the earthquake – so much anguish, so many loved ones at risk – but I also had other things on my mind. This project, headed by Sylvia Schmelkes and Carlos Muñoz Izquierdo, was a great challenge because of my limited university education, but it was compensated by my enormous desire to keep on learning.

During one school term I lived with an evangelical family in a small *ejido* (plot of land owned by a community) in the south of Chihuahua. From Don Mariano, a demanding minister of the Church of God, I learned to respect different faiths. God's word guided his life and that of his family, and this moved me deeply. Although I am more of a superstitious person than a believer, I admired the determination with which, however unsuccessfully, he tried to instill his spiritual sense in me. Ever since then I am not what I used to be. I forgot completely the secret formula for appearing to be innocent. My laughter changed and so did the way I did my hair.

In this small town in the south of Chihuahua, in the framework of action research, I learned to see the school from the inside. I also understood what it meant to be a rural teacher and the many difficulties of the job. I valued the ties of solidarity that held the social fabric of the community together, and I learned the meaning of tolerance. I immediately lost my naïveté: I realized that school is more than teaching and pedagogy. This was also where I received my first death threat. This threat occurred because when I tried to help the families take over the school by supporting their children and participating in the management of the school, I confronted the economic interests linked with corruption within the commonly shared land and the school cooperative.

I was impressed by how hard life is for the peasants. Young people of my age were already old, like Lalo Callo, a twenty-three-year-old illiterate who after four attempts to finish first grade had only learned to misspell his name. His real name was Eduardo Castillo, and like many sons of peasants from the south of Chihuahua, Lalo Callo worked harvesting nuts but dreamed of crossing into the USA. He abandoned his dream when things got better with a job working in the apple harvest and looking after the ranch of *Señor* Amado. I was saved then by my naïveté. Many years had to pass before I understood that those youths who taught me to ride and rescued me from the *cacique* (boss) were not really harvesting apples.

Some time later the project focused on training parents so that they could address the chaotic state of schooling by linking school and community. My responsibilities grew as they now included rural schools in Coahuila and Durango. Organized working sessions with rural teachers and youths made me more aware of what happens in the educational process when the community takes charge of the school. It also represented an extraordinary learning experience for me, including progress meetings with Sylvia Schmelkes at the Educational Studies Center.

Gender stereotypes, power struggles, and the wish to hold on to local customs were deeply felt in this process of action research. The mothers who encouraged any activity that would help their children academically faced the rejection of their neighbors. On their way to weekly meetings, they heard whispers around them and sometimes heard the cry of-

> "There go the *escuelantas* (school attenders)! Women with nothing to do! Better take care of your husbands."
> "Have you made your *tortillas,* Juana?"
> "Let's see if you become less dumb!"

Some could not put up with the pressure, but most learned to laugh and change the meaning of their neighborhood's struggle.

Those were knapsack and sandal times. Wet with sweat and dusty, I walked through the rural misery of the *Comarca*. I ate and drank all the intestinal fauna of the peasants.

To the rhythm of *"Ya llegó, ya llegó, ya llegó, Sergio el bailador"* ("He's here, he's here, he's here, Sergio the dancer"), the rural bus would make its way around the desert of northern Durango. It was my means of transport from one communal land to another, from one school to another. Like many times before, that Tuesday I walked the fifteen miles that separated the ranch from the highway with two rural teachers, Cirilo and Guadalupe. The heat, the stubborn dust that stuck to one's sweat, and the dry wind urged us on. The Coca-Cola delivery truck was our only hope of hitching a ride. The president of the Parents Association, *Doña* Mela, was waiting for me with a big glass of water and her familiar smile. When I thanked her for what I thought was her tamarind water (a juice made from tamarind), she answered me with a roar of laughter. Covering her toothless mouth with one hand, she said, "Teacher, how can you think that it's tamarind water? It's water from the watering hole, boiled, but from the hole. We barely have water. We have very little left, and we share it with the animals. Look at them, poor things; they can hardly bark." Two skinny dogs looked at us, gasping. The dogs and I eagerly drank the water.

I passed many long nights with *Doña* Mela, with Romana, with my *comadre* Concha, and with so many other brave women who taught me the cost of ignorance and submission. Dying "of a pain" or of premature aging, lack of teeth, blows, and humiliations were all part of a destiny that seemed inevitable. I cried in rage with them, and I felt like a revolutionary. Indignation brought me to work with the people and to participate in political activities, both of which complemented the process of action research.

During the weekends I organized women producers in collectives. Some of them felt empowered. Whether as members of weaving co-ops, as oregano harvesters, or even in the failed attempt at harvesting silk worms, they felt immense satisfaction. I can still recall the smell of the *Lagunera* region when it rains and the cracked soil finally gets wet. Sometimes in the midst of my daily life the smell of oregano still awakens sleeping memories.

This was one of the most important stages in making me what I am, and it remains important when I make professional decisions. School, culture, a weak trace of hope, the stubbornness of surviving, solidarity, the ability to laugh at small things: all these brought me close to the simple life. But they also showed me its raw vulnerability. I now call upon the idea of human security to understand that excluded part of Mexico. The lack of opportunities, uncertain future, despair, and apathy that I saw in the faces of those young people who joined me on the road during the eighties still come up when I am exploring new roads.

The Journey

I crossed the ocean and journeyed through the Andes looking for a way out. I was looking for the right words to describe my urge to change the world, to tip the balance the other way.

My next step towards non-governmental organizations (NGOs) came naturally. In two of these, Praxis and Edupaz, I went further in the training process for parents, popular education, and human rights. With Ángel Varela, Beatriz Barragán, Christian Rojas, and Raúl Esparza, all *Lagunera* teachers, we founded an NGO whose objective was education for peace and human rights: Edupaz. We worked on a training project for high school teachers based on existential, rational, and critical values. Our project was based on one created by Pablo Latapí in Aguascalientes some years earlier that had adopted the Spanish model of Education for Peace. We also used a Chilean experience related to human rights education. In Spain I was trained on non-violent techniques, and in Chile, under Abraham Magendzo, in human rights and the design of curricula that problematizes issues.

My encounter with Chile was magical. It was during the spring of 1991 and it was snowing. The experience of human rights, the open wound of a divided people, and the confidence in education as a means to rebuild and channel indignation marked me for life and gave me a unique awareness that I still have. I fell in love for a second time in Conchalí while visiting community buildings that had been used for clandestine human rights committees during the dictatorship. Not much later, I married the father of my son.

At that time human rights were not mentioned in official speeches nor were they something teachers knew about. Frequently the teachers who participated in the training and intervention processes called them "human resources." We faced a lot of resistance in addition to near ignorance of the subject and little awareness of its importance. An argument teachers frequently used to reject training and action for peace and human rights was: "Why should we educate for peace if we are not at war?" Another important issue was the need for better wages for teachers. Once after we gave out the diplomas at the closing ceremony of a workshop, a teacher asked, "Where do we exchange this diploma for a check?"

Twenty years later the *La Laguna* region is still one of the most dangerous places in Mexico. Thousands of people, along with values, peace, and human rights, have been displaced because of the violence. At the moment there does not seem to be much sense in trying to prevent violence or in attempting non-violent solutions for conflicts. When I recall all this, I can't help feeling that we should have done more.

I come back to my memories. Storytellers, innocent brawls, cooking in public places, and many other creative strategies helped us take human rights out of the classrooms and join the teachers in an effort to relate to the community. Whatever useful work we did came from our sense of responsibility to educate those who understood that school was the only option for young people to improve their living conditions and their futures.

Curricula were not my only concern; poverty and violence also left a deep mark on my heart. I can still remember the pain of a student in a high school located in a highly dangerous area, who, after visiting a CERESO[1], said with astonishment and a certain wistfulness, that the living conditions of the prisoners were better than his: "Everyone has a bed, they eat three times a day, and they have work." In his school – now closed by narco-violence – penknives and knives were indispensable when walking up or down the hill to school.

A Round Trip of Human Rights

The evening is gray, and it is raining in the Ajusco (a volcano located outside Mexico City). The shape of my body is strangely reflected in the daily tears the city sheds on my window. I miss the sun and the birds.

In 1993, I left *La Laguna* with my newborn son and moved to Mexico City. Miguel Sarre had invited me to be a part of the Comisión Nacional de Derechos Humanos (National Commission on Human Rights, or CNDH). Since 1992 the Department of Public Education had begun a process of curriculum reform. Citizenship would again be a part of the elementary school curriculum, and because of the importance given the institutionalization of human rights, they would now be explicitly incorporated into the new programs. The CNDH would coordinate their inclusion in the curriculum, and I was given the responsibility for proposing content and suggesting education programs.

For more than two years I faced bureaucratic challenges inside the CNDH that can only be worse in an institution established as a protector of human dignity. How does one create favorable, supportive conditions? How does one strengthen an argument that is losing its meaning because of so many catchphrases? The Zapatista movement shook the country and gave new meaning to the notion of human rights, a meaning very different from the one found in official speeches. At that point, because of the confusion created by daily inconsistencies, I felt the need to look for a new road.

---

[1] CERESO is the Spanish acronym for Centro de Readaptación Social (Center for Social Re-adaptation). It is the Mexican designation for a jail. *(Translator's note)*

I left the CNDH to enter a master's degree program in the Department of Research on Education of the CINVESTAV (Graduate School of the National Polytechnic Institute). Sylvia Schmelkes and Justa Ezpeleta were the tutors that helped me re-enter academic life.

While searching for human rights, I found democracy. My son Jorge, now a first grader who insisted on making his opinions known, taught me how democratic life inside the classroom guarantees human rights. After five long minutes with his hand up, in a class full of restless hands wanting to talk, he took off his shoe and stood up as if wanting to indicate the urgency of his opinion. The teacher listened, heeded, and taught him the difficult art of waiting one's turn without forgetting what one wants to say. This was an essential lesson for democratic life and the practice of freedom of speech, but difficult to understand for a seven-year-old.

Democracy, values, and human rights took me once again to the Secretaría de Educación Pública (Department for Public Education, or SEP) where I was part of a Citizenship and Ethics training team. This work complemented the national vision I first had while working in the CNDH on education, human rights, and the challenges of their implementation. Teacher training and creating teaching materials were the main focus of my new learning process at the SEP. I also managed to understand the institutional logic and came to the conclusion that SEP and I were not compatible. I still liked to watch the horizon and to feel the world spinning, though one can also stand still and observe. Like the clouds, I don't know how to stand still, so I decided to explore the possibility of being an independent consultant.

As an external consultant for the Department for Public Education of the state of Nuevo León, for two years I coordinated a project that aimed at strengthening the teaching skills of supervisors. It was hard work, with great challenges and lots of learning opportunities. Again, I managed with the help and support of Sylvia Schmelkes, who will always be my favorite teacher.

Youth is a shortcoming that disappears with the years. Though I did not think of myself as young in those days, I was young in the eyes of the supervisors who were a part of the initiative. Juan, a teacher and an ethical leader of the group of fifty supervisors and inspectors with whom I began the project, confronted me in the first session. While walking straight at me, he asked, "What can you teach us, if I have taught for more years than you have lived?"

He stopped his heavily built body one step away from me. Since I was much shorter, I was forced to look up to him. I replied, "I am not here to teach you anything. I am here to help you renew your commitment to education."

I faced trials at the Technical Councils of Fomerrey schools and other highly complex places. Soon the supervisors became part of the process to find new strategies for improving the quality of education, to promote the autonomy of schools, and to develop conflict management skills. By the end of the first term, Juan, the teacher, described our achievements in an emotional voice. I still have friends from those times, like Pedro Pablo Villegas, one of those who opposed me but who also was convinced of the value of the process; he became one of the main advocates for change in supervision.

As life traces its journey, it is difficult to fully appreciate every decision. The time I lived in Monterrey signaled a new road in my personal and professional life, for not only did I go through my second divorce and consolidate my work as an independent consultant, but thanks to the help of my colleague and friend Daría Elizondo, I met Ismael Vidales, who showed me the way into the world of textbooks.

New Scenes

Like all "firsts," writing my first book on citizenship and ethics was an unforgettable experience because of the challenge, the new world I got to know, and the difficult but fulfilling work it required. I poured into those textbooks all the issues I had considered for years in my mind, heart, and ethical outlook. I made an effort to create a dialogue with teens, to make it easier to work with teachers, and to promote critical thinking in the face of social and political contradictions. More books would follow, and with them came the opportunity to think more about education in the classroom, even though my own place is probably in a different setting.

In addition to textbook writing, I worked on issues related to students who fall behind, the training of decision makers and counselors, and values education. I undertook this work with the Organización de Estados Iberoamericanos para la Educación, la Ciencia y la Cultura (Ibero-American Organization for Education, Science and Culture, or OEI). While working with OEI, a generous and prestigious institution, I got to know about the state of education in Central America and the Caribbean. I still use Justo (a man's name but also adjective meaning "fair" or "just") as an example of what a good teacher is and as an opportunity to point out good educational practice. Justo ran a center for disenfranchised youth in Puerto Rico, many with legal or addiction problems. Justo told me something that unfortunately is now more than ever true about Latin America: "Here, leaving school before eighteen is almost a death sentence. Many of these kids leave school to die in the streets of San Juan."

The new century was just beginning when Mexico dreamed of being democratic and a First World country. It was then that I became part of the Instituto Federal Electoral (Federal Electoral Institute, or IFE) with the responsibility of designing a program for the education of adult citizens that would reinforce citizenship education in elementary schools. This was how Education for Democracy began in 2003, a curriculum program based on the development of citizenship skills.

In what was an unusual agreement between the IFE and SEP (the Department of Education), I coordinated an inter-institutional group with the idea of turning Education for Democracy into the comprehensive program of citizenship and ethics training for elementary school. It was a complex task and an important learning opportunity for me. I often traveled around the country, debating and planning with teachers about the why, what for, and how to concerning education for values, democracy, and human rights. After a few years, however, I slowly realized that these topics were being replaced by one big concern: violence.

The first time violence interrupted a dialogue on values and citizenship education was in 2005 in Ciudad Juárez. In a comments session after one of many conferences, a teacher asked me, "All this concern about values and democracy is very interesting, but what do we do if our high school students prefer being *mulas*[2] to studying because they get paid five hundred pesos per trip?" This comment generated a string of other questions on the same topic that turned the conversation towards an emerging problem. In the next group of cities – Tepic, Sinaloa, Tampico – the concern was almost the same, though with specific differences, like that of a teacher who asked during a discussion on human rights why teachers could not complain about suffering a human rights violation if a student hits or threatens them.

Violence

I keep silent so as not to remember. I can hear my voice inside me; I do not want to hear it. I keep silent so as to silence the pain.

The professional unease felt by the faculty increased with the lack of discipline within the schools and an increasingly complex social environment that penetrated the school and challenged us. As a teacher form Veracruz once said, "Violence and drug trafficking have changed everything. There are topics we no longer talk about. We cannot establish rules, values, or codes of behavior. We feel threatened and alone."

Social breakdown and the urgent need to help teachers with different resources was even more evident in 2009 when a teacher, also in Ciudad Juárez, said, "All this issue about citizenship and ethics is very interesting, but what do we do when we are losing students because they get paid five hundred pesos for every person they kill?"

Yes, one should be indignant about this. How can I keep on talking about democracy and ignore a teacher who is asking for strategies that will help him guide a student who threatens to kill him? How can one ignore the vulnerability of the educational institutions, of school communities? This reality is impossible to ignore, at least for me. So I turned to the study of the effects of organized crime violence and the possibility of education. I began by exploring the problem, finding out how teachers are able to teach in fear, registering what happens in school communities touched by the crime economy, or the strategies used to attract kids and youths so that they turn into a *punto* (lookout), or a *halcón* (hit man). It hurts to see an armed child in this northern part of the country I feel so close to; it hurts to see the tears of a teacher who watched a student being killed, or the despair of a principal who is afraid of talking because he knows he is being watched. That pain can

---

[2] "*Mulas*" are people who smuggle drugs from one country to another, be it through public transportation or by road. (Translator's note)

only be cured with efficient practices that arise from the particulars of one's community. Some are well known like creating a link within the community, encouraging the participation of students, and creating support nets; other strategies are innovative and even challenging, like establishing alliances with groups who have de facto power.

Today

Dark and deserted streets, the sound of the wind in the tops of trees, and not one soul to be found. Here I am today. I have not abandoned my work in education, in textbooks, or in the planning of programs for citizenship training, but my priority has to do with prevention and risk management. I have received a second death threat. This is how I know this is not a matter to be taken lightly, but I also know one cannot look the other way and act as if it does not exist.

After exploring the problem, I made a record of effective practices and turned to the creation of tools that would help the school community face the challenges imposed by social violence. I formulated Segura, the Guides for School Security for the School Program. I created mini-sites for prevention and risk management in relation to violence, sexuality, and addictive substances for the Citizen Observatory of School Security coordinated by the Facultad Latinoamericana de Ciencias Sociales-México (Latin American Faculty of Social Sciences-Mexico, or FLACSO). I wrote the *School Security Manual* on how to face crises like threats and extortions, response to shootings, the presence of arms, or the threat of explosives in school, among other issues.

These and other issues of school culture related to the problems posed by living together, by the practice of rights and values, can only be faced collectively. So together with other colleagues, we created an academic space for social action called Collective for Education Development, or Albanta. For me Albanta is a luminous sky in constant evolution that allows me to see the horizon. But it is also a safe ground from which we can build, step by step, a road towards a meaningful utopian and humanitarian education based on values. This in a Mexico where, as a girl in the Child and Youth Survey of 2012 said, "Violence will not steal from children their joy of life."

Several years ago my dear and wise friend Dieter Misgeld told me that both in life and work, relationships "are good… or they are not." I follow his advice to the letter and have begun creative, academic, and sociopolitical processes based on a deep respect among colleagues. Their importance lies in helping make this world a better place. One of these processes included my participation in organizing the Child and Youth Survey of 2003 and 2012. Besides being a challenging task, those surveys have been an inspiration for focusing my perspective. Nothing compares with the word of an honest, direct, and concise child who says, "I don't want Mexico to become a drug addict"; who says, "I want leaders to listen and to stop being corrupt" and "I want more schools and teachers who teach, not those who make us dumb." A child's word that translated the most complex moral feeling of a life lesson: "When I think of Mexico, I feel… pain." Together with those girls and boys, I wish for a Mexico that is again a peaceful country, and I hope I will continue to work with teachers in search of a way out of this blind alley.

I have mentioned that I am more fragile than I seem. What can I do? I was awkwardly created. This is why I look in others for what I lack. So my strength lies in the stubbornness that I learned from those that hold on to life, with the certainty that it is possible to emerge stronger from a crisis; from those who have publicly admitted their mistakes and been intelligent enough to begin again; from those that struggle daily against fear, hunger, and ignorance but who do not give up. Love also strengthens me. My partner, Andrés, holds me when I tremble and reminds me that I am still that woman who knows she is small because I fit into his arms, though her spirit might fly to distant heights.

You smell of the winter sun, of a distant cold sea, of the raindrops from the rainbow; you smell of morning coffee, salt in the desert. You smell like always.

I have left many things in my life undone because I lacked the time and energy, like writing a poem or publishing a novel. Many other things I have not wanted to do, and some others I have forgotten with the years, but I hope I will never lose my ability to feel indignation or the freedom of living my life according to my principles and beliefs.

Education for Peace: Signs along the Road

Enver Djuliman (Bosnia, Norway)

> **Enver Djuliman** was born in Mostar, Bosnia and Herzegovina. Since 1996, he has been the head of the Department of Education on Human Rights at the Norwegian Helsinki Committee. Periodically, he teaches at schools and universities in Norway and abroad. He has published several books on human rights and reconciliation in Norwegian, Russian, Bosnian, Serbian, and Croatian. He was awarded the Blanche Majors Reconciliation Prize in 2003.

My original education and professional interests were oriented to the legal sciences. I completed my studies at the Faculty of Law in Sarajevo (Bosnia and Herzegovina) in 1983, and I worked for several years as a young lawyer with the sole aim of becoming an attorney. The tragic part of the history of the Balkans and Yugoslavia, the country where my family and I lived, I accepted as such. I thought that the past was over. However, the wars that happened in my homeland during the nineties of the last century made me realize that the past was not over but was actually continuing. Namely my grandfather lived through two wars, and my father lived through two wars and five years in Communist prisons. My mother also lived through two wars and today is an eighty-year-old refugee in Sweden. I myself also lived through two wars, and my children, at that time, nine and three years old, had already survived one war. We have been refugees/immigrants here in Norway for twenty years already. So the past of my family and my present became one.

Nevertheless, I got through the wars, and now I live in the country that awards the Nobel Prize for Peace. However, I have not been able to leave this last war behind. As will be showed later, that was one of the main reasons I started working on education about human rights, intercultural understanding, and peaceful conflict resolution. In everyone's life there is someone who "pushes our button" at some unpredictable moment and makes us walk on a path "where no one walked before." A twelve-year old girl pushed that button for me by asking: "And why couldn't we prevent the war in ex-Yugoslavia?" And I did not know how to answer her, just as my parents did not know how to answer me. Nothing can change a man like the right question at the right time. I was ready for that question and the moment was right. The meeting with that girl was "a fateful accident" that determined my career, without which I might perhaps have had an easier life.

War and Exile

Although under the Communist regime, Yugoslavia, the country where I was born and lived until I was thirty-three years old, was a happy land. People of different nationalities and religions lived together, practicing their own culture and the culture of "others" as their own. The fall of Communism did not exclude Yugoslavia, where this breakdown was marked by bloody wars in the period between 1991 and 1999. The war in the Federal Republic of Bosnia and Herzegovina (1992-1995), which with the other five republics had constituted Yugoslavia, divided my life between the time before and the time after the war, i.e., the happy life then and this life in exile now. However, I cannot say where in my life the past ends and the present starts nor where the present ends and the future begins. The war brought my life and the life of my family into this "irregular state" in which I now live permanently. Our life in exile required two things from me: to reconcile the losses and the new reality[1] and on the remains of my former identity and competencies to build new ones that would enable me to live a dignified life.

I needed to understand and explain the war experiences and the reality of a refugee and immigrant life. That is how I started to ask myself questions about war, about identity, about culture, and about myself and the "others." Through all those reflections, dilemmas, and answers, there was a red thread: dignity, equality, justice. In other words, human rights. Wherever I was in these reflections, I faced human rights as something that determines and forms reality, but also as something that tells us not only what such reality is, but how it could be. That was the reason in 1996 I chose to study human rights at the Nansen School, the Norwegian Humanistic Academy in Lillehammer.

My fresh war wounds and my life in exile divided my personality. On the one hand, I still had positive relations with people I had lived with before and who had attacked my country, made so much pain, and expelled me into exile. On the other hand, I felt bitterness, anger, and rage towards the same people. I had to do something to understand that and to return human dignity to myself and to these others. I had to reconcile with myself before I could start reconciling with others. The knowledge I had gained during my law studies was not enough. I had to know more about the culture, religion, tradition, stereotypes, prejudices, nationalism, patriotism, "others," about

---

[1] Beside my father I lost eight members of my wider family and many friends in the war, including both those who died after the war and those who survived but in the end took their lives. I lost many important parts of my identity and got a new and lifelong one: a refugee. In my homeland I was a member of the majority, but in this current situation I'm a minority. I lost my social network that I built through the years. All those who were around me, who spoke my language (even an emotional one), who saw me and supported me have disappeared. A new group of people have appeared, and they think and behave differently than I. My language, my competencies, and even my social skills were not valid anymore. I became a reduced person. Because of the war that I was keeping in myself, I felt different from other people. That new reality for me means that I will spend the rest of my life halfway between Bosnia and Herzegovina and Norway, in a no man's land. I'm neither here nor down in Bosnia and Herzegovina. I'm not in either place.

"us and them," and about "acceptance." Thus, in 1997-1998, I undertook the study of intercultural understanding at the University of Oslo. During my previous studies I never had to change myself as I did during these two years. Then for the first time I realized that knowledge, understanding, and even asking questions are not enough: it is necessary to live the positive side of the values we learn about, to practice them in everyday life, and to make them part of our personality (a lifelong process).

At a meeting of young refugees from Bosnia and Herzegovina where I spoke about the war in my former homeland, that young girl asked me the question mentioned above. I realized then that other refugees faced the same challenge as I, and that it was essential to find the answers not only about the past and the present, but also especially about the future where we shall spend the rest of our lives. It was clear that the war had changed us forever. We had to find out how to remember but not to live in the past. We were living one life but looked back to an earlier one, where everything was functioning and where the world and living was more predictable. We knew that forgiving means opening the door to the future and releasing it. We had to go this way, but we did not know how. We had never before gone to a school for war victims or to a school for refugees.

Because of that experience and as part of the Norwegian Helsinki Committee, at the end of 1996 I started a dialogical-educational program intended for refugees from former Yugoslavia.[2] Foremost there was a challenge to build a bridge between the past and the future. This bridge could be called reconciliation: with one's loss, with the past, with the new reality, with a former enemy, with a difficult life, with one's memories, with oneself, and in the end with one's own guilt. At the same time it was a challenge to open the processes that would enable us to re-socialize, to gain self-confidence, to rebuild trust (in ourselves, in others, in the society we had come to), and to rationalize our understanding of reality. The language that led to the wars (Everything begins with a word!) needed to be replaced with a new one that could repair the broken relations between people. That required old concepts to get new content. After a bloody war words such as *truth, justice, guilt, forgiveness,*[3] *acceptance,* and *fellowship* had different meanings than they had had before. We had to use these words to return our dignity. We had to build a language that explains and does not justify, that individualizes instead of categorizing, a language that re-humanizes, a language of relations. This is the language that creates a dialogue between people and not between "adopted words" of religions, cultures, nations, and ideologies. In short a language that would help us to change ourselves.

For such a process we needed knowledge. A different knowledge that:

- would help us to overcome the trauma and to control it, to live with our loss, to build peace and make progress;
- would help us to build new identities;

---

[2] The program lasted for a period from 1996 to 2000 and involved approximately 1000 young people, teachers, and refugees in general.

[3] They say we cannot change the past. By forgiving, in fact we change our past and open the door to the future.

- would tell us why and how we should change our beliefs about ourselves, about others, and about the world;
- would not be experienced as violence against our lives and our realities but instead would liberate us.

In the end, that is knowledge that instead tells us how to remove our inner division between mind and soul (The meaning of *mind* here refers to the values we respect and to our conscience while the meaning of *soul* refers to feelings), where reason says that we should reconcile but the soul refuses. That knowledge combines the political sciences, law, history, economy, anthropology, sociology, and psychology.

At the same time I live through a refugee reality that can be most picturesquely described in this excerpt from the poem *Nightmare* by the Bosnian poet Abdulah Sidran, where the young boy, in response to a question from his mother about the content of his dreams in the aftermath of war, says that he is singing:

> In a voice I haven't got, in a language I haven't got,
> in a house I haven't got, I sing a song, mother.[4]

Children were a special challenge. Not only ours, the Bosnian ones, but refugee children generally. Most of them had a childhood marked with war, hate, and prejudices. They left their country, their homes, their family, friends, and school to begin a new life in a foreign country. The first and most difficult challenge for them was to find/create their identity. Who are they? Who are "the others"? What are their values? What next choices do they have? At the same time the new society sets new, previously unknown challenges before them. On the one hand, they had to learn new social rules about people and relationships that were often in contrast with what they had learned before. On the other hand, they had to relate to their parents, who had difficulty understanding their needs and who wished to keep their parental role and the tradition of their country of origin. So the young people traveled everyday between the two cultures, the country of their origin and Norway. Whatever choices they made were wrong. What choice to make? Something that their tradition, culture, and religion demands from them or something that counts in their new society? Could they choose something else? I thought that the knowledge of human rights, intercultural understanding, and peaceful conflict resolution could help them in reflecting on the relations and challenges of a new life, tradition, culture and religion, and the process of building identity. This knowledge creates a possible choice in difficult situations when society, school, local community, parents, friends, and the others set challenges before them. That is how I started with the program of the Schools of Human Rights for refugees and Norwegian youth.[5]

---

[4] "Nightmare," by the Bosnian poet Abdulah Sidran.
[5] The program, which lasted from 2000 to 2005, was attended by approximately 1000 young Norwegians and immigrants. One of the aims was to integrate them into each other's reality.

Back to Yugoslavia

This new knowledge, the experience of a functioning democracy in Norway, as well as positive educational experiences made me wish to work in both my ex-country but also in other environments where dictatorships or long-term conflicts exist.

From the earlier text one can see that the conflicts in ex-Yugoslavia were trans-generational, transmitted from one generation to the next. Children and youth often inherit the content of the conflict and its unresolved issues. At the same time the educational systems are structured in a way that divides rather than connects them.[6] That is why it was natural to start with youth. That is why I established the program of the School of Human Rights for Youth.[7]

In the Balkans these children now continue their education at universities that are divided by ethnic and ideological differences in the same way the schools are. While they once served Tito and the Communist Party, universities now serve certain ethnic groups and the political elite that stand behind them and to which they are forced to provide a "scientific legitimacy" for their ethno-nationalism. That is how the social sciences (history, literature, philosophy, and sociology) are being "ethnicized," integrating racism, nationalism, and anti-Europeanism itself.

My experiences establishing the study of human rights at Buskerud University College,[8] as well as the need to define the role of the universities in peace building – were the basis for establishment of the program "Build Bridges not Walls" at five universities in Serbia, Kosovo, and Bosnia and Herzegovina.[9]

To Other Conflict Areas

The Norwegian Helsinki Committee, where I am employed, is active in Europe and some parts of Asia. Besides human rights globally, the Helsinki Committee deals thematically with issues of the death penalty, war crimes, and reconciliation. In addition to programs that relate to the monitoring

---

[6] One of the examples is the phenomenon of "two schools under one roof" in Bosnia and Herzegovina. Here Muslim children go to the school in the morning while Catholic children go in the afternoon to the same school without any chance to meet each other. The school curriculum follows these ethnic lines in history, geography, language, literature, etc. That way the schools are used as arenas for "brainwashing" children, teaching "patriotism," and preparing for some new conflict. The children cannot say how it would be if they went together to school because they have been divided since birth.

[7] One school lasts from seven to ten days, and young people of different ethnic background live together and learn about human rights, intercultural understanding, and peaceful conflict resolution. Part of the program are the traveling schools where young people of different nationalities visit the places of suffering and where the witnesses talk about those events. One result is the establishment of youth groups and their projects. Until now around 12,000 young people have passed through this program and thousands of youth projects were implemented. The program was established in 2000 and still goes on.

[8] See www.hibu.no/studietilbud/statsvitenskap/humanrights/.

[9] See www.nhc.no/no/vart_arbeid/prosjekter/Build+Bridges+not+Walls.b7C_wlbM0_.ips.

and promotion of human rights and support the development of democratic processes, in some countries Helsinki Committee has also established educational programs with an aim to support these activities. My jurisdiction was to establish multi-year programs in Northwest Russia (regions of Murmansk, Arkhangelsk, and Kareli); in the North Caucasus (Chechnya, Ingushetia, and North Ossetia: parts of the Russian Federation), 2005- present; in the South Caucasus (Georgia, Azerbaijan, Armenia), 2012- present; in Ukraine, 2005 – 2012; and in Belarus, 2004-present. More than thirty thousand educators,[10] human rights activists, young people, teachers, journalists, persons working in the police force and prisons, and persons with disabilities have passed through these international programs.

I conclude the following observations:

- Education is another name for the activity of building an individual, society, and peace and reconciliation;
- One cannot educate about human rights without educating about intercultural understanding and peaceful conflict resolution at the same time;
- The way one educates is equally important as what one educates about.[11]

Final Reflections

Before all, I would like to clarify that I do not see myself primarily as an educator but – because I have established and developed the above mentioned educational programs – as someone who initiates things and builds arenas for the meeting and discussion between people. The programs in the Balkans and North and South Caucasus emphasize building relations and reconciliation, and that is a part of my engagement, too. For that reason, I would say that to me education is a tool not a goal.

I would say that I work in education because of the books I have read, the movies I have watched, the heroes I have admired, and the people I have met. However, this would be only partially true. Commonly people choose their professions. That is how when I was teenager, I chose to be a lawyer. However, the profession of a human rights educator chose me. In order for this to happen, however, it was necessary that I experience war and exile.

Through education on human rights, intercultural understanding, and work on establishment of relations and reconciliation, I have tried to overcome the war and regain my dignity. I had a feeling of responsibility towards my family, my friends, and myself. Also it was somehow an ethical choice.

---

[10] The educators from all these programs make up the Forum (established in 2009), a professional network that serves to exchange information, knowledge, experiences, and professional materials; it meets every other year.

[11] Education requires a special pedagogical approach, and thus these needs and experiences made me begin writing and publishing books that have been translated into several languages. These writings include: In 2000 *Difficult Reconciliation*, as editor; in 2003 *Introduction to Human Rights*, edited with Gunnar M. Karlsen; and in 2007 *Child, Teacher and School, Selected Texts of Inge Eidsvåg*, edited with Harald Nilsen. In 2007 *Building Bridges Not Walls"*, *100 Methods for Education*, with Lillian Hjorth.

In the first ten to twelve years of this engagement, human rights education was not just an interest but also a direction in my life (sometimes I'm not pleased to say that I'm an educator – but that is a topic for another time). By teaching others I learned myself as well. The knowledge I gained has changed me above all and made me wish to inspire the other people to appreciate and promote these values. Although I still "live" what I do, what I do after all became partially my profession. That is a profession with an aim to contribute to the building of the social resources through education in the countries where I worked, and these resources are the basis for peace, development of the individual, and progress.

In the Helsinki Committee, one of the most respected non-governmental organizations in Europe, I have had the possibility that many educators do not: to teach about all three sides of human rights – legal, ethical, and philosophical; to combine education in human rights, intercultural understanding, and peaceful conflict resolution; to merge theory with practice and real life; to open a place for dialogue; and to connect all that with my own needs.

Finally, come other people without whom I would not be who I am. I will mention here only some of them:

- Lillian Hjorth, my closest longtime collaborator and my sister by faith in what we do and who works today as the Director for Human Rights Academy, Norway;
- Inge Eidsvåg, the Norwegian writer and the educator who introduced me to pedagogy with a humanistic character;
- Sonja Biserko, Branko Todorovic, and Srdjan Dizdarevic from the Helsinki Committees in Serbia and Bosnia and Herzegovina and together with whom even today, twenty years after the war in Yugoslavia, I have lead the battle against nationalism, intolerance, and disregard for human rights;
- Tatjana Reviaka, the courageous fighter for human rights and establishment of democratic processes in Belarus;
- Serhay Burov, my Ukrainian expert;
- Svetlana Ganushkina and Elena Saenkova with whom I collaborate on the programs in the Russian Federation;
- Felisa Tibbitts, the Founder and Senior Advisor of Human Rights Education Associates (HREA), with whom I have collaborated for several years already and who participated in education of my colleagues and educators in the programs I manage;
- Finally, Bjorn Engesland, my boss and my friend through all these years in the Norwegian Helsinki Committee.

In My Own Voice: Stories and Musings to Reflect on Human Rights Education

Mónica Fernández (Argentina)

> **Mónica Fernández** has a bachelor's degree in education, and a diploma in social sciences from Universidad Nacional de Quilmes (Quilmes National University) in Argentina. She also has a master's degree in human rights from Universidad Nacional de La Plata (the National University of La Plata) and a Ph.D. in philosophy from Universidad Nacional de Lanús (the National University of Lanús), both in Argentina. She is a teacher-researcher in the Department of Social Sciences of the Universidad Nacional de Quilmes, where she leads the Ethics of Recognition and Human Rights in Educational Practice Program. She also runs the project Creating Citizenship, Educational and Responsible Networks (CReCER). She is a member of the program Rights for All, A Triple Scheme: Access, Management of Knowledge, and Awareness Practices. She is also the Academic Network Director of the Red Interamericana de Intercambio de Experiencias Educativas para Promover la Educación en Derechos Humanos (Inter-American Network for the Exchange of Educational Experiences to Promote Human Rights Education, or RIIEEEPEDH), which is financed by the Secretary of University Policies of the Ministry of Education of Argentina. She is an advisor to the cabinet of the Undersecretary of Human Rights of the Ministry of Justice and Human Rights of Argentina. She has written numerous opinion articles and academic papers and with other colleagues has organized many national and international conferences and roundtables related to human rights and education.
>
>

By Way of an Introduction

On a typical day early in 2012, I received an invitation from my very dear friend Abraham Magendzo to write my human rights educator story. The request is both provocative and scary. This is because writing about memories laden with the feelings that motivate any teacher is linked to writing about one's philosophy of life. It also has a deep impact on those of us who put into practice educational strategies to create and recreate a culture based on promoting human rights. It is a type of educational motivation that is born out of an ethical and political conviction, profoundly linked to our family history.

Somehow, the main objective of this original proposal is to contribute to the difficult task of teaching and learning about human rights from educational experiences. As a function of the very complex educational theories of the twenty-first century and of new writing techniques, we could argue that personal narrative is like a literary self-portrait. This kind of text or portrait enables one to describe his or her moral inclinations, social competence, artistic sensibility, physical features, professional journeys, ideology, and in a word, his or her story. In that story we can emphasize the features that we consider characteristics of our spirit, of our nature, or of both. The truth is that it is we who face this literary task; specifically, the task is the function of education for human rights.

Even though my history as an educator is brief, the idea of human rights has moved me since I was an adolescent. My educational and political convictions are connected to the experiences of horror caused by state terrorism in Argentina. My life has been marked by the experience of the violation of rights. I have seen how basic rights are violated, even when they are guaranteed by the Constitution.

To go into the field of human rights education, it is first necessary to distinguish it from the teaching of human rights as a juridical discipline. While the former tends to create a culture of respect and promotion of basic rights, the latter is a conceptual, theoretical, or curricular content, and, therefore, any professional with knowledge of the subject can teach it, as is the case with any other subject such as math, history, geography, or semiotics. However, the task of cultural awakening is dubious without the conviction of respect for basic rights. It is necessary to insist on this epistemological, methodological, and ethical-political distinction.

This essay is divided into three parts. The first part of my narrative is completely personal, dealing with a brief history of my family life and my educational experiences. The second part is very different from the first because the narrative focuses on my professional work as a human rights educator. At the end I attempt to open rather than close ways of thinking about educational methodologies that pose problems, that are sentient[1] and critical, with the goal of contributing to this task that we call "the promotion of a culture based on the respect of human rights."

Childhood, Adolescence, and State Terrorism

My school education began at a very early age. At that time few children attended kindergarten, but in my case the school was located near my house. I entered elementary school in 1968. We all had

---

[1] *Sentientes* in Spanish is a concept coined by the Spanish philosopher Xavier Zubiri that poses a link of the same type between intelligence and reality. The conception of intelligence posed by Zubiri should be used in educational tasks. It is used in El Salvador in projects of popular education.

white uniforms. All the boys and girls of the neighborhood attended that school regardless of our social class: the sons of the storeowner, the daughters of the scribe, the sons of the teacher, and the daughters of the dressmaker.[2] Music classes were sublime because during rehearsal we could express our frustrations, as well as love for our family. The reading hours were inspired by a history that branded us and imposed on us "exemplary models" that we were expected to follow without paying any attention to urban realities or stories of everyday life. We were happy and innocent because we did not understand that imposition.

When there was a strike or a work stoppage, everyone stayed at home. We did not really understand why the happiness of the neighborhood seemed to die in those days of general protest. My sister recalls that one particularly cold day when she was walking to school, she became very frightened. She says that she could never erase from her memory that day, when the whole avenue was filled with men dressed in green, similar to the line we made when we crossed the street every day after school, only they carried very big weapons, wore hard hats, and did not let anyone pass through. It was one of those military actions to arrest someone who had protested against the political regime. It was a regime that increasingly crushed the working class, denying them their basic rights. It was a time marked by authoritarianism and by the cancellation of political, social, cultural, civic, and economic participation.

Presidential elections were held in 1973 after yet another military dictatorship, bringing in a new democratic government tasked with the management of the Argentine state. Two years later, on September 11, 1975, my only male cousin lost his life in an explosion that at the time was never clearly explained. He had stopped by to see us the day before the explosion as if he wanted to say goodbye. He shared with me ideas about liberation from sociopolitical oppression that I was not able to understand but to which I listened with great attention because of the great admiration I felt for that seventeen-year-old young kid with the wild curly hair who was about to finish high school. That visit is engraved in my memory. I also remember the horror and crying once I heard the news. He was president of the High School Students Union and a member of the Ejército Revolucionario del Pueblo (Revolutionary Peoples' Army), although I was not completely aware of all this until I was older. The truth is that this event, my rebellious spirit (according to my mother), the social uprisings of later years, and the murders and kidnappings that became part of everyday life were enough to compel my family to send me to a religious school.

On March 24, 1976,[3] the last but most atrocious military coup in the history of Argentina *coup d'état* was carried out against a government elected by the people. I had just begun high school, where I

---

[2] The attribution of gender in this description shows the crude reality of the time. Professions and trades were linked to women and men according to the implicit mandates of society. These tacit educational activities create habits, and that is why we should not lose sight of them. They are the strategies that show the way in which culture is constructed.
[3] In the international context, and as the two international treatises created as part of the Universal Declaration of Human Rights became valid, Latin-American society lived under the terror and cruelty of military dictatorships: Pinochet, Banzer, Stroessner, and Noriega, among others. Most of them were educated at the School of the Americas, which had been established to combat Communism and ensure the fidelity of Latin-American armies to the USA.

had also started a class called "Study of Argentine Social Reality." It is thanks to this class that I had begun to understand my cousin's ideas. That terrific class on social history disappeared from the high school curriculum on that fateful March day in 1976, along with all other forms of political activity, of meetings, of social protests, of ideological criticism, and of elections – all disappeared. More importantly, the forced disappearance of people also started. Yes, people disappeared daily, and no one knew where they were, even though suspicions were clear. My cousin's friends travelled abroad, and some never came back, not precisely because they liked living in a new country, but because state terrorism left them without voice and without a body.

It was the worst, most brutal dictatorship we ever suffered in Argentina. The army, which supposedly existed to make us safe, was the institution that devastated any group of people, even those who took inexpensive buses to get to work. Armed troops came suddenly into any bar, and if it was later than ten PM and you were younger than eighteen, they would arrest you, even if you were with an adult. They came into schools, universities, factories, even your own home, and destroyed everything. They were like a human green tsunami, an army of terror.

The lifestyle of the nineteen seventies was dictated by a group whose actions were the exact opposite of the words they uttered. It was like a double discourse. The implicit message of mass media instructed you on how to buy imported merchandise. At the same time, at school they forced the boys to cut their hair very short and the girls not to wear miniskirts or make up. For all of us the best option was not to get mixed up in politics, not to show solidarity with those who suffered oppression, to keep our mouths shut concerning forced disappearances, and not to ask any questions. The images of the soldier and the police, whom the state had invented but who did not exist, were the models we were supposed to follow. That is why it was crucial not to miss school, not to go out at night, not to congregate on the street, not to forget the document you had to carry. It was critical to "know where one's sons and daughters were"[4] and, above all, to be "right and human."[5] We have to remember that the majority of Argentines because of their silence supported that monstrous plan.[6] How I wanted to erase all that infamy, all that discursive schizophrenia! That scenario marked my adolescent life.

Since for them Communism was a threat to society, any attempt at political liberation, any social protest, or any form of socialism was accused of promoting Communism.

[4] I remember the slogan because it was constantly broadcast on TV: "Do you know where your son is now?"

[5] A phrase coined by members of the Argentine army to welcome a visit from the Inter-American Commission on Human Rights towards the end of the seventies.

[6] I refer to the silence of complicity that arises with terror, which becomes ingrained in ideologies that operated in the political, economic, and cultural domains to generate unseen levels of sociocultural inequality. To go deeper into the subject, I recommend: O'Donnell, G (1984) "Democracia en la Argentina micro y macro," in Oszlak, O. (ed.) *"Proceso", crisis y transformación democrática/1.* Buenos Aires: Biblioteca Política Argentina. Centro Editor de América Latina. The ideas presented in an interview given by Theodor Adorno to German radio in 1966, titled *"La educación después de Auschwitz"* ("Education After Auschwitz") are also relevant. In that interview an epistemic break was shown, which creates a new educational paradigm, according to which the meaning of education is to generate a critical self-reflection that gives particular attention to the abuse of power. (Those of us who have the task of educating teachers should read this text.)

I was able to vote for the first time in October 1983. Things began to change slowly for Argentine society. There were educational conferences, new education laws,[7] and other social and cultural changes.[8] Thanks to the Education Conference of 1986, people began to demand the democratization of education, and with that demand, a fight for the incorporation of human rights into the educational sphere began. By 1994 the Argentinian Congress approved a Constitutional Amendment that placed international human rights treaties on a higher level than local laws. That was how human rights became part of public policy in Argentina,[9] even though they have not been definitively incorporated into formal education.

The current political situation, in which there is an open defense of human rights, is giving us the opportunity to work for the transformation of education. The government supports research, volunteer projects, and university outreach. Some universities now offer human rights classes, master's degree programs in human rights, and programs in human rights education. There is now an Undersecretary for the Promotion of Human Rights, assigned to the Secretary of Human Rights of the Ministry of Justice and Human Rights. Finally, the current education law explicitly makes mention of human rights. In short, there is now a road map for the incorporation of human rights that needs further development.

Within this framework, I will try in the following pages to synthesize the educational ventures in which I participate. I have three objectives. The first is to share a methodological structure (one among the many that exist) that I find appropriate to further human rights education. The second is to comment on the networks of professionals that we established starting in 2006 as part of what we call "Education for Human Rights Colloquiums." The last is to problematize the epistemological distinction between *human rights* and *human rights education*. We should not lose sight of what we aim to do, which is to promote a culture based on respect and the promotion of human rights. This is an educational objective that goes beyond the teaching of a scientific discipline because our very existential perspective is on the table.

Research, Teaching, and University Outreach

My first human rights education project consisted of the recovery of documentary sources in Argentine public universities, such as course programs, forms of political organizations (centers, commissions, institutes, etc.), and research, all of them linked to human rights. The outcome of this search led us to establish general and specific objectives, also related to human rights but now

---

[7] Federal Education Law (1993) and Law of Higher Education (1995). The former was modified in 2006 by the National Education Law. The latter is still valid.

[8] We have to remember that the economic policies of the dictatorship were continued, but the enthusiasm for political changes prevented us from understanding this for a while.

[9] This took place in spite of the economic crisis of 2001, which had terrible consequences for the whole society. After the crisis, a succession of governments took office, but they could not solve the crisis until a new government with a strong popular bent came into power in 2003. The political doctrine of this government is still valid, and one of its main directives is the incorporation of human rights in all spheres of society. For more information, see Klainer y Fernández (2008).

seen from the perspective of educational practice and divided into three complementary axes: the classroom, institutions, and public policies. All this research was informed by the thinking of Paul Ricoeur, in particular the notion of "ethics of recognition."[10]

Based on our results, I selected only those academic programs that explicitly mentioned human rights.[11] The aim was to study the influence that the educational method lends to courses on human rights, both at graduate and undergraduate levels. We adopted for the analysis a hermeneutical perspective,[12] starting from the reading of the curriculum proposals (that is, the course programs)[13] and comparing the programs with international programs about human rights education established by the United Nations. Our main task was to see if the courses and programs for the teaching of human rights were in some way correlated to the educational practices recommended by the international institutions that have as their main task the creation of a human rights culture. It is at this point that we were able to visualize the epistemic differentiation that I have mentioned before between disciplinary fields that attempt to educate and therefore to transform the culture, and the scientific axis derived from international human rights law. This is a research program that demands exploration and problematization.[14] It is a type of specific educational practice that is different from scientific knowledge; Cullen (2004) calls it "practical philosophy," and Freire (1996, 1997) linked it with the notion of "praxis." Both authors emphasize the ethical-political factors more than the disciplinary or curricular aspects of the problem. I would add to these perspectives – since at this point the existential factor plays a specific role alongside the sentient practice characteristic of the human rights educator. It could be said that these are philosophies of life that have existential leanings. It is life itself that becomes the educational experience that is attempted in every classroom exchange.

Nevertheless, theory should not be absent from this study, and that is why there are documentary sources and international institutions that collaborate with education. These are, among others: reports and manuals from the UN High Commissioner for Human Rights, from UNESCO, from the Inter-American Institute of Human Rights, and from Amnesty International. The theory denotes a type of culture that is easy to find in international documents on the protection and promotion of human rights: pacts, conventions, declarations, opinions, committee reports, special rapporteur reports, etc. This is a type of cultural practice that can be glimpsed in the respect and enjoyment of the right to diversity, to identity, to housing, to education, to health, to clothing, to food, to the

---

[10] A phrase coined by Luisa Ripa, Director of the research project Ethics of Recognition and Educational Practice of Human Rights; she is also the director of the University Outreach Program titled The Rights of All. A Triple Scheme: Access, Management of Knowledge, and Recognition Practices. Both are projects of the National University of Quilmes.

[11] Even if this notion was linked to other fields, such as ethics, communication, psychology, education, gender, security, etc.

[12] Technique, art, and philosophy of the qualitative methods or processes that endeavor to interpret, understand, and exteriorize the motives of human action.

[13] Our intention was to analyze the courses and programs to try to understand from their discourse the educational style implicit in each.

[14] I am currently working on my Ph.D. dissertation. Under the philosophical framework I use, I try to problematize this epistemic differentiation while at the same time I try to apply the ontology that Xavier Zubiri describes in his trilogy Inteligencia sentiente to the methodological structure of human rights education.

protection of infancy, adolescence, and youth, to the promotion of women rights, to free election of representatives, to a healthy and diverse environment, to not be mistreated, and to move around freely in the world, among many other rights. These are rights, of course, but with every right we must recall there is a corresponding duty. This, without a doubt, makes us face needs and attitudes that we must clarify through our experiences, our memories, our anxieties, and our feelings.

With the objective of studying the epistemological and methodological factors of human rights education, I began to make a comparative chart. The chart had the following variables: class time, proposed content, whether it was obligatory, major in which it is offered, educational techniques proposed, international documents used, required readings, additional content, type of evaluation instrument, and the goals of the class. With this chart I analyzed graduate and undergraduate courses and made several educational indicator charts. The next step was to compare the teaching proposals, educational techniques, contents, and bibliographies recommended by regional and international organizations for the promotion and protection of human rights.[15]

One of the problems with the teaching of rights is that its theoretical corpus is presented in normative documents of enormous complexity. Since the point of human rights education strategies is the promotion of basic rights, the educational objective is linked with the inversion of its cognitive access.[16] In other words, instead of directly consulting international laws, we suggest that it is important to start with the problems of social injustice that we find in everyday life and work and to study the complex juridical documents later. We attempt to raise awareness about justice and oppression and the importance of being kind and respectful towards others. This element does not appear in international documents, but those who wrote them had to face the most terrible atrocities ever committed by human beings. That is why human rights education demands we consider feelings and emotions. Only then should one proceed to the international documents that came out of these social struggles.

After classifying educational techniques,[17] we developed a methodological proposal that is comprised of three levels (Fernández 2009):[18]

---

[15] I included in the project informal interviews with teachers who, even if they sometimes had not written the course proposals, were able to furnish data on the implied educational objectives. In my dissertation this became Chapter IV, titled "Field of Work."

[16] I gave the title of "Methodological Dimension" to Chapter II, in which I provide a summary of educational techniques used to teach and learn human rights.

[17] The classification of educational techniques was useful in the design of the methodological program developed for the training workshops CReCER (*Creando Redes Ciudadanas, Educativas y Responsables*). Designed by Mónica Fernández, Rosana Góngora, and Néstor Manchini, these workshops have been a very successful experience in human rights education training for teachers. After this training participants design workshops that they apply in high schools. Each session finishes with an artistic exhibition of works in the main University Square that is visited by the educational community that composes the CReCER network. The exhibit is useful as a way to evaluate the process of dissemination. An important member of the human rights community, such as Estela Carlotto, Hugo Cañón, Carlos Cullen, and Marita Perceval, also gives a talk. Through these workshops we can speak about human rights to six hundred people per year. This experience helped produce the Outreach University Program called: "Rights of All."

[18] This material includes the methodological structure for human rights education that I want to compare to the notion of "sentient intelligence" coined by Xavier Zubiri and that gave rise to the ontology of this Spanish philosopher.

- **Problematization/Awareness Level:** debates concerning everyday problems, from an image, a story, a video, conferences, journal articles, games, dramatizations, the lyrics of a song, a case study (hypothetical or real), etc.
- **Theoretical/Normative Level:** an increasingly theoretical study of human rights (e.g., their history, their instruments and mechanisms of protection and promotion at the international, national, or local level, their axiological issues, their challenges, etc.).
- **Active/Multiplier Level:** responsibility, solidarity, and commitment to diversity. Becoming active through debate, analysis, and reflection. One could say that this level functions as a dialectical movement between the other levels and that this movement initiates the cycle of the third level. This is because it tries to engender reflection or considered action. It is usually called practical philosophy.

As a result of my search for documentary sources to frame fieldwork, I established a path of the short history of human rights education.[19] It includes those international records that document the concerns and recommendations that moved experts from the UN and non-governmental organizations to promote the creation of programs (national, regional, and international) to start action on human rights education. Those programs began around 1974, usually promoted by UNESCO. This task made it possible to contextualize the basic principles that involve the teaching and learning process of human rights.[20]

As a function of the technological contribution of the aforementioned work, and in addition to the compiling of recommendations of international organizations for the teaching and learning of human rights, the analysis of the course programs allowed us to understand how university teachers used those methodological recommendations to elaborate their own course programs. This educational coincidence is related to the cognitive difficulty that defines the theory of international human rights law in terms of human rights education. The complexity that characterizes the teaching of human rights as culture, as a creative source of social values, is what mobilized the international community of educators to design diverse educational strategies. The systematization of those educational experiences is the result of consultations with diverse educators around the world and from the compilation of educational practices recovered mainly from popular sectors and from theories of meaningful learning. In other words, the educational recommendations of the World Programme for Human Rights Education derive from the systematization of educational experiences that had been successful in other environments. They are experiences that cannot be absent when it comes to human rights education.

---

[19] I refer to the official history, because the informal history has been developing for a long time, since popular sectors began to demand social justice from the authorities.

[20] I titled this chapter "Normative Dimension" because the international meetings to debate human rights education were also promoted in international meetings and conferences on human rights.

A Closing that Opens Up New Paths

Life experiences have marked many defenders and promoters of human rights. Those of us who live in the complex world of the twenty-first century try to remember those loved ones who have lost their lives in the cruel fight for basic human rights. Our mandate and the motor that propels us to keep fighting for the incorporation of human rights education into the curriculum has the familiar imprint that pushes us to insist on the channels of recognition and on the presence of memory, truth, and justice. We have transformed ourselves, thanks to the familiar and social impressions made by educators for human rights. Some of us can apply the doctrine to the field of formal education because we work in that field. Others participate in different spheres of society, transferring their life experiences to the informal educational field. The truth is that all of us share a common objective: to build citizenship under the framework of respect for and promotion of human rights.

In the framework of a cultural creation of respect and existence of human rights, systematic educational experiences are fundamental educational elements in promoting successful teaching and learning strategies. The skills necessary for the promotion of education for human rights are more cultural than curricular. There is a clear epistemological difference between teaching human rights and promoting human rights education. The former is linked to theoretical transfer. The latter tries to develop cultural habits. The strategies of cultural transformation need an ethical and political commitment with constant criticism and reflection. That is why we call them practical philosophy. We can add to this a moral demand, the need to avoid corporatism and to share this knowledge with all the community. That is how the networks of education for human rights educators, in which educational experiences are always shared, actually function. In this text I have attempted to explore the mutual collaboration between the community and academia, among colleagues, and the constant mutual enrichment that comes from that collaboration. These roads crisscross constantly, opening empirical and theoretical doors and reflecting on both. This is a type of knowledge that is usually called practical philosophy; it is praxis. This is also educational work that is reinforced and amplified with the participation of society in this endeavor. It is not any specific "type" of education but an education based on the defense, promotion, and presence of human rights in the world. The objective is the creation of a culture of respect for otherness, so that atrocities committed by human beings against other human beings are not repeated and so that each person can live with dignity. This is what we Argentines try to remember each March 24th through three concepts: Memory, Truth, and Justice.

BIBLIOGRAPHY

Cullen, Carlos (2004). *Filosofía, cultura y racionalidad crítica*. Buenos Aires: La Crujía Ediciones y Editorial Stella.

Fernández, Mónica (2009). *La educación en derechos humanos en la universidad: método pedagógico y práctica docente en cursos de grado y posgrado*. Tesis de Maestría dirigida por Ana María Rodino. La Plata, Argentina: Facultad de Ciencias Jurídicas y Sociales, Universidad Nacional de La Plata.

Fernández, Mónica (2011). "Experiencias y desafíos en torno a Educación y Derechos Humanos: progresión en internacionalización y en compromiso común." En: *Actas de las XV Jornadas de Pensamiento Filosófico. La primera década del siglo XXI. Balance y Perspectivas.* Montevideo, 13 y 14 de junio, ISBN 978-950-9262-55-3.

Freire, Paulo (1996). *La educación como práctica de la libertad.* México: Siglo XXI Editores.

Freire, Paulo (1997). *Pedagogía de la autonomía. Saberes necesarios para la práctica educativa.* México: Siglo XXI Editores.

Klainer y Fernández (2008). "La educación en derechos humanos en la Argentina: ideas-fuerza de los años ochenta a la actualidad." En: Abraham Magendzo *Pensamiento e ideas-fuerza de la educación en derechos humanos en Iberoamérica.* Santiago de Chile: UNESCO, OEI, SM Ediciones, páginas 33 a 74.

O'Donnell, G. (1984). "Democracia en la Argentina micro y macro." En: *"Proceso", crisis y transformación democrática*/1. Oscar Oszlak, Compilador. Buenos Aires: Biblioteca Política Argentina. Centro Editor de América Latina.

Zubiri, Javier (1980). *Inteligencia Sentiente. Inteligencia y Realidad.* Madrid: Alianza Editorial/Fundación Xavier Zubiri.

Zubiri, Javier (1982). *Inteligencia Sentiente. Inteligencia y Logos.* Madrid: Alianza Editorial/Fundación Xavier Zubiri.

Zubiri, Javier (1983). *Inteligencia Sentiente. Inteligencia y Razón.* Madrid: Alianza Editorial y Fundación Xavier Zubiri.

Zubiri, X. (1999). *Primeros escritos (1921-1926),* Alianza y Fundación Xavier Zubiri, Madrid.

The Road Less Traveled: Odyssey of a Human Rights Educator
William R. Fernekes (USA)

William R. Fernekes taught social studies and Spanish and served as supervisor of social studies at Hunterdon Central Regional High School in Flemington, NJ, until his retirement in December 2010. He received his doctorate in social studies education and curriculum from Rutgers University in 1985. He has published widely in the fields of Holocaust and genocide studies, human rights education, and social studies, including Children's Rights: A Reference Handbook (with Beverly C. Edmonds. ABC-CLIO: 1996) and The Oryx Holocaust Sourcebook (Greenwood Press, 2002). In 2011 he received the Mel Miller Award from the National Social Studies Supervisors Association as the outstanding social studies supervisor in the USA. He is a founding member of Human Rights Educators USA and currently teaches at the Rutgers Graduate School of Education.

When I entered public school teaching in 1974 following my graduation from Rutgers-New Brunswick, human rights was not even a blip on my professional radar screen. More important was securing a job — after sending out over one hundred cover letters and resumes, I was offered three interviews and one position. Luckily, I accepted the position of social studies teacher at Hunterdon Central Regional High School in Flemington, NJ, where I worked for thirty-six and a half years as a classroom teacher and department supervisor. I was fortunate to work in a school district that supported professional growth, encouraged innovation and creativity, and provided the necessary resources to develop programs that challenged students and adults to seriously examine human rights as core elements of an issues-centered social studies program.

My undergraduate education occurred from 1970-1974, which comprised one segment of a period of tremendous social upheaval in the United States. With the benefit of hindsight, it is clear that the professors I encountered and the books I read, along with the activist climate that existed on the Rutgers campus, planted seeds that would later develop into a career-long commitment to helping young people examine controversy and social issues in their pre-collegiate education. Attending a teach-in at the Rutgers gymnasium about the bombing of Cambodia, as well as reading the vigorous debates about US policy in Vietnam and Southeast Asia raised my consciousness about the impact of government policy on the lives of innocent civilians, something that I had not considered important growing up in a quite conservative New Jersey suburban household. Sam Baily, who taught courses in Latin American history and who was the advisor for my master's degree, challenged my assumptions about social revolution and opened my eyes to the enormous – and often very negative – influences of the United States in Latin America. During my senior year, the elected Allende government in Chile was overthrown by a coup that was supported by the United States, and I had the unique experience of being taught by the expatriate former Chilean ambassador to the United Nations and poet, Humberto Diaz Casanueva, who chose not to return to Chile after the Pinochet coup (He eventually returned to Chile in 1983). With the Watergate conspiracy unraveling and the eventual resignation of President Nixon, abuses of human rights were front-page news, but I was still relatively naïve about how widespread the daily violations of human rights were around the globe.

As I became more knowledgeable about historic and contemporary human rights issues during my master's degree program, I made a more concerted effort to engage these topics in my daily teaching. In addition to my increasing engagement with professional social studies organizations, I started my doctoral program in social studies education at Rutgers, where I became a student of Jack Nelson, a major figure in the field who not only advocated issues centered approaches, but who also set an example for his students as a committed activist-scholar. Jack's influence on my thinking about rationales for social studies education and how scholars can and should serve as committed public intellectuals has been enormous. His work on academic freedom spanned both publications and support for individuals whose jobs were threatened, while his commitment to open debate and the consideration of ideas from across the ideological spectrum demonstrated that one could be an effective teacher while advocating policies and practices that could improve the quality of life for people in all walks of life and across all boundaries. It was inspiring to learn from someone who not only encouraged the critical examination of social experience, but whose scholarship was inseparable from the broader struggle for social justice.

My interests in social justice intensified as I conducted research for my doctoral dissertation, which examined non-traditional curriculum theories and their relationships to the study of United States history in American secondary schools. In particular, my research into the works of Paolo Freire, Michael Apple, Henry Giroux, and the Frankfurt School's critical theorists such as Herbert Marcuse and Jurgen Habermas sharpened my perspective on how schooling too often reflected patterns of domination by powerful interest groups who had little or no interest in social studies programs focusing on the critical examination of issues related to social justice. In contrast, many textbook publishers, state curriculum designers, and professional organizations were content to sustain mainstream narratives of history that omitted any serious consideration of human rights concerns and emphasized the "banking" concept of education so effectively critiqued by Freire in *Pedagogy of the Oppressed*.[1] In this context, I now felt better equipped intellectually to engage my students with

---

[1] Paolo Freire, *Pedagogy of the Oppressed*. New York: Continuum Books, 1993. Reprint of the original edition on the 20th anniversary of its publication with a new preface by the author.

issues that would help to "counter-socialize" them (in Shirley Engle and Anna Ochoa's words) and help them develop the knowledge, skills, and attitudes to become active, engaged citizens.[2]

The vehicle for doing so became study of the Holocaust, which in New Jersey was given impetus by the policies of a committed Governor, Thomas Kean, and the creation of a state Commission on Holocaust Education. As I became more knowledgeable about the history of the Holocaust and its contemporary implications, my teaching about the Holocaust and genocides emerged as a prominent aspect of not only my work with students, but also my professional activities, such as workshop presentations, seminars, and publications. I gradually came to the realization, albeit a sad one, that (1) many educators lacked a strong command of the history of the Holocaust and (2) few had given serious consideration to how average human beings had been willing to engage in the destruction of human rights which was a central focus of the Nazi regime. For me it wasn't sufficient to include a unit on the Holocaust in a US History class and view it solely as an historical episode — rather, study of the Holocaust was an opportunity to raise fundamental questions about human behavior, challenge stereotypes and patterns of prejudice that were central to the development of genocides, and examine how the struggle to support human rights was an ongoing challenge in the contemporary world. The more I worked on how to integrate study of the Holocaust and genocides into the required social studies curriculum, the more I recognized that my students lacked a coherent intellectual framework to make sense of those historical cases, as well as how they related to my students' lives. Meeting this challenge opened doors for me to the serious study of international human rights, which I saw then, and continue to see today, as a critical conceptual framework for understanding the struggle for social justice in the United States and around the globe.

A key event in my developing understanding of human rights and its central focus in the social studies was the publication in September 1985 of a theme issue on human rights of *Social Education*, the most important professional journal in the USA for social studies educators. Edited by Samuel Totten, the issue contained a highly stimulating set of articles and resources, one of which quickly caught my attention – an article on how to initiate a campus chapter of Amnesty International (AI). With a small group of interested students, we created a high school Amnesty chapter at Hunterdon Central in 1986, and I'm proud to say that the chapter has remained active for more than twenty-six years. The chapter's student members were dedicated "activists in formation," and we soon established a reputation for consciousness raising about human rights through the use of letter writing projects, poetry readings, benefit concerts, guest speaker presentations, and a host of other programs in the school and community. The energy and commitment of the students was inspiring to me, while the students learned how hard it was to develop and carry out projects in an environment where the understanding of international human rights issues was quite limited, and in some instances hostile. Bringing former prisoners of conscience to the school as guest speakers and providing fellow faculty with resources about human rights issues and how to engage students in social action was very rewarding, and gradually the climate of the school became more accepting of our work.

---

[2] Shirley Engle and Anna Ochoa, *Education for Democratic Citizenship*. New York: Teachers College Press, 1988.

In August 1987, I was chosen as the new supervisor of social studies, succeeding the person who had hired me. The timing of my appointment coincided with the approval in the late 1980s of a required third year of social studies in New Jersey's public high schools, which was mandated to focus on world history/cultures. In consultation with department faculty, we developed a thematic design for the new course as well as a three-year integrated curriculum framework that positioned human rights as a central component of not just the new course in world history and cultures, but as a core theme in US History. Informed by Willard Kniep's scope and sequence design for a global social studies curriculum,[3] our new eleventh grade course, entitled Comparative World Studies, incorporated units on tradition and change in the modern world, global security, international human rights, and the global environmental challenge. With modifications that were instituted as the school moved from a traditional eight-period day to a four-by-four block schedule with eighty-four-minute instructional periods, this course remained in place from 1990 to 2011. During these two decades, between 400 and 750 students annually learned human rights concepts and norms, investigated case studies dealing with rights in conflict and the international responses to human rights violations, examined the purposes and functions of the United Nations human rights system, and developed social action strategies to raise consciousness about human rights issues in the USA and worldwide. Additionally, the critical roles of NGOs regarding human rights were a central component of the course, and the school's Amnesty International chapter served a vital role in supporting the development of these social participation projects. Faculty teaching the course enthusiastically embraced its issues-centered approach, and a number of them became presenters at social studies conferences in the USA, in addition to working closely with our Amnesty chapter students to implement in-house programs on human rights issues.

In the late 1980s, I was invited by the Amnesty International office in New York City to participate in the newly formed Human Rights Education Steering Committee of Amnesty International USA (AIUSA). Traveling to its first meeting in Chicago at the AI Midwest Regional office, I had no idea how this initiative would develop, but it is clear to me now this was a critical turning point for my development as a human rights educator. My own ideas about what constituted human rights education would be informed and refined through the stimulating dialogues and activities of this wonderful group, which included Nancy Flowers (then teaching at the Castilleja School in Palo Alto, CA), David Shiman of the University of Vermont, Cosette Thompson of the AI San Francisco Office, Ellen Moore of the AI Urgent Action Network, and many other committed educators from around the USA. We quickly recognized the scale of the challenges facing us in trying to raise the profile and improve the delivery of human rights education in the USA, not only because of the historical ambivalence towards the full range of human rights guarantees in US society, but because effectively we were the "only game in town" that was making such an effort. It also became clear that K-12 educators who embraced human rights education as a priority for their daily practice were a small but dedicated group, so the development of a support network was clearly needed.

From the beginning, we recognized that any effort like this would require a long-term commitment of support from AIUSA and possibly other organizations, and for a time we were able to make progress in

---

[3] Willard M. Kniep, "Social Studies within a Global Education." *Social Education* Vol.53, No. 2, October 1989, 399-403.

curriculum development, delivery of workshops and programs to educators, and establishing connections to professional organizations and other resource networks. But by the end of the 1990s, the formal "steering committee" had dissolved and other groups had taken up the slack – notably resource centers at the University of Minnesota and elsewhere, while AIUSA's focus on K-12 education diminished.

Through my work with the AI Educators Steering Committee, I came into contact with Beverly Edmonds of Berkeley, CA, who became a dear friend and colleague. One of the lasting impacts of the AIUSA initiative in human rights education was its positive reception by the National Council for the Social Studies, which supported the inclusion of workshop sessions and major speakers at national conferences on human rights, as well as publications on human rights issues. In 1992, Beverly and I co-edited a special theme issue of *Social Education* on the rights of children, and this was the impetus for ABC-CLIO publishers to invite us to co-author *Children's Rights: A Reference Handbook* in 1995.[4] This project was another key step in my personal development as a human rights educator since it opened my eyes to the daunting challenges which children face every day in having their human rights guaranteed. It further reinforced my conviction that the United States was far behind in the field of human rights education – not only because the USA refused to even consider Senate ratification of the UN Convention on the Rights of the Child, but also because of the impressive efforts being made around the world to improve the rights of children and educate them about the full range of human rights embodied in the Convention.

With the election of George W. Bush in 2000 and the development of administration policies that emphasized American exceptionalism and disdain for international cooperation through the United Nations (for example, the "unsigning" by the Bush administration of the treaty establishing the International Criminal Court in the mid-1990s), it was obvious that any movement forward on human rights education would have to occur at the state and local level. Ironically, the period from 1990 to 2010 saw the emergence of the "standards" movement in US education, and by 2007 over thirty-five states had some inclusion of human rights content and themes in their state social studies standards. Simultaneously with the development of both voluntary national standards documents and state educational standards that mandated what should be taught and learned by students in public schools, a parallel development occurred which has helped to raise the profile of human rights education in the USA: the inclusion of required content for study of the Holocaust and genocides in selected states and the creation and rapid development of the United States Holocaust Memorial Museum into a significant national educational institution.[5]

At the invitation of William S. Parsons, then a consultant to the emerging Holocaust Museum education department and since the mid-1990s the Museum Chief of Staff, I served on a team of

---

[4] See William R. Fernekes and Beverly C. Edmonds, guest co-editors, theme issue on "The Rights of Children" *Social Education*, Vol. 56, No. 4, April/May 1992; Beverly C. Edmonds; William R. Fernekes, "Children's Rights in the Social Studies Curriculum: A Critical Imperative," *Social Education*, Vol. 56, No. 4, April/May 1992, pp. 203-204; and William R. Fernekes and Beverly C. Edmonds, *Children's Rights: A Reference Handbook*. (Santa Barbara CA: ABC-CLIO Press, 1996).

[5] Dennis N. Banks, "Promises to Keep: Results of the National Survey of Human Rights Education 2000," updated November, 2007. Accessed from www.hrusa.org/education/PromisestoKeep.htm October, 2012.

experienced educators who advised the Museum's educational programs. This was a transformative experience as I was afforded the opportunity to pursue my interests in both Holocaust/genocide studies and human rights while helping raise awareness about the Museum's programs and activities in the United States and overseas. My own research and writing became more focused on examining the historical and contemporary intersections between Holocaust history and the struggle for human rights in the twentieth century. I have been gratified that over the past twenty years the Museum's own programs and activities have displayed a much greater emphasis on genocide prevention and issues of human rights.[6] Additionally, as we developed new courses at Hunterdon Central dealing with study of the Holocaust and other twentieth century genocides, students responded positively to these opportunities, and the courses have been consistently enrolled for many years.

At the close of the first decade of the twenty-first century, my wife and I made the decision that it was time for me to bring closure to my work as a school administrator and begin a new chapter in our lives. Thus, I retired from my position as supervisor of social studies at Hunterdon Central Regional High School at the end of December 2010 and began working as a part-time college professor, first at Rider University in Lawrenceville, NJ, and now at the Rutgers Graduate School of Education, where I had completed my doctoral studies.

Simultaneous with my shift from working in K-12 education to university teacher training, and based on my publications and the professional affiliations I had sustained over the years, I was invited by Nancy Flowers and Felisa Tibbitts of Human Rights Education Associates to participate in the newly formed Human Rights Educators USA consortium, which is dedicated to making human rights education a top priority in US schools and educational settings. Among those gathering at Harvard in September 2010 to organize the consortium and move it forward were long-time friends in the field, including Nancy Flowers, David Shiman, and Kristi Rudelius-Palmer of the University of Minnesota, and other leaders in human rights education drawn from around the USA. Based on our work so far, I am quite optimistic that this consortium will make a substantial, long-term contribution to the development of human rights education in the USA, and I'm doing my part by integrating human rights education content and concepts into my teaching of pre-service social studies educators at Rutgers. In the spring of 2013, I began teaching a new course on "Human Rights and Education" at Rutgers, a very positive development and one that has brought me back to where my journey began in 1970. Although it's true that "you can't go home again," I'm continuing to make a contribution to advancing understanding of human rights through the schools, and, by influencing teacher education, I hope to plant seeds that will be nurtured for many years to come. So, my journey continues, and I'm excited to see what the future holds.

---

[6] See William R. Fernekes and David A. Shiman, "The Holocaust, Human Rights and Democratic Citizenship Education," *The Social Studies*, Vol. 90, No 2, March/April 1999, 53-62; William R. Fernekes, "Education for Social Responsibility: The Holocaust, Human Rights and Classroom Practice." In F. C. DeCoste and Bernard Schwartz, editors, *The Holocaust's Ghost: Writings on Art, Politics, Law and Education*. Edmonton (University of Alberta Press, 2000), 496-512; and William R. Fernekes and Samuel Totten, "Human Rights, Genocide and Social Responsibility." In Samuel Totten, editor, *Teaching About Genocide: Issues, Approaches and Resources* (Greenwich CT: Information Age Publishing, 2004), 249-274.

The Integrative Power of Human Rights Education

Nancy Flowers (USA)

Nancy Flowers has worked to develop Amnesty International's education program and is a founding member of Human Rights Educators USA, a national human rights education network. As a consultant, she has helped establish international networks of educators, develop materials, and train activists and educators in many countries. She is the author and editor of articles and books on human rights education including Acting for Indigenous Rights: Theatre to Change the World (Minnesota, 2013); Local Action/Global Change: A Handbook on Women's Human Rights (Paradigm Press, 2008); and Compasito, a Manual on Human Rights Education for Children (Council of Europe, 2007).

The first time I heard the words *human rights education*, I had to ask, "What is it?" Some thirty years later I am still learning what human rights education can mean in the lives of societies and of individuals, including my own. I now appreciate how becoming a human rights educator has served to unite disparate aspects of my life into a coherent whole, not only the professional and political, but also the intellectual and spiritual. From this perspective I can also recognize how seemingly unrelated experiences prepared me for this work.

Recognizing Injustice, Without and Within

I was born in rural Mississippi, a place as starkly racist as South Africa under apartheid. Sunflower County was 80% Black, 20% White, with such strict segregation that even my poor country town had two of everything – schools, churches, toilets, drinking fountains – though those for the Black majority were always inferior and inadequate. Only very small children escaped this social chasm: until we started school, we could play together freely – at least out of doors.

The summer I was five, I was playing "house" with two other little girls, Sylvia, who was Jewish, and Deena, the daughter of Sylvia's Black nanny. After we made our playhouse in a hedge, we had to decide our make-believe roles. Sylvia claimed mommy, the most-desired part. "Okay," I said, "I'll be the daddy, and Deena, you can be the maid." Deena stopped still, crossed her arms, and said, "I ain't gonna be nobody's maid. Ever!" It was a searing epiphany. Why had I automatically assumed that she would be the maid? Why were white people the bosses and black people the servants? It wasn't fair. Although only a kindergartener, from this moment I was no longer able to accept the world without question. Everyone I loved endorsed this system. Could they be flawed as well? It was a true loss of innocence.

I wish I could report that Deena went on to leadership in the Civil Rights Movement, but in fact, I never saw her again after that summer. In September our worlds parted forever when we entered first grade in segregated schools. Shortly thereafter I moved away to an entirely different community and never thought again of Deena until many years later as I began to confront my own unconscious racism.

That painful personal process of bringing into awareness and owning my own biases has made me recognize a most difficult and yet essential challenge of human rights education. Rage and revulsion against the torturers, the tyrants, and the bigots come easily but do nothing either to transform them or to foster reconciliation. Instead, it reinforces a false dichotomy between evil doers as a despised "Other" and ourselves as the self-righteous "good guys." How do we cultivate the courage and generosity to stand up to injustice but still acknowledge the humanity of its perpetrators, as well as our own potential to hatred and evil? How do we distinguish between accountability and vengeance? How do we instill self-reflection and moral imagination in a society, a community, or even an individual?

Assuming Responsibility

When the Korean War broke out in 1950, my father was recalled to the army and we began the nomadic life typical of military families. As a result, I grew up without a true hometown but exposed to many different cultures and values. The lessons were multiple, but one stands out starkly.

In the early 1950s we lived in "occupied" Germany, still physically and emotionally devastated by World War II. When I was thirteen my father took me to see Dachau. Although later transformed into a museum, this former death camp was then off limits to the public, a bare place with its barbed wire, barracks, and ovens still intact. He said, "I want you to see this place and understand that it's not about bad things that Germans did. It's about bad things that all human beings can do. Even in our own country."

I protested that this could never happen in America. "No," he insisted, "just think about the way we treat colored people in Mississippi. This could happen anywhere unless people stand up for what is right."

This early lesson has come to shape many decisions in my life. I am convinced that one essential goal of Human Rights Education (HRE) is the understanding that "injustice anywhere is a threat to justice everywhere."[1] HRE must empower individuals to believe they can make a difference, to

---

[1] Martin Luther King, Jr., "Letter from a Birmingham Jail."

accept the responsibility to do so, and to have the knowledge and skill to act with both effectiveness and integrity.

Preparing for Informed Action

A third formative experience came when I was an undergraduate at the University of Georgia. Although I considered myself an atheist, I had joined a small study group organized by Hardin "Corky" King, the Presbyterian chaplain. We met weekly to read and discuss contemporary theology. Dietrich Bonhoeffer's *The Cost of Discipleship* impressed me deeply with the challenge to live one's beliefs.

Suddenly the Civil Rights movement made that challenge concrete. When the University admitted the first African-American students in 1962, riots broke out. Encouraged by racist groups like the Ku Klux Klan, mobs stoned the students' residences; armed federal soldiers were sent in; the university closed. This was no time for passive liberalism; one was either for or against racial segregation.

I claim no heroics in this crisis, but it dramatically taught me that it takes more than courage to take a stand. I experienced firsthand the importance of having examined principles to guide action and the power of non-violent leadership like that Hardin King provided. If people are to defend human rights, they need to have understood and integrated those rights into their own lives. Facilitating this process toward informed action has become a primary goal of all my work as a human rights educator.

Relearning Learning

After university I became a teacher, and like most teachers, I began by trying to replicate my own educational experiences. Inevitably I reproduced the traditional classroom in which I had grown up. However, in mid-career I was jolted out of complacency by the National SEED Project (Seeking Educational Equity and Diversity). The vision of the project founder, Peggy McIntosh, led me to a new understanding of inclusiveness, active learning, the role of the teacher, and even the purposes of education.

I saw for the first time how the existing educational system failed so many, especially ethnic minorities, the poor, and women and girls. By the time I was introduced to human rights education some years later, I had already radically altered the goals of my teaching and developed new skills and perspectives much more suited to human rights learning. I had learned to be a genuine collaborator in learning and to value my students' questions and experience as much as my own presumed "right answers."

At this time I also began to write textbooks and develop curriculum that reflected this new conception of learning, as well as a collaborative approach to creating new resources.

Finding an Ethical Framework

In the Deep South of the 1940s my parents were considered liberals, both politically and religiously. They were serious, ecumenical Christians and life-long Democrats (I was nearly named *Eleanor* for Eleanor Roosevelt!). They truly lived the Biblical moral that "Everyone to whom much was given, of him much will be required."[2] Although their sincere example established life-long values for me, I was unable to share their Christian faith or find any other established religion that spoke to my spiritual needs. However, the better I understood human rights, the more I found in them another, more inclusive ethical framework that could unite people of many different beliefs or no beliefs at all. Human rights are no substitute religion, but they offer principles that honor the dignity of humanity and address basic human needs. They can provide a moral compass not only to guide the individual conscience, but also to guide the state and to relationships among states.

Because they are not divine ordinances demanding obedience but an evolving human construct, human rights require intellectual engagement and continual questioning and reassessment. One of the most compelling aspects of human rights education has been the inherent invitation to engage people in analysis and debate, to apply their intellect, emotions, and experience to some of the most profound problems of our human life. It requires continual engagement in fundamental questions about what it means to be human and what is essential to justice and human dignity. And in this pursuit I have genuinely been not the teacher but the co-learner.

Late in life I have found in the meditative discipline and ethical tenets of Buddhism a practice that not only complements but also enhances my work as a human rights educator. Especially the Buddhist emphasis on compassion and non-violence in word or action has had a profound influence on my understanding of genuine peace building.

Acknowledging Good Fortune

One of the great good fortunes of my life has been finding in human rights education what the Buddhists call "right work," which integrates my intellect and my heart, my highest aspirations and my deepest commitments. And for all people this unifying power of human rights creates a common language that expresses our shared humanity and at the same time honors our differences.

As I enter my eighth decade I am increasingly aware that accidents of birth, geography, and history shape our lives more than do our individual talents and efforts. Certainly we make choices, but the range of choices open to any one of us is very much a matter of fortune. One aspiration of human rights is to improve the fortunes of the whole human race, enabling everyone to achieve the promise of the Universal Declaration of Human Rights: "the full development of the human personality." Human rights education is essential to make that aspiration a reality.

---

[2] Luke 12:48.

Closing the Gap of Dignity

Shulamith Koenig (Israel, USA)

>
> **Shulamith Koenig**, founding President of People's Movement for Human Rights Learning (PDHRE), is a recipient of the 2003 United Nations Human Rights award. In 2011, she also received a Gold Medal from Mikhail Gorbachev, former president of the Soviet Union, as "Woman of the 21st Century." For the last twenty-five years, she has developed international public policy and facilitated worldwide actions for learning human rights as a way of life across communities. She has been working as a facilitator to evoke critical thinking and systemic analysis with a gender perspective about political, civil, economic, social, and cultural concerns within a holistic human rights framework that leads to action. To develop viable models of learning and acting, she is facilitating the development of human rights cities around the world.

My life is the evolution of purpose and often-uncontrolled commitment to join in transforming the world. Isaiah is my prophet, Martin Buber is my teacher, Eleanor Roosevelt is my hero, and Nelson Mandela is my idol; and the thousands of people I met in the last twenty-five years in more than sixty countries are my true guides, not to mention my family and friends and those who have joined me, caused, and supported my evolution throughout my life. As was said more than 1500 years ago with great insight by Rabbi Ben Zoma, who was quoted in the biblical *Chapters of the Fathers*[1]: "Who is the wise person? The one who learns from everyone?" As was stated: from all my students I have gained wisdom.

In this book that calls on pulling together the aggregate of insights, knowledge, and praxis gained during the many years of commitment and dedication of human rights educators, I appeal to you, the reader, to contemplate and take action to close the gap of dignity, to add a missing link to your efforts now and in the future. I believe it to be an imperative to: (a) introduce throughout the world an ongoing process of learning human rights as a way of life; (b) integrate such "learning" throughout all sectors of civil society; and (c) offer it as a "new," re-imagined, and re-crafted guiding worldview. Human rights education (HRE) does not reach 95% of humanity, the women, men,

---

[1] Pirkei Avos. *Ethics of the Fathers* (Artscroll Mesorah Series). New York: Matsudah Publications, 1984.

youth, and children – those who need to know and own human rights to meaningfully transform their lives. I hope that my humble contributions in the coming pages will inspire some of you to make a promise to reach those left behind in your current HRE efforts. It is urgent that all of us join in a world movement of MENTORS, to encourage and facilitate such learning in every community around the globe. Let us not "educate" or "inform" anyone, but with the people in their communities design ways and means that will secure a process whereby all people, wherever and whoever they are, will learn, know, and own human rights, discovering how it is relevant to their daily lives, to the future of their families, communities, and humanity as a whole. Simply, I believe that people should empower themselves by making their choices drawn from the knowledge stored in the comprehensive human rights framework as a way of life. We, all of us, need to hold in our hands a tool to construct a powerful strategy for economic, societal, and human development. We can do it! I have been trying for all my life through the many endeavors I chose to engage with about which I was asked to write.

In our fast-moving, tumultuous lives, much of it imposed on us with the many guided today by social networking, we can search and find moments of unexpected transcendence that can liberate and inspire new ideas – the gift of real, meaningful hope that leads to action. Capturing these magical moments – as I always try – can move us to re-envision our lives as one vibrant link in the chain of humanity's expectations for dignity, equality, and life void of all forms of discrimination. Such a journey is one of social responsibility reinforced through integration of the learning of human rights that leads to action. As the learners join in the eradication of poverty and liberate themselves from violence, a "new political culture based on human rights" starts emerging, as called for by Nelson Mandela, where the learners chart and own their future guided by the holistic vision and practical mission of human rights as a way of life.

Such an extraordinary moment in time took place in 1948 when Eleanor Roosevelt, joined by men and women from more than eighty countries, gave the world the Universal Declaration of Human Rights (UDHR), a "gift" meant to remove the chains of colonialism and to *never again* have humanity experience genocide. The UDHR delivers a holistic worldview, a space to belong in dignity in community with the "other," as said by Franklin D. Roosevelt: "Freedom from fear and freedom from want." Yet it is very sad! Most of the people around the worlds know little about it.

Every year on the tenth of December and every day, we must continue to ask: How does the meaning of human rights add to our daily lives and to the lives of people in our community? Can human rights become the guiding light for crafting a better world by all for all? And if so, why are there so few of us who know the meaning of human rights as a way of life? What can we do about it? This has been my search for the last twenty-five years.

We must note that transcendence did not end with the event of the UDHR. It gave the United Nations its overarching purpose and foundation that forcefully radiated the vision for economic and social justice. It was translated by UN member states into human rights' norms and standards that are relevant to the lives of all women and men, youth and children in all places of all cultures and religions. They are articulated in the two Covenants on political, civil, economic, social, and cultural human rights and in the conventions on the elimination of racism, the human rights of women and of children, and recently of Indigenous Peoples, people with disabilities, and soon of migrants, the elderly, and more to come. This is an overarching powerful framework that more than 150 of the 192 UN Members have ratified – the other forty-two have ratified a few. Ratification means synchronizing the laws of the specific state with the very specific human rights norms and standards. Again: very few people in each of the 192 countries know them to request that indeed these covenants and conventions – even with the reservations – become the law of the land and furthermore, be able to claim them. So please do tell, what are most human rights educators doing about the here and now, for forceful community action?? This is not blame – this is just a call to bring about soul-searching, for change to close the gap of dignity.

Case in point: Bangladesh, a Muslim country, upon ratification of the Convention on the Elimination of All Forms of Discrimination Against Women (CEDAW) made five reservations out of the sixteen articles; these five articles were considered by religious leaders to contradict Muslim laws. A movement of women in the cities and around the countryside introduced discussions and learnings that examined the meaning of CEDAW to the lives of women in Bangladesh, analyzing the consequences of these reservations to their lives. As a result of ongoing learning, reflecting, and lobbying through the democratic political system, women were successful in having their government eliminate three reservations. The pressure by and for women is still mounting to eliminate the other two. Women are demanding to be treated as full human beings!

We all know but always must remember that these carefully developed human rights instruments attempt, at least officially, to move humanity from the oppression of vertical and hierarchical institutions to newly constructed horizontal spaces where all people can move freely, able to make horizontal, creative choices in and for their lives. Where all people with new insight can walk, without or with partners of their choice, towards the horizon that they have selected. Many know this intuitively, yet so few know about human rights as a way to be with one another or how to integrate them into their lives. I made it my task with those who joined our organization to move this sense of decency from intuition to putting in the hands of people the power of human rights.

It is painful and a wonder to me why many working to change the world do not use this powerful tool for action. Is it because many international human rights organizations and human rights educators focus mostly on violations and do not bring a comprehensive message to all of us who yearn to realize our hopes and expectations imbedded in the rich, invigorating, and fully comprehensive human rights agenda? (Indeed, patriarchy and economic colonialism are alive and thriving. Genocide did not vanish, as we never stop to evoke historic memory.) There is much to be cynical about, including a process of learning human rights as a way of life where immediate "outcomes" cannot be recorded. This, fortunately, does not prevent me from being a fanatic. On the contrary! I continue to flag the imperative of introducing and facilitating, in as many places as we can reach, a never-ending, on-going process for all to learn and know human rights as a vital and viable inevitability for people's lives.

As I continue to ponder, I know that such efforts must go beyond time-bound pedagogy, lesson plans, and methodologies applied in the form of "education" and "information." We need to engage the communities in a dialogue about the meaning of human rights in their past, present, and future. Have them get in touch with an inspiring worldview for which we have no other option. For example, in Argentina during an intensive, very lively discussion with police cadets conducted by Susana Chiarotti, one of the cadets stood up and spoke about his human rights being violated; then the chief of police, who came to observe the "happenings," interrupted the cadet and ordered him to sit down. The cadet turned around, faced the chief and said: "I have learned here that we all have human rights to express ourselves freely. I will therefore not sit down before I finish my complaint." After the session, Susana believed that she would never be allowed to hold another session with the police. When she returned to her office, a call came from the chief of police. "Please," he said, "find time to hold such learning sessions with the entire police force in the region." Visiting Rosario, I was told by the director of the police academy, "We have no other option but human rights," which has become my mantra ever since.

In our work we find it so gratifying and often amazing how people develop systemic analysis when introduced to the holistic human rights agenda, holding in it the many details that can step-by-step transform their lives. People spontaneously decipher between cause and effect as they hold honest, often brave, discussions between women and men about patriarchy as a major cause that underlies human rights violations. Thereof, critical thinking flourishes – setting the way for sustained realization of human rights. (I recall, with much delight, the young man from a small village near the City of Kai, the first Human Rights City in Mali. He introduced himself as the oldest son of the local religious leader. Amidst the second week of discussions on the meaning of human rights as a way of life, he called me out of the room to let me know in secret that as a result of thinking about what he has learned, he told his father that his mind was made up to marry only one woman. It was his personal conclusion. We had in no way spoken of polygamy or even hinted at it. To me it was a wonderful gift for hard work!)

The French philosopher Levinas wrote:[2] "If one person was missing from the world, the absolute truth would be different." Allow me to look up with humility at tall trees such as Levinas and say: "If one person was missing from the world, human rights would be different." Human rights are the living TRUTH that all must know. It is ever evolving. It is ever discovering and redefining our being in the world in equality and without discrimination. We each bring with us the moment of transcendence and uniqueness-of-being for which human rights was created. We must learn to act with human rights as a living organism, indivisible, interconnected, and interrelated. And ALL the people must know them! The discovery of human rights as a way of life through learning and dialogue at the community level brings moments of transcendence, moments of trust that carry in them respect and acceptance of others as full human beings.

---

[2] Emmanuel Levinas. *Nine Talmudic Readings*, trans. Annette Aronowicz. (Bloomington, Indiana: University Press, 1990.), xvi.

Young people around the world are taking to the streets and squares, challenging the status quo as young people have always done. The significant difference today is the genuine fear about limited opportunities to a generation that will be worse off than their parents. Governments and NGOs decades ago designed systems to deal with post- Second World War generations. Today these are ill equipped to address the needs of seven billion people, with more than 45% being under twenty-five years old. Allow me to repeat: *It is obvious that we need to re-learn, re-imagine, and re-craft a new vision that can meet the needs of today towards a better tomorrow.* The human rights framework, the learning in communities that human rights stands to contribute to restructuring our lives, will unfold a new thinking of who we are in the world with others and hopefully act upon it. This is where our energies are called for.

In many countries the university campus, always a hot spot for protest and a base for generational change, is the ideal place to organize corps of faculty and students that will together investigate how to introduce a new way of viewing the world, learning and integrating human rights as an integral part of daily life. Thus the work undertaken by human rights educators, the Office of the High Commissioner of Human Rights, and UNESCO, must not be conceived and designed as "training" and/or time-bound studies, but as an integrated process of ongoing learning in every academic discipline. By introducing into their immediate communities ongoing learning and dialogue, the university as a whole can become a pioneer in bringing forth a new vision of the UDHR. This needs to be coupled with a well-designed cultural, religious strategic plan to ensure that within a given community every woman, man, youth, and child will know, claim, and be able to act upon human rights as an integral part of their daily life, enriching their cultures and religions with a new way to embrace their future. The question is how to develop a participatory appraisal tool that helps people express their concerns and simultaneously makes them aware that they are linked to a global initiative/movement. How do we stand to motivate them to see that their concerns and lives are linked to others around the corner and around the globe? The idea is that everyone living on earth needs to know their human rights in order to claim their rightful place in the "household of humanity."

I ask myself day in and day out: How do we achieve this most ambitious and necessary undertaking? Where do we begin the learning about human rights? In the words of Eleanor Roosevelt, we have an answer. She said: "Where after all do universal human rights begin? In small places, closes to home – so close and so small that they cannot be seen on any map of the world. Yet, they are the world of the individual person: The neighborhood he/she lives in; the school or college he/she attends; the factory, farm or office where he/she works."[3]

Human rights visionaries around the world have echoed these words in their call for men and women, youth and children to know, own, and claim their human rights. These women and men have understood human rights learning (HRL) as a transformative process, one that awakens

---

[3] Eleanor Roosevelt, "In Our Hands," (Speech delivered at the UN on the 10th anniversary of the UDHR, March 27, 1958).

the consciousness to a new perspective, a different way of viewing the world, and charts their future. Eleanor Roosevelt refers to the transformation from within, thus allowing people to see the relevance of human rights in their daily lives. This new perception is then carried out into the greater world where the "I" becomes the "WE" and the "WE" becomes "HUMANITY."

I was asked to tell the story about my life that led me to making this commitment. So I will, with the hope that young people searching to make this a better world for all may find some parallels that will lead them to become "mentors." First allow me to describe what I mean when I speak of a mentor: It is a person, a woman or a man, who is capable of evoking critical thinking and systemic analysis about civil, cultural, economic, political, and social concerns with a gender perspective within a human rights framework that leads to action. It is a woman or a man who believes that all people have a deep sense of justice, dignity, and thus of human rights. It is a woman or a man who believes that "human rights" is a universal worldview that transcends cultural and religious disagreements to render culture and religion a space in which we can live together. And, most importantly, it is a member of the community who does not teach but with the people creates an ongoing process of people interrogating the meaning of human rights to their lives, to know, own, and be guided by them.

My personal story and some varied narratives that, at the young age of eighty-two, keep me going to leave a legacy so that in five to ten years, all people learn and act upon human rights as a way of life that is moral, political, and protected by law. Using the short version of the UDHR to start the mentoring, design and develop insights that lead to belonging in community in dignity with others.

I do not know what specific qualities make one a ceaseless human rights mentor. One who believes and acts with the conviction that there is no other option but for all to know and be guided by human rights as a way of life? Well, having called myself a fanatic who repeats mantras, the keystone events throughout my life might explain my actions for the past twenty-five years.

At the age of two, I was told that my name, *Shulamith*, means a woman from Jerusalem, a woman of peace. (Later, I learned, it's a name from the *Song of Songs of King Solomon*, a woman from "Yeru-Shalem" – and people will see fulfillment.) At the age of six, while complaining to my parents about the teacher who said that the Jews are the "Chosen People" and not my Arab friends, I was told, "Yes you are, chosen for social responsibility." At seven, I was writing poetry and teaching children of European refugees to read and write Hebrew. (At that age, I also remember a print of the *Praying Hands* by Dürer hanging above my bed.) By the age of nine, I thought of myself as a child of the Holocaust; the Italians were bombing Tel Aviv, and broken-up families of refugees from Europe were invited to live in our home. Then at fourteen, I joined the Underground; and at the age of sixteen, I instructed fifteen-year-olds how to be secret messengers against the British in the streets of Tel Aviv. In 1948, I joined the Israeli Army, and in 1949, as an officer and the women's commander of Jerusalem area, I resigned my post in protest of having orthodox girls relieved from service in the army for no cause but merely because of being religious. (This was the beginning of the tragic manifestation that we see today of perpetrating injustice by religious groups in the illegal settlements, apartheid, and the uprooting of hundreds of people and thousands of old olive trees – an important historic symbol in the West Bank.)

At the age of twenty, I came to the USA to become an engineer, hoping in the future to be able to chart a different journey for Israel, new Jews in our new country. As I was learning about the Salem Witch Trials in my introductory classes to the English language, I was meeting groups at Columbia University who called for a world government. At that time to make a living and to try to effect change, I gave speeches about "Integration and Discrimination in Israel" and "Sex and Femininity in the Israeli Army." The Israeli Embassy did not like it, but I did not stop. I got married and had a son, divorced, remarried, and had two more sons. Back in Israel I joined Shulamith Aloni, the leader of the civil liberty movement and "Kol Koreh": a voice calling from the desert! I assisted in developing the Alfred Adler Institute in Tel Aviv, where I have learned from the students of Adler much of what defines my commitments to human rights learning. I worked with Arabs and Jews, learning together the meaning of civil rights to our combined lives. I established "Peace Now" in our home in Tel Aviv, manufacturing water-saving products in a factory in Jerusalem with Jerry, my wonderful husband, where we employed Arab women who came to work with chaperones. I joined and organized the first Israeli-Palestinian dialogue in Washington, D.C. I was called a traitor in Israel for saying in a television interview that I will not have my sons fight unjust wars. It was a never-ending search for justice. After seeing Israeli's enlightened future falling apart around us and losing our sense of humor, realizing with great pain that we could not contribute any longer to stopping the endless vicious cycle of humiliation in the West Bank, we left Israel and came back to New York with the hope that we could find some ways to make some difference.

In retrospect these pivotal experiences generated my fanaticism and my commitment. Now I stand only to quote the following by Thomas Isidore Noël Sankara (December 21, 1949 – October 15, 1987): "It took the madmen/women of yesterday for us to act with extreme clarity today. You cannot achieve a fundamental change without a certain amount of madness."[4] I share this quote of "madness" to give you the reason why I have dedicated my life to try to move the world to learn human rights as a way of life. Today, I reach out to young people to take over this legacy.

As we settled in the USA, I wrote several articles questioning whether Israel could be both democratic and Jewish, while calling and demonstrating to put a stop to house demolitions and land grabbing in the West Bank. On a spring day during a drive with my family along the Hudson River, we discussed the meaning of the only modern option we knew: democracy! A spark was ignited: "What if all people in the world knew human rights as a way of life? Wouldn't democracy become the fulfillment of a holistic vision and mission that will create a new journey for humanity?" "Yes!" the family agreed! Thereafter, for many days my husband and three sons encouraged me to use the energy I was endowed with and call for an international effort of human rights education. (To add

---

[4] From 1985 interview with Swiss Journalist Jean-Philippe Rapp, translated from *Sankara: Un nouveau pouvoir africain* by Jean Ziegler. Lausanne, Switzerland: Editions Pierre-Marcel Favre, 1986. Used with permission in Sankara, Thomas. *Thomas Sankara Speaks: The Burkina Faso Revolution 1983-87.* trans. Samantha Anderson. New York: Pathfinder, 1988. 141-144.

to the story: the source of energy that drives me, as I was told, is as follows: I was born in Jerusalem on a Friday night, as the Sabbath entered the city of the prophets, during the longest day of the year, June 20, 1930.). Thus, PDHRE – People Decade for Human Rights Education – was born, now the People's Movement for Human Rights Learning.

The twenty-five-year voyage started at the Center for Human Rights at the UN where I learned from a wise woman, Elsa Stamatopoulou, the meaning of human rights. In her office I discovered the many details of the Covenants, which are guided by a moral authority, derived from the covenant Abraham made to observe the sanctity of life, and Conventions, which are guided by political, civil, economic, social, and cultural concerns. Having been a socialist, I was taken aback by the obvious lack of understanding and very little effort being undertaken in the field to advance economic, social, and cultural human rights. In 1990, with a grant from the Norwegian Development Corporation, PDHRE laid out a plan to reach thirty countries around the world to introduce civil society groups and organizations to the Covenant on Economic, Social and Cultural Rights. From the outset I personally chose not to work with human rights organizations that centered at the time only on political and civil issues and looked at human rights as mostly a legal paradigm. I made this decision after having met Amnesty International leaders in London, along with other human rights organizations, and those few who at the time worked as human rights educators. Recognizing that there is an absolute need for the Covenant to be introduced to and known by an array of civil society organizations in every country in the world, I took another road. We looked for groups whose community work centered on issues such as labor, women, education, religion, health, housing, etc. – identifying twenty-three such issues (See www.pdhre.org/justice.html "Call For Justice," where human rights commitments and obligation to each of twenty-three issues and groups are detailed.) With the small amount of support sent to a development organization identified in each of thirty countries, we advised that they convene a two-to-three-day retreat with local leaders working on these issues. They were instructed to identify five main overarching concerns in their community. Each of these five organizations was invited to write one page detailing their profile and the story that described their specific concerns and provide analysis, including the hopes and expectations for change. These five pages were given to a local human rights expert who was asked to prepare the first day's learning and discussions why these are indeed human rights issues. The second and third days were designated to echo the first day, where participants learned to connect their specific issues to human rights.

It was in Nairobi, Kenya at such a workshop that something happened that has guided PDHRE's work ever since. There was a Kenyan development worker who devised a way to stop the burning of wood to cook food in the market place: she exchanged the wood for solar lenses – even now it is very progressive. When she heard about our initiative, she offered to hold such a meeting in Nairobi, but was told by the authorities that the meeting could not be held in the city. So she moved it to take place out of the city. As participants arrived at the meeting space, they noticed and tried to ignore, a policeman who was already sitting in the back of the room. As the morning proceedings progressed and the expert very carefully wove the meaning of economic and social human rights as relevant to the five issues presented to him, the policeman rose suddenly to his feet and called out with excitement, "Stop it! Stop It!" All looked around, worried (These were bad days in Nairobi). The expert asked, "What have we done?" The policeman smiled and said softly, "If this is human rights, come and teach it in my village."

This single statement became a major milestone that sets our commitment to this very day. With many colleagues around the world, we never stop promoting and facilitating the integration of an ongoing process in the villages for all to learn, know, and own human rights in a new viable way to achieve sustainable change. At PDHRE we continue to answer this policeman's request in every region around the world. We continue to facilitate learning with local community leaders to have them become mentors of human rights for people to internalize them as a way of life and to carry with pride the vision of Eleanor Roosevelt.

In Israel I was a member of a committee created by our Prime Minister at the time, Izak Rabin, to implement in Israel the Decade of Women, which, as we know, gave tremendous impetus and thrust forward to the issues of women and equality around the world. Telling my friend and colleague Robert Kesten about my decision to work at having all people know human rights and own them as their own, he suggested, "Why don't you work with people at the UN to declare a Decade for Human Rights Education?" Indeed, I did.

In 1993 in Vienna, I approached single handedly (forgive again the lack of humility) sixty UN missions, convincing them of the need to declare the UN Decade of Human Rights Education, which thereafter was called for in the Vienna Declaration on Human Rights. Then through the end of 1994 we worked feverishly with the support of civil society groups in Asia and others to put through a General Assembly Third Committee Resolution that set international public policy on human rights education. (This was also a follow-up to the UNESCO 1990 event, organized at the time by Stephen Marks, who later with other members of our board offered Member States the language of the Resolution that set forth the essence and creativity for the Decade.) It was my "fault" calling it *education* rather than *learning*. I did not realize what we stood to lose. In my bad translation from Hebrew to English, we lost the meaning of the word *learning*, which allowed the narrowing of the vision and mission of the Decade. The word *education* in many ways was a "trap," since it engaged in this effort mostly teachers, experts, and students to teach and study human rights, mostly in schools and academic institutions. Indeed, it also reached local authorities and law enforcement agencies and informal education (Don't misunderstand me, this is very, very important!! but hardly enough). Education of human rights uncovered human rights as a legal paradigm, mostly as a set of "norms and standards" in the relationships between the people and their governments; even though in a very precise language, the resolution named many civil society development groups and organizations, calling on them to engage and integrate HRE in their work. Alas, it did not happen as we envisioned. The objectives and goals of the Decade were misunderstood, and HRE is still locked in chains as is manifested in the recent Human Rights Council's Declaration on Human Rights Education and Training.

In the first four years of the Decade we organized several meetings with top leaders from around the world and were also active with the group that created Human Rights Education Associates. However, we were still not answering the call of Eleanor Roosevelt or the policeman from Nairobi.

In 1997, we facilitated with Susana Chiarotti (who complained that I dream and she has to work hard) the development in Rosario, Argentina, the first Human Rights City in the world. Staying true to our vision and mission, Susana invited 120 representatives of groups from around the city, called to sign a declaration of the city's becoming a human rights city. In the audience were representatives of the Toba people –100,000 Indigenous People in a city of one million, those who were isolated and marginalized in the city. At her insistence, they joined in the formation of a steering committee that planed the various campaigns. These were designed to introduce learnings throughout the neighborhoods for the purpose of engaging inhabitants in the planning and future development in the city – at one point quotations from the UDHR were printed on every bus ticket in the city.

Here, to further answer the request of Abraham Magendzo to contribute narratives about the "learning process," allow me to share a story from the human rights city Rosario. The Civil Society Ad Hoc Steering Committee in Rosario, after learning in depth about human rights, had developed campaigns for members of the community to learn about the meaning of human rights to their lives. In this process they asked the various neighborhoods to report on violations and realization of human rights as identified by them. These guided to mapping the human rights in the city, which led to the development of alternative budgets presented to the city. At one of the Committee's weekly meetings a group of Toba women told their painful story: When giving birth and crying out loud in pain, they were humiliated by nurses and doctors who told them: "Shut Up!" and "Stop having sex if you cannot stand the pain of giving birth." These women, having learned that human rights celebrate dignity and respect, told the committee, "Our human rights are being violated." The committee, many of whom were familiar with the Theater of the Oppressed, decided to call for a meeting at the public theater, inviting all the nurses and doctors who were free that evening. Many came as requested by the director of the city's hospital who said, "After all, this is a human rights city." On the stage several members of the community role-played in "The Scene in the Delivery Room." A hush fell in the theater during the performance. Toba women sitting in the front row covered their faces in the memory of pain and insult. As the curtains closed, the chief of the hospital walked over to the representatives of the Toba women and apologized loudly, saying earnestly, "Anyone, nurses or doctors, who continues to behave the way we just saw on this stage, will be instantly fired!" Within a few weeks, Susana introduced the learning of human rights at the medical school, which is now a required course throughout the medical school. Human rights learning as preventive medicine!

We have documented this and other very exciting innovations from around the world in a book called: *Human Rights Cities: Civic Engagement for Societal Development* (See www.pdhre.org/Human_Rights_Cities_Book.pdf).

Almost in every region around the world, as we facilitated this process, we kept hearing: "Come and teach it in my village" and "There is no other option but human rights." It is because of what we learned that we moved to speaking of *learning* rather than *education*; we realized it is an ongoing, necessary process to be integrated into the work of every segment of society, including local authorities and the private sector. Human rights learning leads people to participate as equals, women and men alike, in the decision that determines their societal destiny.

In 2008, alongside the sixtieth anniversary of the UDHR, the "Elders" led by Nelson Mandela, sent out a clarion call proclaiming: "Every HUMAN has RIGHTS." Recalling Voltaire, who was asked "What should we do about human rights?" – to which he answered, "Let the people know them." – and having facilitated the learning and integration of human rights as a way of life in more than sixty countries for twenty-one years at the time of the Elders' call, I sent them a note saying, "But do the "humans" know them? Most do not!" It is therefore imperative to add to the Elders' call, and be loud and clear: *And every human must learn, know them, and own them as a way of life!* It is essential that all people be guided in their day-to-day life by the knowledge they still need to gain, enabling women and men to work towards meaningful, sustainable economic and social transformation. We have no other option!

Having been in hundreds of communities around the world, facilitating dialogue and introducing a process of learning about human rights as a way of life, I choose not to engage in the discourse about diversity and/or intercultural dialogue, neither about peace, not to speak of not calling our work human rights education, which it is not!! I believe that such discussions distract us from holding the necessary and essential conversations that can lead to the planning of meaningful ways and means to facilitate the learning of human rights as a way of life throughout the world. Such efforts, when implemented, will evoke a sense of ownership of human rights instead, put in the hands of the learner a powerful tool for positive action, enriching people's ability to live with and within diverse cultures in trust and respect of the humanity of the other. This is not a mere dream. As people pursue equal participation in the political decision-making process, in the decision that determine their lives, women and men alike, they join in weaving a new foundation of equality for all and the elimination all forms of discrimination. Basically, as already said, this is what human rights is all about.

The awareness of communities that all human rights concerns and effective movement towards the realization of human rights – be it political, civil, economic, social, and cultural – are indivisible, interconnected, and interrelated, with a gender perspective, have people accept how we are all different from one another; yet yearn to belong in community in dignity with others. Any place in the world, we each have different and diverse cultural affiliations and inclinations and several personal identities, yet we all belong to the same humanity bound by the vision and mission of human rights as a way of life. We may all have different interpretations of belonging and how we relate to subjective historic memories that frame our pride and uniqueness within our families, villages, towns, and cities, not to mention religious and national identities, yet, all must be bound and guided by the fully comprehensive human rights framework. We can all overcome these diversities and break through the vicious cycle of humiliation by assuring that every community in the world designs and adopts an ongoing learning process where the humanity of the other is at the center of such learning, to join in closing the vicious cycle of humiliation where people exchange their equality for survival. The litany of human rights education, to which this book is devoted and with all good intentions, does not go fully this way. To have people discover that they have full ownership, that they are the bearers of these inalienable "commandments," and that they must cautiously appraise what it means to their lives.

To move from theory to practice, it was quite evident to us when school children in Thies, Senegal, a community of 250,000 inhabitants being developed as a Human Rights City, learned that "education is human rights," interconnected and interrelated to other concerns in their lives. They innocently asked: "If education is a human right, why do some of our next-door neighbors not go to school? Why are their human rights being denied? Who is denying their human rights?" They were told that the parents of these children did not register them at birth. Students between the ages of twelve and sixteen teamed up spontaneously. In three years, going from door to door, they registered 4,312 children. Simultaneously, they lobbied with the authorities to expand the capacity of their schools and add more teachers. (It is important to note that this success story encouraged UNICEF further to do the same around Africa where fifty million children are not registered. As said: learn, know, own, plan, and act!) When the efforts of registration was completed, the teams, who were energized by their accomplishment to bring human rights to their community, called on the neighborhoods to collect the garbage off the streets and move it to empty lots; they asked the mayor to create a garbage collection service as a human right to protect the city's health. Visiting Theis, I met the mayor and shared with him my mantra "There is no other option but human rights." He called in his assistants and ordered them to write it on the wall above his desk.

In the village of Malikunda, Senegal, as a result of ongoing conversations about the meaning of human rights, men and women declared an end to female gentile cutting. At the celebration of this unique community decision, a brave old woman, who did many of the cuttings, stood on the stage declaring that she will never cut girls again as she was lamenting the past. The first girl in the village that was not cut was named by her mother "Sen Sen" or "human rights." Learning human rights as relevant to the lives of children in Thies or to the future of the women and men of Malikunda, and now throughout Africa, handed them a powerful tool to overcome oppressions of all kinds, enriching their lives to *never again* – as already reiterated – barter their equality for mere survival.

In an introduction of the learning process in several communities, I recently launched a discussion about human rights as a HOME. When you are a child, "home" is the place where you feel safe "out of the rain," protected from the burning sun, and loved. As you grow older, home can be the memory of a lullaby, the stories you were told or overheard, the clothes you wear, the earth you till, a book you read, the yearning for dignity, including the good or painful memories that instruct our daily lives. In short, the world we live in and wish to be able to claim our own. People learning about equal, horizontal choices of decency, acceptance, trust, and respect are so well-articulated in the holistic human rights framework. As we translate its meaning to our lives, we learn to walk towards a new horizon, to restore or build new homes, internalizing the human rights language as a path of freedom in our HOME.

The word *home* holds a whole universe of meanings. Basically it is a "space" where people can be free from fear and free from want and often a refuge from persecution. It is a "place," a mindset, an insight to wisdom, paving the road for walking securely with the human rights language for our hopes to become a reality and sometimes even transcendence. Many of us hold onto painful histories, often current memories of being "evicted" and violated and/or evicting our enemies from their homes to secure ours: this is a path to mistaken freedom. Human rights offer a home where the dignity of all people is being celebrated, the ultimate habitat of and for humanity, where no one human right can violate another – as in Article 30 of the UDHR.

This may be seen as Utopia in a world – a home – that in sixty years, from 1950 to 2010, grew from two billion people to seven billion, all needing a home of their own. This is also a world where "social networking" undermines value systems, spreads contradictory definitions about decency and trust, and leads many aimlessly in many different directions where they feel anguish but don't know how to relieve it.

These often conflicting observations lead us to follow Nelson Mandela and ask all to join in weaving a political movement that will carve a new future for humanity. In a Dalit village sharing with women that "food, education, health, housing, and work at livable wages are inalienable human rights," they clapped their hands, danced, and repeated these five human rights imperatives as a mantra. When I asked with humor, "Why are you dancing?" They answered: "We thought the government is being nice to give it to us from time to time. Now we understand the meaning of human rights! It is ours to have!"

It encompasses it all: Such a dance needs to be danced in every village.

The development of a "political culture" is an ever-evolving phenomenon of being in community with others – of belonging; of defining the other as being fully human; of choosing or having been born into a specific culture and/or religion; and most importantly, of creating human rights political movements. The price of bread is political. A human rights political culture holds in it a critique of the patriarchal system. A system that both women and men participate in: that must be done if the comprehensive vision and mission of human rights is to be realized. Women as well as men must fully recognize that patriarchy is a system where injustice is justice, a system that allows imposed marriages and human-trafficking, the many forms of discrimination against women (just to expose the tip of the iceberg). Life IS political in all its forms. Human rights, as my friend Loretta Ross describes it, and as was noted earlier, is political and moral protected by law. Understanding it as such, we can indeed create a movement that will transform the world to a political culture based on human rights.

Will it be overreaching or too ambitious if we call on every single civil society organization, all local authorities, and the private sector to integrate ongoing, never-ending process of dialogue, discussions, and learning about human rights as a way of life? Women, men, youth, and children empower themselves, moving from slavery to freedom, from self-righteousness to justice, and from charity to dignity.

Churchill said that democracy is not the best solution, but we have no other. Democracy became a structure rather than a living organism that allows the participation of all in searching for the solutions and decision-making practice, in equality and without any form of discrimination. As a result of touching the lives of so many people – and with all modesty – I came to see the simple truth: a real democracy is a comprehensive delivery system of human rights that can be realized through a never-ending, ongoing process of learning and integration at all levels of society of human rights as a way of life. There is no other option!

On the day the Governor of California Arnold Schwarzenegger – who was born in Graz, Austria – allowed to be put to death a prisoner who forty years earlier had killed a policeman in a demonstration of Black people who were calling for equality, the Mayor of the Human Rights City of Graz personally took off the name of Schwarzenegger from the top of the Sports Arena. When asked why, he answered, "Because Graz is a human rights city!" (The death penalty is vehemently opposed in Austria by law!)

A final note: human rights learning should not be understood as another description of human rights education. These are two very different categories and approaches. In five to ten years we hope to evolve movements that will have all people in the world learn, know, and own human rights as relevant to their daily lives, using the gained knowledge for planning their lives and taking relevant actions. Doing so they will be able to use human rights as a powerful tool for change, as a strategy to economic, societal and human development – joining in changing the world.

Human rights educators can, indeed, contribute very creatively to this essential process. Taking a step towards implementing a process of learning, let's listen to what I have learned from Professor Abdullahi Ahmed An-Na'im, a Sufi who was exiled from Sudan, now at Emory University. He asserts that the only universal state of being is DIGNITY! Those of us who want to stay away from the statement that human rights is an imposition by the western countries on the rest of the world have those who make this statement listen to women and men in the village. Ask them to share with you their lullabies, legends, and personal historic memory. Every human rights mentor will be able to identify the yearning and celebration of dignity, decency, and trust in these stories and songs. This will affirm the fact that the international community listened, accepted, and honored these hopes and expatiations for dignity by creating the UDHR to confirm and celebrate human DIGNITY! Many of my colleagues move through communities in their own countries using Abdullahi's insight to evoke discussions about the meaning of human rights as a worldview relevant to people's daily lives.

One of my mantras describes human rights as the banks of the river where life flows freely. And when the floods come, people who know and own human rights strengthen the banks of the river to prevent the floods and maintain freedom. Knowledge is power! Learning about human rights as relevant to people's daily lives has us all move from slavery to freedom every day – every hour – every second of our lives. In conclusion allow me to share a pledge that I have originally composed for the Economic Human Rights Movement in the USA. We had one thousand men in Japan hold hands and repeat it out loud, both in English and Japanese, and on many other occasions around the world, including recently at a UN Program of 3400 high school students from twenty-four countries holding hands and saying:

> We are the human rights generation.
> We will accept nothing less than human rights.
> We will know them and claim them.
> For all women, men, youth, and children,
> From those who speak human rights,
> But deny them to their own people.
> In our hands human rights is a way of being.
> We will move power to human rights.
> We have no other option!

Having taken this voyage, I am grateful to have been given the chance to share these pages with others who have contributed their wisdom and experience. I see this as a mere beginning in the search of the meaning of life – the meaning of human rights to our lives – of a journey that you the reader may choose to take, to have every human being learn, know, own, plan, and act guided by human rights as a way of life for which we have no other option. It is our duty to close the gap of dignity!

Why Did I Become a Human Rights Educator?
Elena Ippoliti (Italy, Switzerland)[1]

> **Elena Ippoliti** works at the Office of the United Nations High Commissioner for Human Rights, where she is responsible for various human rights education programs and activities. She previously worked as assistant lecturer at the Human Rights Chair of the International Free University of Social Studies (LUISS) of Rome, and as a consultant to the Department of Sociology of the University of Rome, "La Sapienza." She has collaborated with the Human Rights Commission of the Italian government and been involved with a number of NGOs, including Amnesty International-Italy, Amnesty International-USA, Human Rights Watch (USA), and the Italian Refugee Council.
>
>

For me, becoming a human rights activist, and a human rights educator in particular, was a natural step once I got to know that "human rights" – a kind of "universal social contract", i.e., a set of internationally agreed-upon principles promoting dignity, equality, and solidarity – existed. A key moment for me was my first "encounter" with the Universal Declaration of Human Rights at the time I was starting university education. In those days, I was searching for a value system to root myself and to use as a basis for helping others less privileged than myself.

Going back to my personal history, I can recall two main factors that have probably influenced my future involvement: the education I received from my parents and a strong innate sense of equality and justice.

I had a happy and protected childhood, being the only daughter of Italian parents who upon their marriage migrated from their small villages in the countryside of central Italy to the Italian North – Milano – searching for a better life. They had lived through the last part of the Second World War and were determined to give me a better life, moving away from their background of poverty to a "developed" environment – the city– and investing in my education.

---

[1] The views expressed herein are those of the author and do not necessarily reflect the views of the United Nations.

My father was a *carabiniere*² – as a matter of fact, he was playing the clarinet in the Milano *carabinieri* band (actually, this background helped me a lot later on in "breaking barriers" when delivering human rights training to law enforcement agencies). My mother was a seamstress and then employed in a cleaning enterprise. Despite their modest origin and the fact that the words "human rights" had never been spoken in our family, a central principle of my education was the respect for others, without any distinction, to the point of putting the wellbeing of others before our own – not as a sacrifice but in solidarity and with a caring attitude.

The second factor that facilitated my involvement in human rights was my innate – but, I guess, also related to the education I had received – strong sense of justice, as well as desire to take action against injustice. I remember since childhood being deeply touched and disturbed by children's bullying – whether the victims were overweight or shy children, or children with slow learning paths – and wanting very much to take action. I remember getting angry at those behaviors and feeling somehow powerless, not knowing how to address abuses in a non-violent way.

I attended middle and secondary education in schools managed by religious Catholic institutions. By enrolling me in private schools, my parents wanted me to focus on formal education and spare me from the political tensions, which caused a lot of turmoil in public schools due to a major wave of violence striking Italian society in the '70s, the so-called "terrorism" period. So, unlike some of my peers who were attending public schools, I did not get involved in Italian politics. But I was looking for opportunities to take some action for justice and solidarity in my context. In middle school, I got active in the "missionary group," which dealt with projects assisting African communities. This experience lifted my understanding of justice (and injustice) from my playground and stories I had read in books to current world realities.

Through my adolescence, I looked for a value system to support my desire to help others and to contribute to justice. I was not satisfied with the framework proposed by the Catholic Church, which I was offered both at school and at home, where my parents were practicing Catholics. I considered it to lack a universal ground. As the Internet did not exist at that time, my quest for a universal value system geared me towards the reading of philosophy, but this exercise gave me more questions than answers.

In the meantime, my family moved from Milano to Rome, and I enrolled at Rome University. Despite the advice of many, who foresaw a future of unemployment for me, I chose to study sociology. I felt it could provide me with tools for social action and allow me to explore humanity in a holistic manner as it included subjects ranging from cultural anthropology to social psychology, political science, and so on.

In the second half of the '80s, Amnesty International and human rights were gaining visibility thanks to a series of human rights concerts, in particular the "Human Rights Now" tour that included a concert in Italy. I had heard of Amnesty International in Milano and had visited its office

---

² The *Arma dei Carabinieri* is a branch of the Italian Army that performs law enforcement functions.

as it seemed to me that they were doing interesting work, but I had had no time to deepen my understanding until I moved to Rome.

In connection with the forthcoming human rights concert in Italy, the Italian Section of Amnesty was circulating human rights leaflets and materials. I remember one in particular that reproduced on its back the text of the Universal Declaration of Human Rights – yellow words against a black background.

As I was reading the Declaration's text, I was thinking that I could absolutely agree with everything written in there. I was struck by the fact that it was a text which had been developed internationally by persons from many different countries gathered at the United Nations and that somehow it belonged to all, beyond any religious or other background. I immediately felt I wanted to learn more about this. On my own I started to do research on human rights, for I did not want to take for granted what one organization, Amnesty, was proposing. The more I learned, the more I got interested. My self-learning exercise about human rights inspired me to take two main steps.

The first one was re-orienting my university sociology studies, with the kind support of my professors, in order to focus them on human rights-related topics and materials, which at that time were not so many as nowadays. I did my final university dissertation on Amnesty International and decided to deepen my legal understanding of human rights with a master's degree in international human rights law at the University of Essex, one of the very few human rights programs existing at that time.

Secondly, I became a volunteer within the Italian Section of Amnesty, doing a bit of everything at the local (a student group) and national (section-wide) level. In particular, I felt that it was important to have the human rights framework more broadly known as it could inspire constructive activism as it had done with me. I started participating in the Human Rights Education Committee of Amnesty, in particular speaking in schools, as Amnesty was very much solicited for this type of input. I was passionate – and, by then, quite knowledgeable – about human rights, and therefore I was effectively engaging my audiences.

This is how my involvement with human rights education started. Then, through the years, I continued pursuing it as a volunteer but also in more professional settings, for instance at the university level.

It is more recent history that I joined the United Nations and that my contribution to human rights education continued in this setting. Related developments in the past twenty years or so have been quite amazing though, particularly looking at them from a global perspective. We have witnessed an exponential growth of the human rights education movement at all levels – local, national, regional and international – in terms of policy and methodology development as well as institution building, programming, and networking.

But this would be the topic for another book!

Empowerment! A Dialogue on Why We Are Involved in Human Rights Education

Judy Gummich and Claudia Lohrenscheit (Germany)

Judy Gummich is a diversity trainer and consultant. Currently, she is also employed as a researcher at the Department of Human Rights Education, Inclusion, and Diversity at the German Institute of Human Rights. For more than twenty-five years she has been active in grassroots organizations and contexts dealing primarily with issues related to the African diaspora, especially in Germany, and anti-racism, migration, asylum, gender, sexual identity, (dis)abilities, inclusion, and intersectional life realities and discrimination.

Claudia Lohrenscheit is Professor for International Social Work and Human Rights at the University of Applied Sciences in Coburg, Germany. An educational scientist and intercultural pedagogue, she completed her Ph.D. in Human Rights Education in South Africa. Previously, she was head of the Department for Human Rights Education at the German Institute for Human Rights and Co-Leader of the Centre for Educational Studies in the North and South at the University of Oldenburg. Her current projects focus on children's rights, women's rights, and lesbian, gay, bisexual, transgender and intersexual rights (LGBTI), as well as human rights education.

Introduction

When Abraham Magendzo's invitation to reflect on the motivations and foundations of our educational practice in human rights reached us, we decided to combine our two narratives into a dialogue. We were skeptical at first: what's so special about our lives that they need to be shared with others? And although Abraham's initial question about why we are involved in human rights education was attractive in a stimulating way, what's so interesting about us? At the same time, both of us were curious to learn about each other's narrative. And both of us felt everything that helps to find ways of learning to promote an understanding of universal human dignity is a welcomed opportunity we'd like to share.

We are lucky enough firstly to have the luxury to reflect on what we do because we live in a safe environment where we don't have to deal with bread-and-butter issues on a daily basis, and secondly we share the same great luck to be working in the human rights field professionally: we earn our living teaching and learning about human rights. There's nothing better and there's nothing more necessary today.

This text is written at a time where in Germany some people remember the *pogrom*[1] of Rostock, where twenty years ago a violent mob led a mass movement of citizens to burn a house of non-indigenous Germans. Meanwhile beer and *wuerstel*[2] were being sold, and people were enjoying themselves singing and shouting racist and fascist slogans. Rostock was only the first of numerous racist and anti-Semitic attacks that followed the time when the two Germanys were newly re-unified. Twenty years later, the country is confronted with the fact that the domestic political system is still blind to racism. For a period of ten years, the so- called NSU[3] has systematically murdered nine German-Turkish and German-Greek citizens as well as a German police officer, unnoticed, ignored, and hidden by the responsible authorities and encouraged by celebrities like the former Minister of Finance in Berlin, Thilo Sarrazin, who publicly fuels fears and stereotypes against everybody who doesn't fit into his narrow understanding of Germany and the Germans.

Although a majority still likes to think that the racist and anti-Semitic attitudes that form the basis of violent action and hate speech are only virulent at the right-wing margins of society, it becomes more and more obvious that an anti-democratic attitude can be found right in the middle. How is it that people and structures teaching the denial of human rights are still successful? And how can we initiate learning to counter this? Human rights as a legal system helps a lot, but it is clear that the law alone won't do the job.

In human rights education, we speak of a "culture of human rights." In fact, this is the only understanding of culture we are able to share. This is a culture we both want to belong to. But what is it that makes us want to belong to a human rights movement? Why do we want to learn what many others deny? What makes the difference between a person wanting to share human rights values and a person wanting to deny them? Which resources and learning processes would be necessary to help build a network of human rights learning that is as open as possible for everybody to access? And, finally, what was it that helped us personally to develop an understanding of human rights that we are able to share through teaching and learning?

---

[1] A term used to describe an organized massacre or persecution of a particular ethnic group, in particular that of Jews in Russia or Eastern Europe. (Editor's note)
[2] Sausage (German)
[3] NSU: Nationalsozialistischer Untergrund (National Socialist Underground), a right-wing terrorist organization in Germany.

To conduct this dialogue, we sat down with a little tape recorder in our office at the German Institute for Human Rights in Berlin. We talked for an hour and a half, trying to find some answers to the question of why we are involved in human rights education based on our own social and family backgrounds, our childhoods, and our school years, as well as our first steps to develop a political consciousness and its continued evolution as adults. Later, we transcribed and edited the text a couple of times before we sent it to Abraham Magendzo, whom we would like to thank for this opportunity: it was a wonderful occasion for reaffirming ourselves in what we do and why we do it.

Empowerment with People Who Share the Same Experiences

Claudia: We both agreed to start our conversation with the keyword we've chosen as a title: *Empowerment*. Would you like at the beginning to explain what you understand by empowerment and why it is so important?

Judy: For me *empowerment* means to be capable to fight for your own rights and for human rights, not only as an individual but also as a group. You cannot do it all by yourself. You need support from other persons, other groups, and comrades. You have the possibility to fight for your rights. But when we talk about human rights, it's not only for you; it's for others as well. You can't really separate it. And why is it so important? Good question! In a way we as human beings should live in such a way that we respect and accept each other and also live in peace.

Claudia: When talking about such beautiful concepts as living in peace, having solidarity amongst us, or being comrades, sometimes I almost feel embarrassed about my longing for peace. Sometimes it seems ridiculous to talk about it because we'll never reach it anyway. But it's true; it's there, the longing. Why should we be ashamed of it? Empowerment is often used as a heading or a buzzword. Everybody's talking about empowerment. But I'd like to see us also take a deeper look at what empowerment practices really are. For example, I like the differentiation of the Black women's movement between empowerment and power sharing: Empowerment is something I do for myself. At the same time, it's something I share with people who have the same experiences of exclusion, discrimination, etc., that I do. This has to be distinguished from power sharing, which is something that might be done by others, by people in more powerful positions. But nobody can empower me. It's really something I do with people who share the same experiences.

Judy: This is something that empowers: to share with people, to feel that you are not the only person experiencing this. You are not crazy. This is reality, and you share this with other persons. Then it comes from inside. The power comes from inside.

Claudia: It's this feeling: I'm not alone. I'm not the only person experiencing this, and I'm not the only person who found a way out of it. We can also share the strategies and techniques we used to become strong personalities and to stand up for our rights.

Judy: If we do this together, at a certain point it makes me feel stronger.

Claudia: Yes. I found it interesting when you said that empowerment is connected to solidarity. Sometimes I'm worried about solidarity as we're living in a time where empowerment is practiced by closed groups. For example, here is a group of Black lesbian women, next to a group of gay migrant men, next to a group of indigenous gay men, etc. They all work for their own empowerment, but it's hard to share and sometimes hard to work collaboratively. I'm sure we sometimes need exclusive groups, and it's important to have a safe environment to be able to talk freely. But I wonder how we then open up those closed groups again?

Judy: But for me it's not only opening up those spaces because you need them. But you have to find allies. If I really mean empowerment seriously, then I think discrimination as well as empowerment affects everyone, not just me. Therefore, I have to work with everybody. I have to fight alongside everybody but maybe in different ways. But it should be an issue for every person not only for me as a Black, a lesbian, a gay, or whatever. And that makes the change. I remember a speech of Audre Lorde where she said, "If you don't use the power you have, others will use it against you."[4] That's what I really learned from her: To see, to perceive what I have, and really use it. This is empowerment.

Claudia: Nicely said, thank you. What our topic really is here today is Abraham Magendzo's question about how we became involved in human rights education, to somehow tell a story of why we are here doing what we do. We've agreed to share our biographies in order to identify our own teachers, guides, or comrades or find some kinds of "triggers" that maybe lead the way.

Judy: O.K. Let's start with the early years, with our own family and social backgrounds, with that question in mind: How does it happen that we are involved in human rights education? Would you start?

Claudia: What I could say concerning my family background is that early in my life I developed a feeling of not belonging or a feeling of being different or poor. My mother, born in 1944, worked as a hairdresser and in a pub; my father, a chemistry worker born in 1944, died young as an alcohol addict who regularly beat up his wife. We didn't have much money. Later on they were divorced. That was not very common during that time, so I was the only one from a divorced family in my early school years. Sometimes I was labeled a "latchkey child" (*schlüsselkind*), which was used for children whose parents or mothers weren't home. So people looked down on me: "Oh, that poor kid. She doesn't have a mum who cares for her." My family was known in the area, and I was "that kid from that family." Today, I would say I felt in a way that there was a stigma, a negative stereotype.

Judy: Was it a small town or village?

Claudia: Yes. So the feeling of being different was instilled in my consciousness early in life. That feeling stayed with me, not only from the outside world but also from within, in the family context,

---

[4] Audre Lorde. *The Berlin Years 1984 bis 1992* (n.d.): n. pag.
http://www.audrelorde-theberlinyears.com/studyguide/AL_studyguide_eng.pdf

because in our family I was the sensitive and clever child. I went to high school and later also to university, something no other member of my family had done. My mother had tried to take me out of school because she wanted me to become a hairdresser. One of my older sisters talked to my teachers to persuade them that I must do my "matric," my *Abitur*.[5] We did that behind my mum's back, and she was very angry about it. But in the end we succeeded. Concluding, I would say these early encounters with feeling different or not belonging were important for what later then developed in my life, as important as the early support I got from my older sister and the school.

Judy: It's similar with me because I grew up in a children's home. I came there when I was eight days old, so really from the beginning. When I was three or four years old, I started to realize that I was different. In the children's home, I realized I was different because of my skin-color as a Black German. And outside, especially in school but also in the streets, I was different both because of my skin color *and* because I came from a children's home. You could tell us by our clothes; they were second-hand. Also, by what we ate at school. We only had bread with jam while the others had cheese and everything. We couldn't afford the sweets others had. We didn't even have small change to spend. That was when I realized I was different.

But for me, it was not only being different. There was another kind of being different: other people were better, and I was lesser. It was not the same. I didn't have the same worth as other people. That's what I experienced as a child. Everybody, including I myself, said to me, "It's not your fault," but between the lines I always read that it's my fault. I knew it was something I could not change. I often wanted to change it, but I couldn't really change because it was me. In the children's home, I felt O.K. I was different but not as different as outside.

And like you, I always had to fight for my education. I had a teacher who would always downgrade me. She didn't want me to attend high school. And I had to fight with my family, too. I always kept contact with my mother and her family. But there I had the same fights as in other contexts. I think, on the one hand, these contacts gave me strength, but on the other hand, it was a double bind somehow. I was loved by them, but also got the same attitudes and stereotypes from my family as from other people in town, teachers, and people on streets. Sometimes I didn't know which was better.

Claudia: This is something that we obviously share, this feeling of not belonging, of being different or lesser in the family or children's home as well as in the outside world.

Judy: That's true. But I always felt that the way I was treated was not right.

Claudia: This early feeling of justice. I was always wondering where I got this from. It's certainly not from my family. I wonder where I picked that up.

---

[5] Abitur is a designation used in Germany for final exams that students take at the end of their secondary education. (Editor's Note).

Early Supporters Who Lit the Flame

Judy: That's an interesting question for me, too. The children's home where I grew up was run by Catholic nuns. And there was a special nun there. She always tried to make clear to me that I have the same worth as others. She was one of my early supporters in a way. But again, there was this double bind situation. I got the same bad images about Black people from her as from the others. But nevertheless she also taught me: everybody is equal; you have the right to be here. Something like this.

Claudia: That's interesting. We could say they were early supporters. They were not always free from ambivalence or a double bind as you call it. They were not perfect, but they succeeded in giving us resources.

Judy: Yes. Giving us strength and also some kind of empowerment, consciously or subconsciously. When I look back, this was very important for me.

Claudia: I think it's not possible to survive without some kind of support. It's also an important concept in psychotherapy. For example, this is something people with a borderline diagnosis must find: Who were the early supporters, resources, or facilitators in their lives?

So, maybe we could leave it here concerning our family or social backgrounds. Shall we move on to our early school years?

Judy: Yes, but may I go back just a little bit? The information I got about myself was: You have nothing, you are nothing, you can do nothing. Very often, if I look back, this was the message I received.

Later on this started to change. After the children's home, I was in a boarding school only for girls. I had an English teacher. She was the first person who I felt saw me as a whole person, not just my skin color, my social background, or whatever. She saw my positive sides. She really supported me and told me that I had the potential for a better education, that I should really do what I wanted to do. So after the boarding school I went to Munich and tried to get my "matric" (*Abitur*). I was not successful at that time, but at least I did what I wanted for the first time. I wouldn't have done it without her. I wouldn't have tried to get a higher education. I wouldn't have trusted my context or myself. She gave me the strength to fight against my family. I was successful in the end.

And there was another teacher, a young German teacher I had the last year. She also tried to get me in touch with Black history. I couldn't take it at that time; everything that had to do with Black people, Black history, Black music, etc., so I rejected it. But she tried in a very soft way, presented material to me, and encouraged me to look at it: If you like it, take it. But at that time, I wasn't able to do that. Later on, I was, but she lit the flame for it. Let's put it this way. But that was a time when

Martin Luther King was making his speeches, and Cassius Clay, today Muhammad Ali, was boxing. She also supported me to choose my own way. I think without these teachers, well, you never know what might have happened, but without them ... they supported me so that I was empowered.

Claudia: Well, I could say that in school something that really struck me, that really developed my early political consciousness, was learning about the Holocaust, the Shoa, for the first time. I remember we had a history teacher, such a strong guy with such strong opinions. For weeks we had fights with him in class. There was a small group of us who couldn't understand how all this could have happened without a resistance movement. He taught us about the totalitarian system and how each and every one of us at that time would have happily been involved, too. We girls would have loved to be members of the BDM (*Bund Deutscher Maedel*).[6] We all would have been *Mitläufer*, or collaborators. But then in our free time after school we found out about Anne Frank. We came back triumphant: Yes, there was resistance. We would have been like Anne Frank. Totally naïve! But it stood for the feeling or the longing that there must have been a way. No matter how dark it may seem, there must always be a way to belong to the right side. I think it was at that time that I really developed a desire to make sure that I would stand on the right side. I was not persuaded that this could never happen again. And, in fact, it happens again and again – exclusion, discrimination, violence. So that was a question leading me through my school years: how can I make sure that I am on the right side? And would I really stand up for human rights?

Judy: As far as I remember, I wasn't ever taught about the Holocaust in school. I have no memory of that.

Claudia: Here, it's obvious that you are older than me. In my school days it was the norm to be taught about World War II; in your time maybe not. I was lucky enough not to have any teachers who themselves had been part of the terror regime of the Nazis.

Judy: I definitely had those teachers, definitely one in particular. And the nuns didn't talk about it. They didn't talk about the Nazi regime or the role of the Catholic Church at that time. This came later when I tried again, for the second time, to do my "matric." In this school, I developed what I call political consciousness. It was really a mind opener; and by the way, it was again through a German teacher. With him I learned to read between the lines, for example, not only to look at years and numbers in history, but also to see the backgrounds and different perspectives of history. For example, to question what the Nazi terror had to do with colonialism. He really tried to make us see where the connections were. He also encouraged me to write because I still had this opinion about myself from my schooldays: "You can't write." "Don't try it." "You cannot use the German language properly." I had internalized these messages. He was the one who really taught me, "Yes, you can write." I wish I had had more teachers like him. Maybe, I would have begun to write books.

---

[6] BDM, *Bund Deutscher Maedel*, was a National Socialist organization infiltrating fascist and racist values into young girls' minds. Involved were all girls aged 10-18 years who hadn't been excluded through Nazi ideology.

He also encouraged me to not always believe what people say: Make your own ideas about it! Think about it! What is your own opinion?

Claudia: Critical thinking. At this stage, we can see that school and individual teachers can play an important role either way, as supporters or …

Judy: Destroyers.

Claudia: Yes, but also as provocateurs. What I liked about my history teacher was how he provoked us. This perhaps says something about the way we learn. I think I love to learn through provocation. So that teacher, he didn't really mean that there was no resistance. But, of course, he had a point. Hardly anything was possible without risking your life.

Judy: Sometimes, I also ask myself, especially with this Nazi teacher I mentioned, how I managed to deal with these attacks on my person, on the core of my personality. I think it's all those little steps I took to become stronger, to develop self-confidence. Otherwise these attacks would have destroyed me. As a child, I didn't have much support. In the children's home, there were more than thirty children for two caretakers. They didn't have the time to look after each and every child all the time.

Claudia: That's a question for me too: I wonder how I managed, coming from that family background, to develop such a wonderful life.

Judy: And also to love life, to love to learn. Despite conditions in that school and in school life generally, I still have developed a love of learning.

"Despite" as a Motivation

Claudia: It's interesting that we both say "despite": despite the family background, despite conditions in the children's home or school, we are now where we are. What I can say is that this "despite" later on became a guiding principle: to do things despite obstacles that seem to be impossible. I can only live this life, although from a global perspective, this life is horrible in so many ways. Humanity needs transformation so desperately. I cannot understand how anyone in this world can be happy when there is so much hunger, violence, etc. in the world. I have no choice but to live here, but I'm sure nobody can be happy as long as there is hunger. If people ask me why you do what you do, I always answer that I'm doing it although I know that perhaps I won't succeed in this life. I know I won't change this world. There won't be peace tomorrow. But what else can I do but act despite the odds.

Judy: Yes, because working for human rights makes change. Maybe sometimes you won't be able to see it making a change in your life, at least at the moment. But every moment which is different, every moment where you have a different perception or interaction with people, changes your life, in fact.

Claudia: Hmm. What I mean is that this world really is in a state of violence; there's so much hunger and injustice. The struggle for human rights hardly ever really succeeds. For example, we have had two hundred years of the women's movement. Are we women really free now? No, we are not. So why are we activists or educators? Why don't we just say, "Leave it! I'm enjoying my life"? The only explanation I can give is that I know we are not always successful. I know this world is in a miserable state; we have more hunger and violence than fifty years ago.

Judy: But we have improvements.

Claudia: Do we really have improvements?

Judy: Sometimes.

Claudia: I'm not so sure about that, but nevertheless, I'm fighting for human rights *despite*. It's like this guy from ancient Greek philosophy, Sisyphus – Camus later wrote about him.[7] He keeps rolling a stone up the hill, and the stone keeps rolling back, but he's doing it anyway.

Judy: You cannot just do nothing. It's not possible. I can't just leave things like discrimination and other human rights violations as they are. That's also no solution, but at least I tried.

Claudia: At least I tried to be on the right side.

Judy: There's a very good saying of Vaclav Havel that really fits here: "Hope is not about the conviction that something will end in a good way but that it makes sense no matter how it will end."[8]

Claudia. Nice. Shall we move on? So we both found out that school life and individual teachers were quite influential. And they stimulated somehow the early development of a political mind or awareness. For me, I can say that, as a young adult, I really started to develop political thinking. It all started with the discovery of the meaning of my sex and gender. I started step by step to realize that as a girl or a woman, I was not equal. Sexism was in the language, in the perception of my body, in the fear of leaving home at night, in the fear of being raped.

I had the great luck that the women's movement in Germany at that time during the 1980s was not yet dead. It was almost dead, but in this little town where I lived, there were still some women's groups around. For the first time in my life, I had this fantastic feeling of being part of a group that shared the same experiences of injustice. We could share and discuss how we could deal with it. There were the women's parades on March 8. For the first time in my life, I was part of a demonstration. I saw all these wonderful women. I was part of them. We were on the streets,

---

[7] Camus wrote about the absurd state of life human beings are confronted with: Trying to make sense in a world that seems senseless (Albert Camus: *Der Mythos des Sisyphos. Ein Versuch über das Absurde* (*Le mythe de Sisyphe*, 1942)).
[8] In German: "*Hoffnung ist nicht die Überzeugung, dass etwas gut ausgeht, sondern dis Gewissheit, dass etwas Sinn hat, egal wie es ausgeht.*" *Auswärtiges Amt.* N.p., 29 Jan. 2014.

shouting. We built night groups. So we were running around the streets at night, loud and ugly, with the aim of protecting other women, accompanying them home, and preventing rape. But we also followed men. Whenever we met a single man at night, we would provoke him, trying to make him feel as we do at night. Of course, this was not possible. No, it really was an ugly practice. But we didn't know any better. That was the time when I first got information about abortion rights in Germany and about how the police treat victims of rape. I was an angry young woman at that time, lucky enough to find other angry women to share with. That really brought me into the sphere of political activism and also education.

Judy: I started my political work, my political consciousness, and working in political groups linked to the stationing of US Army Pershing II missiles in Germany. For example, I was part of the human chain (*Menschenkette*) in Ulm, which was part of the greater peace movement, the Easter Marches. I was very shy at that time. I didn't talk in discussions but only listened.

I remember the first time I had the courage to speak in front of this big group. And I was astonished that they listened to me. They agreed with what I said. That was the first experience for me of being able to move things and have influence over what people discussed. I had sat there one year without saying a word, but, from that time on, I started not only to bring in my perspective, but also to listen to others more intently and to talk to them.

My gender consciousness came very late because I grew up mostly more or less amongst women only. In the children's home, I was amongst girls; in the boarding school, I was amongst girls. Later on, I was in a residential home for girls.

Claudia: So, you had enough of women?!

Judy: No, I learned to love them. Therefore, when I was in the street as a teenager, for example, as a Black teenage girl or woman, I realized very quickly that people treated me differently from other teenaged young women. I knew this had to do with my skin color. It was always both for me, skin color and gender. I cannot separate them.

Later on, in the peace movement, I remember this big event. There was a lot of paper and rubbish around. I asked one of the big speakers there, "What happens to the rubbish when everybody has left?" And he said, "The cleaning women will take care of this." I was shocked. How can he speak so well, and in the next moment be so unconscious about other things? After a while, I understood: it's only part of the package. These peace activists focus on their issues, but at the same time, treat others like shit. But from then on, I joined the women's peace movement. They were different. I was participating in women's peace camps. It was an interesting experience for me, but still I didn't really feel that I belonged there.

The first time I really had a sense of belonging was when I met other Afro-German women, Black German women. That was in the mid-1980s when we started ADEFRA,[9] the organization of Afro-German women. This was the first time that I really felt I belonged. Before then, there was always something missing. There was always this – how can I put it? – There was not a perspective on human rights as a whole but only on different single issues, single aspects. That was what I missed. With ADEFRA I had the feeling that here I can be as a whole person, including my social background, my biography, my gender, my sexual identity, my skin color. Everything had space there. But I also realized that there was still something not included: Black people with a disability. That was before I had my daughter with Down Syndrome. It was a good place to be and to share thoughts with people who had the same experience of being Black and German, but still something that was important for me was not there. It was not addressed. It felt as if I always had to choose among things when I was there. For me, this was exclusion in a certain way. And more and more, especially after I had my daughter, I started to look at human rights as a whole and not just look at single issues like racism or sexism.

Claudia: What you say there is interesting because I remember those early encounters with the women's movement. There was a group of lesbian women as well. At that time there was this slogan, "Feminism is theory and lesbianism is the true practice". I wasn't a lesbian, and I was so annoyed by that slogan. Why can't I be a feminist and heterosexual at the same time? So lesbians were complaining, wanting to have their own space. But I was the one who was lobbying for cooperation because there were not so many of us. But in the end we split. Whereas I had the feeling that here I can be as a whole person, people really see me, I don't have to have fear because I'm not at risk of being attacked by men or whatever. But others had the feeling that they were not seen, that aspects of them were not acknowledged. They had to fight. That's why we have this development of having smaller and smaller groups with clearly marked identity characteristics. This is empowerment but also exclusion at the same time.

In a way, you had to find your Black, lesbian, persons-with-disabilities peer group. I do understand, and I am completely convinced that this is what we need to be able to empower ourselves. But it's also so sad that you obviously have to find somebody equivalent to you in all aspects to be able to identify yourself. I wish sometimes we as human beings could be more open than that. In Berlin, for example, we have a fight amongst Turkish-German gay men, and they fight against indigenous white gay men. So there are two minorities fighting for the same thing but fighting against each other. How mad is this?

Judy: The question is how can we fight together?

Claudia: How can we practice solidarity? How can we be allies?

---

[9] ADEFRA is the acronym for *Afro-deutsche Frauen* (Black German Women).

Judy: At the same time, how can we have our own spaces, which are also necessary? We need to have both. But how do we get there?

Claudia: I don't know.

Judy: We teach human rights! Really, that's one of the core issues. We should focus on the mechanics of discrimination instead of focusing on particular groups or singled-out aspects of identity like gender or skin color. We need to identify the ways ideologies, laws, and social structures reinforce racism, sexism, ableism, etc. This is what human rights work means. This is how we can analyze how people are excluded, how their human rights are being violated, and how they don't have equal access to human rights.

Maybe, I don't know, this will help to develop more solidarity. And it may also be helpful to accept our differences as well as our commonalities. You always have to see both.

Claudia: Have you ever heard about the so-called trickle-down effect? It means something is pouring down and spreading. Maybe there is a kind of trickle-down effect. We start maybe with a single-issue group such as women. We are getting strong; there's a strong movement. But then we realize it's not enough to be a woman. I'm also Black, I'm also disabled, I'm also gay or lesbian or whatever. So maybe as a group we are empowered already. Can we take the next step from there and include not only gender, disability, etc.? Maybe it is a natural process that these groups are getting smaller. We are not yet here to be able to know what comes next.

Judy: I don't know.

Intellectual and Physical Processes

Claudia: O.K. There is something else that was very important for me, the discovery of my body. Feminism was not only an intellectual process; it was a physical process as well. One book was very instrumental at that time. It was a book to learn about the bodies of women.

Judy: I think I know exactly which one you mean.

Claudia: Yes, it was that big pink book called *For Ourselves*.[10] I must tell you this now because I was shocked at that time. In the book, there were pictures of the vagina, black and white pictures, many of them. Somehow, at that time, my sexual organs were completely unknown to me. The book argued that as women we usually know more about the penis, the male body, than about ourselves. I was around twenty. I had had sex already at that time. But with that book, for the first time in my life, I heard that I had a clitoris. I didn't know it. I didn't realize it. I was so angry: how come I was already so old without knowing my own organs? We had a small women's working group on that

---

[10] Anja Meulenbelt: *Fuer uns selbst. Koerper und Sexualitaet aus der Sicht von Frauen.* Frauenoffensive 1981

issue, trying to learn all about our bodies. Up till then, I had learned in school, for example, or in those magazines that young people read; I heard all about sexual reproduction but nothing about my sexual desire or pleasure. It was such an eye opener. In a way, I believe women today are not any smarter about these issues. That's shocking.

This story repeated itself in my mid-thirties when I read another book by Claudia Haarmann.[11] Like Anja Meulenbelt more than twenty years earlier, she argues that despite the over-sexualized media, women today still don't know their bodies and are full of shame in relationships to their bodies and not at all free to choose a sexuality they really want. In this book, I saw a picture of the clitoris. And that was again shocking. What I believed up till ten years ago is that the clitoris is a small little thing. Now for the first time in my life, I saw a picture of the clitoris, ten centimeters long, with two flanks. Only the head is visible; the rest of the organ is internal. Again: how come? I'm a feminist, and at the age of thirty-five I am learning this? Of course, there are political reasons for this. I'm saying this to make the point that the development of critical thinking was a physical process as well as intellectual.

Judy: Yes. I had this kind of process with Black women. I couldn't have done it with White women. I needed this space to be open to talk. At that time, I couldn't understand the lesbians. They discussed whether ADEFRA, the Organization of Afro-German Women, should be an organization only for Afro-German lesbian women. But if you say women, you mean *every* woman. We also had discussions about who is going to define who is lesbian or not. The same question is who is going to define whether I'm Black or not.

We learned a lot about men but not much about women. We learned a lot about White history but nothing about Black history. A real discovery for me was the book *Farbe bekennen (Showing Our Colors)*.[12] For the first time I read about Black German history. History here, not in Africa where some White Germans were. There had been a Black history here in this country hundreds of years. I was in my mid-thirties.

Claudia: You were shocked about this suppressed knowledge?

Judy: Yes. We always learn about the oppressors but not about ourselves.

Claudia: That's interesting. The second really important issue for me besides gender was racism. I was part of a church that was also providing a so-called "Third World Shop," where you could buy literature and other things from Africa, Latin America, and Asia. I was a member of that "Third World Group" and would sit in the shop and sell fair-trade coffees. There were also political groups focusing on Nicaragua, El Salvador, and South Africa where I became a member. We started to

---

[11] Claudia Haarmann: *"Unten rum..." Die Scham ist nicht vorbei*. Innenweltverlag. Koeln 2005
[12] Katherine Oguntoye, May Ayim, and Dagmar Schultz (Hg.): *Frabe behennen. Afro-durtsche Frauen auf den spuren ihrer Geschichte*. Orlanda Frauenverlag 1981. *Showing Our Colors: Afro-German Women Speak Out* (University of Massachusetts Press, 1992).

develop political action to free Nelson Mandela and oppose Apartheid. I remember we lay down in front of the Deutsche Bank and spilled tomato sauce onto the street to demonstrate that the bank was financing and profiting from Apartheid. This link to South Africa has stayed with me for the rest of my life up till today. Later, as a student, I had the chance to travel to South Africa and meet people there. That was the first time that I met human rights people. O.K., there was Amnesty International (AI) before. But at that time, AI was a single-issue political group fighting for political prisoners. But then in South Africa, there was this huge, dynamic, colorful, diverse human rights movement. I knew then that all my longing had a name: human rights. It felt like home. This was what I wanted to do. Then, I started to look for human rights people here.

Judy: For me traveling was important, too. My first time in Ghana, I was concerned with development issues. But I always had the feeling that I was working against myself. I had a scholarship for three months but stayed six months. After that, I knew I didn't want to work like that, not in those kinds of still colonial structures. I couldn't say that some projects or networks aren't really good things, but it's very difficult to change these kinds of structures. I didn't want to be part of them.

Claudia: I totally agree.

Judy: That was a time, not the first time, when I was in a more or less Black environment. I lived there, I had contacts there, I felt free. It was the first time really that I had this feeling. They could identify me as a foreigner, but nevertheless I belonged. That was a strange situation. How can you be a foreigner and at the same time belong? It took me some time to accept that. But when I came back from Ghana, I started with the Afro-German movement. I had a call from a Black German whom I already knew from the women's peace movement. However, at that time we hadn't talked to one another. It was common at that time that Afro-Germans didn't talk to other Black people if they were not connected to their family or their environment. After that, she had already contacted May Ayim.[13] At least we had exchanged our telephone numbers, and she called me at the right time, and I said, "YES!" So we founded ADEFRA in Munich and also an office for Germany, first with the support of the White women's movement. Later on, the more empowered we became, the more difficulties we had with the White women's movement.

Claudia: Here we are again. That's the process that happens.

Judy: I still have the feeling that those six months in Ghana are a source of my power. It's never ending. It's still there.

When I met Audre Lorde and read her books, this was also important to me. She was the one who was not just focusing on a single aspect of identity. Paraphrasing Audre Lorde, who stated more than once, "I'm a Black warrior, a woman, a mother, a poet, a lesbian, etc." She taught us that we had to work together, that we had to fight for human rights all together in the end. What I also really loved

---

[13] May Ayim, Ghanaian German poet, was the first researcher focusing on Afro-German history.

about her was that you could joke around with her at the same time. To love life, to enjoy life, that we as Black people have the right to enjoy life: that's also what I learned from her.

Claudia: That's true. Of course, I also love to enjoy life. But we are so privileged. I'm so rich. I'm so well educated. I'm living in the rich part of the world. These privileges must be linked to the responsibility to use them to promote human rights.

Judy: Yes, but I also learned to appreciate the gift I have from life. It's important to not only see myself but to use the privileges I have to fight for human rights.

Claudia: We need to come to an end soon. I would just like to mention one point that we didn't touch on yet: LGBTI (Lesbian, Gay, Bisexual, Trans- and Intersexual) issues. This was important for me at a certain point of time in my life. After I came out, I desperately wanted to be amongst lesbians: lesbian parties, lesbian political groups, lesbian bookshops, lesbian bakeries, etc. My whole world became lesbian, and I was so excited about it. During this time, I developed a real joy in being different. Remember what we said in the beginning about being different? I tried to be different; I would always want to be different from "the others." Being a lesbian, I could really celebrate this. I had a fight with my family. My sisters were shocked, and one didn't want to talk to me at first. But this changed. Today, I feel it's a completely private thing for me. And I also find that the struggles of lesbians and gays in Germany today are a bit too conservative sometimes. The community once was so innovative, so colorful, and so diverse. But in a way, they have lost that, or I've lost it. Today, my solidarity is strong for the rights of intersexual people who need all our support to be what they are. Their human rights are denied simply because they don't fit into the polar system of "male" and "female." If they succeed with their struggle for human dignity, they will give society as a whole the gift of getting closer to a true understanding of humanity and what it means to be human.

Judy: For me it was my Black coming out: to really say that I'm Black, live that I'm Black. I have my dreads now, and they are also a sign of standing up for who I am. Is it joyful for me to be different? Yes, but not as a single person. It's joyful for me especially in groups. It was very different when we were a group of three or four or five people, but when we were twenty or when we had our big meetings with more than a hundred Black people, I really enjoyed that.

I remember a situation where we were driving a big car. There were seven of us, seven Black women. We were at a service station and got out of the car one after the other. You should have seen how they looked! They couldn't believe it: another one, another one, and another one. We felt that together we were strong and self-confident. That was a joy. And joy for me is also that I won't let anybody take away that I am who I am, and also can choose whether I show it or whether I don't show it. The interesting thing about my generation of Afro-German women is that we grew up very isolated. There would be one Black child among hundreds of White children. I discovered after a while that we had to learn not to be the single Black or single different person but to get together. It was really a process to fight together, to have fun together, but not to be an exception. I am the rule not the exception. This was a new experience. Nowadays, I can also play with it sometimes. It's funny.

Claudia: If you are at that point where you can play with it, you have won. You are not as vulnerable anymore. Of course, we are always vulnerable, but it doesn't have such destructive effects anymore.

Judy: It's about self-confidence, meaning to be sure about myself, knowing who you are and where you belong. For me it's as though I still haven't found the place where I belong, but I can well live with this reality. I have learned from my outsider experience as an Afro-German female child, from growing up in a children's home, as well as from being a Black lesbian single mother with a light-skinned daughter with Down Syndrome. And I have learned, lastly, from the disappointments I had within the Black community, not only in relation to disability. I have accepted that this one place of total belonging will never exist.

Claudia: Yes, I have accepted that this place does not really exist.

Judy: For me.

Claudia: In fact, for anybody. If we all realize that there is not this one place or one space or one group where everything is right for me, then maybe cooperation amongst different groups will become possible.

Judy: Yes, I think so too because then you are open, if you don't just stick to your own personal situation, if you really have human rights in mind, all people in mind, then you can cooperate.

Human Rights Educators: Subjects of Their Own History

Abraham Magendzo K. (Chile)

Abraham Magendzo Kolstrein is a Chilean educator, researcher, and specialist in curriculum, human rights education, citizenship education, and anti-bullying. He is a Professor of Education and an educational and vocational counselor at the Education Institute at the University of Chile. He holds a master's degree in education and history from the Hebrew University of Jerusalem, Israel, and a Ph.D. in education from UCLA. In the nineties, as Chile returned to democracy, he promoted the analysis of the educational curriculum, as well as the professional development of educators in education and human rights from the Programa Interdisciplinario de Investigaciones en Educación (Interdisciplinary Program in Educational Research or PIIE). He remains involved in these issues today. He is currently Director of Doctoral Studies in Education and coordinator of the UNESCO Chair in Education and Human Rights at the Academia de Humanismo Cristiano University in Chile. He has published widely in his fields of interest.

From My Own History

I will begin by attempting to identify those defining moments that, in my opinion, made me become a part, consciously or unconsciously, of the community of human rights educators. This exercise in introspection is not easy. It requires among other things an effort to reveal events that still have significant meaning. They may be events that did not seem important at the moment but that left an indelible print and constructed a history in which these events now have great significance.

As I select and resurrect the most relevant facts, I will try to explain what they mean in terms of "turning me" into a human rights educator. They are important and intimate moments and are therefore subjective and emotionally charged. I will also take a conceptual review of my history, trying to give it a theoretical base. I will refer to some authors, but above all, I will be creating my own frame of reference that will explain how I have been constructing my identity as a human rights educator. I will also establish certain relevant periods of my life that seem to be the building blocks of my identity as a human rights educator.

Inside my Identity

I was born in Chile in the thirties to a family of immigrant Jews. My father was the first rabbi of the Jewish community. There can be no doubt that this context left an important imprint on me. In those days, even more than today, one could feel the extremely crude and dramatic poverty in Chile. Misery and suffering, especially the suffering of others, slowly crept over me and left its mark. My family was small. There were only three brothers in my family. The rest of the family had remained in Europe. We lived in a neighborhood where poverty was a daily fact of life.

This *barrio* (neighborhood) of my childhood also bore the marks of World War II and the Holocaust. As a Jewish family, all of us were left with indelible marks. The fact of belonging to a religious minority in a predominantly Catholic country made one an "outcast." This is something that can serve to reaffirm one's sense of identity and belonging, but at the same time it can alienate. Belonging to a group that is the object of discrimination and historical persecutions defines you. I can still remember being insulted in the street as an "exiled Jew."

A Communist Brother

My older brother became part of the Communist Party at the age of eighteen. The impact on our family, especially on my father, was enormous. It was not an easy fact for a rabbi to accept. He was fully aware of the persecution suffered by Jews in the Soviet Union, particularly during the times of Stalin, when many Jewish-Communist intellectuals were accused of being "cosmopolitan," "Trotskyists," and "Zionists"; and many of them were killed. In addition, more than three million Jews living at the time in the Soviet Union were not allowed to practice their religion and their culture.

In any case, justice as a discourse entered our house. My brother continuously talked about injustices. He brought newspapers and books featuring arguments for class struggle. In spite of the fact that we disagreed on important issues, he had a strong influence on me. He opened my eyes so that I was able to reflect on and become sensitized to social issues.

When we finished high school, my twin brother and I had to go out and work because our economic situation was dire. Our father had died a few years before, and our mother did everything she could to make ends meet. I worked as a secretary in a women's clothing factory. There, I witnessed how female workers spent hours and hours glued to the pedals of their sewing machines for the most meager of wages. When I mentioned this to my brother, he immediately said, "The injustice and exploitation of the rich is responsible for creating a surplus based on the work of the poor." This emphatic statement remained engraved in me, and I wondered if this state of things could be changed.

The Religious-Marxist-Religious

In the beginning of the fifties, I went to Israel to participate in a seminar and course for Jewish leaders who came from all over the world representing movements or parties made up of youth. I belonged to a religious youth movement. I looked for and found references in the Bible and the Talmud that strengthened my concern about social issues, for justice, truth, respect for life, assistance and responsibility to others, solidarity, freedom, etc. My friends and colleagues in this religious movement referred to me as the "religious Marxist." On the other hand, those who belonged to the left-wing youth movement considered me a "Marxist religious," pointing out, as was the case of my Chilean friend, Sergio Yulis, that from a social and humanitarian perspective Biblical tales had important inconsistencies for they accepted slavery, wars, eye-for-an-eye justice, and private property, among other things. These inconsistencies have always resided inside me, for as a believer they create conflicts and problems in me at both the rational and emotional level.

The Holocaust Slaughter

The Holocaust marked all of us. We could see up close the blind hatred, extreme and unfounded intolerance, sick racism, xenophobia, and the anti-Semitism that ended up in the most brutal dehumanization, in the use of barbarism, in unlimited atrocities, in Dantesque scenes, in the extermination of millions.

Studying in Israel at the Hebrew University in the beginning of the sixties, I got to know Holocaust survivors. With Érica, my wife who had lost her mother and a large part of her family in the Holocaust and who had been confined to the ghetto in Budapest, Hungary, we witnessed the Eichmann trial[1]. The testimonies of the concentration camp survivors cannot be described; they belong to a phantasmagoric and terrifying reality. They depicted scenes which seem unreal, beyond imagination. The Holocaust strengthened my Jewish identity, but also instilled in me a deep empathy and sensitivity for suffering and pain and a commitment to "Never again," to "Remember and do not forget."

Changes

By the middle and end of the sixties, social changes were perceptible in both Chile and the rest of the world. Stagnant and old-fashioned schemes were called into question, as was the prolonged history of injustice, inequality, and abuse that had been reproduced and perpetuated. The most excluded and dispossessed groups – such as workers, students, women, and Indigenous Peoples – felt that the time had come for them to claim the rights they had been denied for generations.

---

[1] Adolf Eichmann (1906-1962) was an SS officer responsible for Jewish deportation to extermination camps. After the war, he escaped to Argentina where he was captured in 1961, and brought to Israel to stand trial for crimes against humanity and against the Jewish people. He was found guilty and hanged in 1962.

Political parties, both center and left wing, implemented these demands. So began "the freedom revolution." With the appearance later during the sixties of Unidad Popular (People's Unity or Popular Unity), a coalition of left wing, socialist, and communist political parties, radical changes were implemented, both in the means of production and in some structures of the state apparatus. Nobody, much less me – of course – could remain indifferent. But though I believed in the changes, I felt that they were going too fast. In spite of personal tensions and contradictions, I felt transformational and emancipatory thoughts and attitudes rising up inside me.

Denied Rights

This desire for change was violently interrupted on September 11, 1973, with the establishment of a cruel, despotic, and merciless military dictatorship. Basic human rights were denied, a regime of terror was established, and many people were tortured and disappeared. Little room was left for freedom; hopes were delayed and disappeared.

Slowly, I gained awareness of how basic liberties were being restricted. In my work at the School of Education at the Catholic University, I realized I was censoring myself. There was fear. Little by little, more instances of people being tortured and disappeared emerged. Many friends had to leave the country. The desire to bring back democracy increased as the dictatorship stomped around like a giant monster.

Popular Education and Critical Pedagogy: The Entry to Human Rights Education

We created the (Interdisciplinary Program in Educational Research, or PIIE) as an opportunity to rethink democracy. It was an academic undertaking that enabled us to act in relative freedom and recover democracy. We knew it would arrive one day, but we had to fight for it. The military would not give it back without a struggle.

Within this program, which was inspired by Paulo Freire, we developed popular education initiatives. We worked in towns empowering people, delivering conceptual and procedural tools so that they would feel and act as subjects of dignity and rights. In addition, little by little, and with international cooperation, we introduced the language of critical pedagogy. It was the beginning of my participation in human rights education.

First Steps in Human Rights Education

During the dictatorship we did not call our work "human rights education," for this language was considered subversive and dangerous. It must also be noted that it was only during the middle of the eighties that talk about human rights education began to be heard of in Latin America. During those times, when dictatorships befell our country and other Latin American countries and we could see only a glimmer of light at the end of the tunnel, I received an invitation from Jorge Osorio to deliver a talk on human rights education as part of a class on popular education for adults. Jorge is a friend, an intellectual, and a tireless fighter in the struggle for democracy. We met at Punta de Tralca, near the sea, far away from the sight of the military and repressive forces.

Almost everyone who attended the course had suffered humiliation and degradation of their dignity. They had been incarcerated, tortured, and threatened. They spoke of their suffering and pain, their losses, their torments and sadness, and their frustration, but also of their hopes. I sympathized deeply with their suffering and anguish.

A question that began to arise in me: Why was it only the victims who had to reestablish democracy? Why should they be the only ones tasked with rebuilding this long-suffering society? Why should they be the only ones who had to think about human rights? I felt quite strongly that once we recovered democracy, if we intended not to repeat what had happened, we should, as a necessity, as an imperative, educate about human rights, educate for "remembrance" and for "never again." I remembered my earlier promise to "Remember and do not forget."

In 1990, with the slow but firm rebirth of democracy and with the help of international agencies like Diaconía from Sweden, we began to work with teachers to organize workshops, and to communicate with educators from other countries who were already involved with human rights education.

Human Rights Education in the Curriculum

Once democracy was reinstated, I thought, naively perhaps, that the experience of the dictatorship meant that human rights education would be a priority and become part of the curriculum without difficulty. But things did not turn out as we had envisioned. Contradictions emerged, a policy of consensus prevailed, and a fear of using human rights language explicity or even subtly arose. I remember a high-level government official of the new coalition government who called me into his office and almost imploringly said, something like, "It is true that we have recovered democracy through a historic plebiscite. Most Chileans, if not all, voted 'No' to Pinochet, expressing through their vote that the seventeen years of dictatorship had been enough, and he had to abandon the power he had taken by force. Nevertheless," he added, "we cannot include a school subject called human rights education in the curriculum. You must remember that Pinochet is still here, the military violators of rights are still here, and so are the politicians who supported the dictatorship." He paused and asked me, "Why not call this new subject Education for Love?" I smiled at him sarcastically and told him that I was in no way opposed to love, but the name human rights education was universal; it was not my invention. Language creates reality. The phrase human rights education has strong connotations that enable the construction and consolidation of democracy, so that human rights will never again be infringed upon in Chile as state policy, as well as to leave a clear and unmistakable legacy of human rights for generations to come.

Cross-Curricular Approaches to Human Rights in the Curriculum

The previous account, which is mostly anecdotal, became more complicated and contradictory as we got closer to curriculum reform. After the intervention of several human rights organizations, it was decided that human rights should be a part of the curriculum but included under "ethics education" as one of the Objetivos Transversales Fundamentales (Basic Cross-Curricular Objectives, or OFT) along with three other areas: "growth and personal assertiveness," "development of thought," and "the individual and her/his environment." In other words, the idea to create a separate human rights course was rejected in favor of an approach that would permeate all other subjects and require these school subjects to be oriented towards a human rights education approach.

During the mid-nineties, the Ministry of Education invited me to become a part of the Unit of Curriculum and Evaluation (UCE), responsible for the creation of new curriculum and programs so that I would be in charge of the OFT. From this post, I defended and supported the idea that human rights should be infused in the entire curriculum. I asserted that human rights education should not belong exclusively to human rights educators; on the contrary, it should be a part of all subjects in the curriculum so that within their specific content and disciplines all teachers would support the creation of students as subjects with rights.

Nevertheless, I have to admit that in my research, visits to the classrooms, and workshops for professors on OFT, I realized that, with a few exceptions, teachers were not fully accepting the cross-curricular nature of human rights education in the curriculum or even the very notion of human rights. There were several reasons for this, such as the emphasis that the Ministry of Education placed on time and resources and the fact that national and standardized tests had to focus, preferably on language, science, mathematics, and history. This relegated the OFT and human rights to a secondary status. In addition, teachers acknowledged that they were not prepared to take full ownership of human rights, and even less to infuse all their subjects with human rights. They claimed they had not received professional development for this. It was then I thought that somehow we had failed. Above all, there was and there is a need to incorporate human rights education in institutions dedicated to the training of teachers and in the curriculum, as well as a need to improve the skills of working teachers as human rights educators.

Creating Networks of Human Rights Educators

It was and it still is a long road, but we were not alone. Networks of human rights educators were created both in Latin America and other countries. It was the beginning of a world movement of human rights educators and sponsors. I would like to acknowledge the work and encouragement of the Inter-American Institute of Human Rights of Costa Rica (IIDH) and of the Latin American Council of Adult Education (CEAAL), which established the Latin American Network for Education for Peace and Human Rights. In addition, on an international level, the Global Human Rights Education Network was created as a part of Human Rights Education Associates (HREA).

I have had the privilege of participating actively in these networks. We have met many members at several events, conferences, colloquiums, and symposiums that have enabled us to discuss ideas, methodologies, reflections, materials, and publications and, why not add, to learn about the multiple problems, dilemmas, and conflicts faced by human rights education (some of which still exist), while at the same time proposing solutions. In addition, thanks to the technology tools that are now available, we have been able to strengthen the networks and to communicate easily with one another.

More importantly, I want to highlight that these networks have allowed me to get in touch with a great number of human rights researchers, educators, sponsors, and activists. I cannot name them individually because there are so many, and I would prefer not to omit any of them. Little by little, I have established intellectual and, above all, emotional and friendly connections that I deeply value. Trust and emotional connections are essential for human rights education. This human rights community is an authentic community linked by a common purpose: supporting the creation of a culture of human rights through human rights education.

Workshops with Teachers

From my first steps in human rights education in the eighties, I thought I should put my knowledge and experience – which I had gained in academic life and by working in popular education – in the service of human rights education. We began by organizing human rights workshops for teachers along with Patricio Donoso, Claudia Dueñas, and the Santiago Workshop of Community Animation. In addition, we worked with María Teresa Rodas, of the Interdisciplinary Research on Education Program (PIIE), a non-governmental organization to which we all belong and which later joined our collective efforts.

To be honest, we hardly knew how to organize them. Because we understood the body was like a door to human rights violations, we incorporated body culture studies[2] along with music, the human rights legal framework, and a participatory, critical, and constructivist methodology. We created opportunities for speaking and other forms of expressions that enabled participants to discuss what they thought human rights should be, share violations they had suffered, and express their emotions and pain. We discussed how to incorporate human rights into the curriculum and how to create a practical pedagogy.

In terms of body culture studies, I remember that one of the specialists asked the workshop participants, about thirty teachers, to walk about the room without bumping or walking into each other. At the end we asked, "What does this physical exercise have to do with human rights?" A teacher answered, "I realized that in spite of the small space, we respected each other without

---

[2] Body culture studies describe and compare bodily practice in the larger context of culture and society, i.e. in the tradition of anthropology, history, and sociology.

incurring any violence. We took care of each other. There is enough space for all of us. The rights of all can and should be respected."

The workshops became an opportunity for sharing individual and collective understanding on human rights. The awareness was there in the minds of each teacher. There was an infinite, imperative need to communicate, to talk, to recall, and to discover that one's knowledge also belonged to others. It was knowledge and experience that was now finally heard, that was not silenced any more, that was not hidden by fear. There was an understanding that "the others" were both in me and with me. This awareness had a collective objectivity. Teachers met each other through a process of interpersonal communication. Step by step, in daily personal experience and with the others, in personal stories and collective stories of human rights violations in the body of real human beings, teachers began creating a language of common meaning. Teachers discussed the indignities they had suffered as Chileans, as persons, and as teachers. Again and again, sometimes compulsively, they told how their ability as teachers and educators had been denigrated, how they had to remain silent, and how with that silence they became accomplices of the violations and thus part of those violations. Long held blame, recriminations, looks, and hidden sentiments emerged.

From this experience in the workshops with teachers, in 1994 we published *Educación en Derechos Humanos: Apuntes para una nueva práctica* (Education in Human Rights: Notes for a New Practice) with the help of PIIE and the National Council for Reparation and Reconciliation. This publication included papers from several Chilean researchers, thinkers, and educators.

Researching, Publishing, and Promoting Human Rights Education

The need for research, writing, publishing, and promoting human rights education grew with the appearance of new ideas that were generated by political, social, and cultural circumstances and challenges posed by both national and international colleagues. This need also grew because of the different Latin American and international institutions with whom we had established close working and personal relationships. We were frequently invited to participate in different events, conferences, and workshops to discuss issues related to human rights education. This, of course, required us to research, think, discuss, study, and to write.

A challenge arose which required that we relate human rights education to a series of new and significant topics that emerged from the changes, contradictions, and tensions experienced in our societies. I began to work and publish on several topics and their relationship to human rights education: the challenges faced by the curriculum, cross-curricular themes, critical pedagogy, problematic and controversial content and methodology, tolerance, and discrimination, as well as social and cultural diversity as founding elements of human rights education. I also explored the being of others (otherness), dilemmas, and tensions faced by human rights education, generic skills required by human rights education, citizenship education, a human rights perspective on preventing school violence and bullying, redistributive social justice, recognition, and representation.

Undoubtedly, writing is not an easy task; as is well known, it requires a significant amount of thought, dedication, and perseverance. It also demands reading many diverse authors and bibliographies, research, close observation, questioning, and especially dialogue and discussion of ideas. Luckily, colleagues and educators both from the Academia de Humanismo Cristiano University, the UNESCO Chair, and those belonging to networks of researchers, activists, and educators on human rights encouraged us to write. They read our first drafts and gave us valuable feedback. I had the opportunity to discuss human rights education at conferences, workshops, and seminars outside Chile. Occasionally, someone would approach me and say, "I wanted to meet you personally. I have read several of your papers, and have used many of them in my work as a teacher." Of course, I always thanked them for this show of affection with humility and modesty. If what is written is not read, it is the same as if it had not been written. The written word doesn't exist without a reader.

A New Century, A New Task

By the end of the first decade of the twenty-first century, I took on the challenging task of capturing thoughts and ideas about human rights education which had been produced in Latin America from multiple and diverse experiences, practices, and materials. I have to say that it has been a long road. Nevertheless, I thought that if we wanted to advance human rights education, to strengthen the theoretical base, and to establish a paradigm that would enable new practices, we had to necessarily and immediately systematize those ideas so that we could produce a Latin American body of teaching. The prevailing consensus indicates that human rights education has grown in complexity and there is a need to organize different concepts that have emerged during the last years. We therefore needed to build a Latin American discourse, inclusive and common to all.

There are of course questions and ambiguities related to the character and specific meaning of human rights education. There are questions about how it complements or distinguishes itself from other, related fields: education for peace, citizenship, and democracy; ecological education and sustainable development; education for tolerance and non-discrimination; and acknowledgment of social and cultural diversity; education on gender, and so on. There is no clear-cut definition, nor are there precise limits and parameters for human rights education.

With this aim in mind, at the beginning of 2008 I invited a group of distinguished and experienced human rights researchers and educators to conduct an analytic review and evaluation on the development of human rights education in their respective countries. The idea was to identify the most relevant and meaningful ideas prevalent during this development.[3] The final twelve monographs were published in 2009 by the publishing house Editorial SM Chile in a book titled *Pensamiento e ideas fuerza de la Educación en Derechos Humanos en Iberoamérica* (*Thoughts and Ideas to Strengthen Human Rights Education in Latin America*).

---

[3] Argentina: Rosa Kleiner and Mónica Fernández; Chile: Marcela Tchimino; Colombia: Manuel Restrepo; Brazil: Susana Scavino and María Vera Candau; Costa Rica: Ana María Rodino; Spain: José Tuvilla; Mexico: Gloria Ramírez; Perú: Rosa María Mujica; Portugal: Carlos Esterao; Puerto Rico: Anita Yudkin and Anaira Pascual Morán; Dominican Republic: Cheila Valera and Mónica Bajaj; Uruguay: Mariana Albistur, Gabriela Juanicó, and Graciela Romero.

In the year 2012, I worked on a research project with María Isabel Toledo, a colleague from the Diego Portales University with whom I have shared for years an interest in the topics of pedagogy of collective memory and human rights, school violence, and bullying. We wanted to learn about how history professors teach the unit related to the military coup and the transition to democracy, which are part of the official history curriculum. Several questions arose from this research:

- Why do fifty percent of the teachers not teach this unit? (passive neutral attitude);
- Why did many professors hold two opposing views on the military coup and the infringement of human rights, but they did not have a personal stand on the subject? (active neutrality);
- Should teachers confront the topic of human rights and their violation more vocally and accurately; this is to say should they take an unequivocal stand?

These questions allowed us to face fully the subject of neutrality and indoctrination on controversial topics like human rights and others. We have several publications on this subject.

The Harald Edelstam UNESCO Chair on Rights Education

With Gloria Ramírez, who heads the UNESCO Chair in Human Rights Education at the Autonomous University of Mexico and with whom I have a close academic relationship and friendship, and with Patricio Donoso, we decided that we should create a UNESCO Chair and thus become part of a network of many chairs around the world. Some of them had already been established in Latin American countries such as Uruguay, Costa Rica, Colombia, and Puerto Rico. Finally, in 2003, after much effort and some red tape, UNESCO allowed us to establish a Chair on Human Rights Education in Santiago, named for Harald Edelstam, the Swedish Ambassador to Chile who rescued and protected many politically persecuted people after the military coup and was called the "Raoul Wallenberg" of the seventies.

This UNESCO Chair has allowed us to promote a series of initiatives in research, extension, and teaching. In this last sphere we have improved a didactic pedagogy for the teaching of human rights and collective memory for college students. Its main features are critical, constructivist, and participatory perspectives that, above all, restore students' daily concepts and experiences of human rights. In terms of public events, the Chair has organized colloquia on topics such as collective memory, recent history, and their relationship to the arts.

A feature I wish to highlight about the UNESCO Chair is that it consists of a small group of volunteers, which has grown in strength due to mutual trust both in academic and personal relationships and through collectively addressing issues when tensions arose. Above all, this is thanks to their unlimited commitment to human rights. In my view, this is an indispensable and unalienable condition if one wishes to further enhance the topics of human rights and human rights education.

A Conceptual Reflection

Considering the events I have mentioned, I can see clearly that the reason for my involvement in human rights was not accidental. We are the result of our identity, contexts, and circumstances. We are social persons, children of our own micro history. I believe the core of my motivation has more to do with the emotional sphere rather than the rational one although, of course, the latter is always present. Nevertheless, what prevails are feelings of belonging within my own identity as well as feelings of empathy for suffering, pain, and the anguish of the "Other." In this sense, I feel a close link with the thought of Richard Rorty, a pragmatist philosopher from the United States, and Emmanuel Levinas, an ethical thinker on otherness.

Rorty would argue that human rights are not founded on the exercise of reason, but on a sentimental view of humanity. He would suggest that human rights are not rationally defensible. He would maintain that one cannot ground the doctrinarian basis of human rights on reason and a moral theory, for moral beliefs and practices are ultimately not motivated by reason but by an empathetic connection with others. Morality, he would state, has its origin in the heart, not the mind. Rorty is quite skeptical about the philosophical basis of human rights. This would mean that the existence of human rights is something "good and desirable," something we can all benefit from. He is in no way hostile to human rights doctrine, but he believes that human rights have a better chance when an appeal is made to emotions and the unnecessary suffering of others, rather than from the precise arguments of reason.

Emmanuel Levinas' ideas have to do directly with the experiences and vicissitudes, the sufferings and deprivations he endured during World War II. Except for his daughter and wife, who managed to hide in a French monastery, his entire family died in the Holocaust. For Levinas, ethics go further than Being. It could be said that after Auschwitz, his concerns could not refer to "manners of being" or to "the comprehension of being"; the question has to do with ethics, the relationship between the being and the Other, the responsibility to the Other, the encounter with the Other. He argues that responsibility goes to the level of even being responsible for the responsibility of the Other. This is my concern. Because responsibility to the Other is part of the essence of being an individual, it cannot be relinquished: the "I" is a "hostage" of the Other. Levinas explains that, "I am responsible for the Other with no hope of reciprocity, even though it might mean giving my life." He quotes Dostoyevsky, "We are all guilty of all and for all men before all, and I more than the others."

Levinas identifies the Other with the "Face." The Face cannot be seen; it can be heard. The Face is not the countenance; it is the print of the Other. The Face does not have a reference; it is the "living presence" of the Other, pure meaning and meaning without context. Usually, the meaning of something depends on its relationship with something else. On the contrary, in this case Face is only meaning. You are you. This is why the Face cannot be seen, but heard, read. The Face is the word of what the voice lacks, the word of the orphan, the word of the widow, of the foreigner. The Face is an ethical imperative that says: "You shall not kill!" This is the first word of the Face. It is a command. With the Face comes a command, as if a master had spoken. Nevertheless, the Face of the Other is unprotected; is the wretched for whom I can do all and to whom I owe all.

So, looking back at my personal history – both authors bring me back to it – my involvement with human rights education, and perhaps that of many other educators, is the result of an identity, of a history, of circumstances that are more emotional than rational. Human rights education is for me a way of expressing my empathy, commitment, and responsibility, my watchfulness of others, to recognize in them that we are all subject to rights and dignity.

Human rights education is the place for learning to be aware of the Other, to "take care of" the Other, to learn not to turn one's back, to say, "Yes, I am my brother's keeper." It is the place that allows us to recover our memory and commit ourselves to "Never again"; to teach new generations about the atrocities committed during the Holocaust and during dictatorships that must never happen again, to anybody, under any circumstance. Human rights education is the sphere that teaches to eliminate prejudices, intolerance, and discriminations of all types that have caused so much suffering through history and that still cause pain. Lastly, human rights education is an opportunity for dreaming of a better future.

BIBLIOGRAPHY

Levinas, Emmanuel (1974). *Humanismo del otro hombre*. Mexico: Siglo XXI.

Rorty, Richard (1999). "Human Rights, Rationality and Sentimentality" in *The Politics of Human Rights*. London: Verso.

Why I Am a Human Rights Educator?
Edward O'Brien (USA)

Edward O'Brien was a lawyer and longtime educator who founded the Street Law program in Washington, DC, in 1972. He was the author of a number of books, curriculum materials, and articles on law and human rights education. He served as Executive Director of Street Law Inc., which has worked to spread teaching of law, democracy, and human rights across the United States and to over forty other countries. More recently, he was a professor at the University of the District of Columbia in Washington, DC.

My mother was from Virginia. She grew up in the segregated South and espoused strong racial views at the dinner table. Once she said that the Daughters of the American Revolution had a right to forbid Marian Anderson from singing at Constitution Hall in Washington. Another time she told me, "Never call colored people by their last names or they will take advantage of you." Fortunately, my father countered her views. He was a lawyer and a liberal Democrat from Brooklyn. This experience led me to believe in human rights, though I never heard the term growing up.

In 1968, I was in danger of being drafted to go fight in the Vietnam War, and I left law school to teach high school social studies and gain a draft deferment. I still didn't know the term "human rights" though that is what opposition to the war was all about. In 1971, I returned to Georgetown Law School and enrolled in every public interest course I could. Even in those courses, I never heard the term "human rights" though that is what my study there was all about.

I enrolled in a course called "Public Interest Law in the District of Columbia," where we learned that citizens there did not have a vote in Congress. They still don't. This is a gross human rights violation, but we didn't call it that. In that course, I was involved with starting the first Street Law program. We went into the inner city high schools of Washington and taught criminal, consumer, torts, family, housing, and constitutional law. We taught human rights, but we still didn't use the words.

In 1975, the national Street Law program, Street Law Inc., was born and published the first *Street Law* high school textbook, which is now in its eighth edition, having sold over two million copies. The words "human rights" didn't appear in the early editions. In 1985, a momentous event happened in my life. I was invited to South Africa to share the Street Law program and materials. I met up with Professor David McQuoid-Mason, Dean of the University of Natal Law School (now University of KwaZulu-Natal). Others said if we tried to do Street Law, we would be arrested. He said, "We can do this." He took the American *Street Law* textbook and adapted it for South Africa, adding South African law and examples and wonderful illustrations. He said to me, "Why are there no human rights in this book?" I said I didn't know much about human rights and that we only used those words in the USA when we were talking about violations in other countries. He convinced me of the importance of human rights domestically as well as internationally, and we decided to jointly write a human rights textbook that would be simultaneously published in South Africa and the USA. This book is called *Human Rights for All*. I believe it is the only human rights textbook to be published for use by students in those two countries.

After the publication of that text, I began to investigate the field of human rights education (HRE) in the USA and found that there was a small band of educators – including Nancy Flowers, Bill Fernekes, and Janet Schmidt of Amnesty International, Kristi Rudelius-Palmer of the University of Minnesota Human Rights Resource Center, and Loretta Ross from the Center for Human Rights Education in Atlanta – who were doing pioneering work in the field of HRE. I also found out that there were many other people in the USA and around the world doing the same. I joined forces with these US folks and formed a coalition we called Human Rights USA. Funded by the Ford Foundation, this project was designed to spread HRE nationwide. It selected pilot cities, trained teachers, and educated school (K-12) students and people in communities.

Street Law Inc. sponsored the US publication of the *Human Rights for All*, text in the early 90s and adopted the organizational slogan "Education about law, human rights and democracy." It shared the South African experience and over the next twenty years adapted it for use in Latin America, Eastern Europe, Russia, the Middle East, and other countries in Africa. Under the leadership of Richard Grimes of the University of York, it spread to forty-four law schools in the UK. At one point South Africa was using the *Human Rights for All* text at eighteen law schools, where law students went into schools and the community and taught law, democracy, and human rights.

I have learned that to teach law or democracy without teaching human rights is vastly inadequate. Human rights are a value system and a foundation on which law and democracy rests. Young people must be taught ethical behavior, and human rights are a set of ethical standards the world has agreed upon. In *Human Rights for All* we centered learning on the Universal Declaration of Human Rights as the principles therein which allow us to measure practices by any government, including the USA, against universally accepted rights.

If only I had known about human rights when I was sitting at the dinner table and my mother was expressing her views!

Widening Educational Horizons: Critical Plans for Education for Peace and Human Rights

Greta Papadimitriou (Mexico)

> **Greta Papadimitriou Cámara** attended the Autonomous University of Aguascaliente (UAA), where she received a bachelor's degree in psycho-pedagogical counseling, with a specialization in human rights education and a master's degree in educational research. Her master's was completed with a scholarship from the National Council for Science and Technology of Mexico (CONACYT). For twenty-three years, she was a member of the Education for Peace and Human Rights Program at UAA (1989-2012). She founded the Association for Education and Human Rights of Aguascalientes and the Education for Peace Collective, A.C. Starting in 2007, as a member of the latter, she developed educational programs on peace, human rights, conflict resolution, and gender perspectives. She has also been a coordinator for various programs on crime prevention and social safety in cities. She has been an external advisor for several government agencies dealing with human rights, women, and education both in the State of Aguascalientes and in Mexico City. She has authored more than thirty publications, the most significant of which are textbooks for civics and ethics.

Before the Program for Peace and Human Rights Education (1964-1989)

I come from a nomadic family with deep spiritual and artistic influences. My father, Christos Jorge, and my mother, María Teresa, met on a theater stage. They were engaged in Campeche, where my mother was born and lived. At the end of the fifties, they started a family in Mexico City, where my father was born. My siblings, Jorge Luis, Martha Teresa, and I were born during the sixties in the city of Querétaro. My brother Carlos Eduardo was born in San Luis Potosí.

I was born in a decade of student and peace movements, some of which I recall from family discussions and from gatherings of intellectuals at our house, as well as from the little I could gather from television. At the end of the sixties, when I was five, we moved to Aguascalientes. It was there that I attended elementary school, high school, and college from 1969-1986.

I spent my childhood and teenage years on the stage. As soon as school was over, I took drama, classical ballet, and singing lessons. Theater was my main after-school activity during my elementary and high school years. I toured all around the country – we sometimes also visited foreign countries – with the Aguascalientes' Teatristas Company, which was directed by my father.

My family owned a bookstore in the Cultural Center of Aguascalientes where all the family worked together. This is how I became familiar with the literature from what was then called the "Latin American Literary Boom." Before I was intellectually mature, I had already soaked up the Latin American literature available at that time.

My father's life as a promoter of culture and my mother's patience enabled us to meet a group of renowned writers, musicians, performers, artists, and actors from all around Mexico and Latin America. All of them were followers of *el Che* (Che Gueverra), Fidel Castro, and Salvador Allende. This is why I have never forgotten the pain we felt when we learned about the coup d'état in Chile that ended Allende's life. I was nine years old at that time.

In college during the eighties, I began to venture into the field of education. I read about the ideas of great educators and social science scholars, the most influential of whom was Paulo Freire.

I did not learn about Freire in a classroom, but rather as a consequence of the fact that in my family we were all avid readers. It was my sister Martha who initially gave me his first books. Teachers like Chava Camacho allowed me to write essays on Freire's pedagogy, even though it was not at all part of my academic curriculum in psycho-pedagogical counseling, and writing these essays enabled me to develop my own perspectives.

My marriage during my fifth semester of college meant a significant change from a liberal and progressive life to a conservative even retrograde one. I say this with some regrets, but not shame. It was the first path I found to distinguish myself from my family environment. I kept on studying nevertheless. In the mornings I played the role of a perfect housewife while in the afternoon I was a student with all the ups and downs of student life. I became pregnant during my last year of college, and Jesús, my oldest son, was born in 1987. I finished my studies when Jesús was one year old.

In 1989, María de los Ángeles Alba Olvera, one of my college teachers, knocked on my door to ask me to help her create groups for a research project that she would lead. This project would continue for ten months with the help of María Jiménez Loza, the teacher who had recommended me.

When I was twenty-five, with my husband's consent – for I had to ask his permission – and with a two-year-old son and pregnant with my youngest child, Jorge Eduardo, I enrolled in the Education on Peace and Human Rights Program at the Mexican Association for the United Nations (AMNU) and the Autonomous University of Aguascalientes (UAA). I did not realize then that this was the beginning of an immense life project that, inevitably, meant my emancipation.

During the Education for Peace and Human Rights Program (1989-2012)

From "Theirs to Ours" (1989-1994)

Under Pablo Latapí Sarre, the Education for Peace and Human Rights Program (EPDH) began at the basic education level, elementary school, with a team of university researchers as well as a team of teachers from each of the six elementary grades. This project would go on to have a tremendous impact on human rights education in Mexico. It was created with material and support from two Chilean institutions: the Vicaría de Pastoral Social (Vicar for a Social Pastoral) and the Interdisciplinary Program for Research on Education (PIIE, mainly from work developed by Abraham Magendzo). We also received support from the Peace and Justice Service in Uruguay, thanks to a proposal by Luis Pérez Aguirr and recommendations from UNESCO.

As I have described elsewhere:

> The Mexican Association for the United Nations (AMNU), with the assistance of the Autonomous University of Aguascalientes, was the first Mexican association to create an explicit education for peace project. Their work has continued since 1988, first as a project and later as the Education for Peace and Human Rights Program.
>
> The main objective of the research program was the design and application of an educational methodology that would introduce human rights into elementary-level classrooms. Together with the Education, Peace and Human Rights Association, AMNU also encouraged this program at the high school level in Torreón; in Mexico City it was also undertaken at the preschool level.[1]

It must be acknowledged that the program benefited from the contemporary political situation as the government, wishing fervently to incorporate Mexico in the Free Trade Agreement (NAFTA), had decided to promote a development plan that sponsored human rights education from a values perspective.

In 1989, the year I began participating in the program, the coordinator, Ángeles Alba, and her team of teachers (founding members of this program: María Elena Ortiz García, Gabriela Asunción Barba Martínez, Francisco Águila Rivas, and Esther Barba Ávila) had participated in a course at the Universitat de Sant Cugat del Vallés in Barcelona, where they met with a group of educators for peace who would later enable us to define our own perspectives on education for peace. Collaborative agreements were signed with members of the Seminar on Education for Peace at that university, such as Paco Cascón Soriano and Rafael Grasa, who would become influential in our program. Paco would be especially important in my life as an educator for peace and human rights.

---

[1] Human Rights Commission (2004). *Marco conceptual educativo de la CDHDF* (Educational Conceptual Framework). Human Rights Commission. Mexico City.

Both Latin influences in the program, the Latin American and the Spanish, balanced the tension generated by the confluence of human rights education, the participatory methodologies influenced by Freire, and the socio-affective methodologies from the workshops of Paco Cascón. So the program began to develop its own identity, never losing its focus on the values of human rights, based both on the legal aspects of human rights, as well as the right to education (unlike the emphasis on historical and political aspects, which became emphasized years later).

It was during this time that I reclaimed my nomadic roots and travelled around my country, sharing the project in other states and cities. As a consequence, my family life began to fragment, and I realized that I could "no longer hold up the walls of my house." The year 1991 marked an important period for the program both internally and in terms of local, national, and international visibility. This was the first year of a summer workshop taught by national and international teachers that continued for sixteen years. I was able to meet people who were essential for the program and consequently for myself.

In 1993, María de los Ángeles, a member of AMNU in Mexico City, invited me to join her at a Latin American conference at the Servicio Paz y Justicia (Justice and Peace Service) in Uruguay. Though she was no longer coordinating the program and I still had not obtained tenure at my university, my personal interest as an educator for peace and human rights was established, and I began to more or less lead the academic development of the program. At the end of the conference I was in charge of planning a second Latin American conference in Aguascalientes.

After this trip the program was included in the Latin American Network for Education for Peace and Human Rights of the Latin American Council of Adult Education (CEAAL). The following year, 1994, in the midst of an indigenous uprising, we hosted a conference in Aguascaliente with the support of the governor of the state, Otto Granados Roldán. That same year I participated for the first time in an assembly of the Latin American Network, and by the end of the year my political and educational position, which was strengthened by the struggle for indigenous rights, led me to take a less ambivalent position about my professional and personal life: I decided to separate from the father of my children.

During this time we began to realize that the government's promotion of human rights, such as the creation of the National Commission for Human Rights and its branches in the individual states, was a response to international interests based on unequal economic relations. As a result, concern for the rural areas had almost disappeared, and what little remained was in its death throes. This was evident from the segregation of social classes in every city in the country.

Re-focusing and Re-planning from inside the Education for Human Rights Program, (1995 - 2003)

At this point AMNU requested us to stop in order to clarify the focus and reorganize the project so that it could be implemented throughout the whole school system: preschool, elementary, and high school. The team in Mexico City headed by Ángeles Alba was in charge of preschool. I was in charge of elementary school along with a team in Aguascalientes. Silvia Conde and a team in Torreón coordinated high school. The Latin American Institute for Educational Communication (ILCE) published an anthology comprised of international documents and basic readings for the EPDH program, as well as two methodological guides for preschool and elementary levels.

Influenced by Rafael Grasa and Paco Cascón, who questioned the lack of a gender perspective in our work, the work of both Lawrence Kohlberg and Carol Gilligan were incorporated in the program. Though we lacked methodological tools, we began to engage with gender perspectives. We received the support of many specialists in this field, such as Marcela Lagarde and Marina Subirats, as well as countless materials donated by the Seminar on Education for Peace in Spain.

During this period, with the support of the team from EPDH, I created an academic concentration on education and human rights at the Autonomous University of Aguascalientes. Abraham Magendzo has noted it as the first of its kind in Latin America. Due to lack of resources and a reduced academic staff (since it relied mostly on external academic experts), the concentration offered only three academic classes. For more than a decade we only had Bonifacio Barba Casillas, counselor and collaborator with the program, as well as Jesús Antonio de la Torre Rangel. This work encouraged all the participants of the team in Aguascalientes to pursue graduate study.

From 1995 to 1996, we worked with the National Liberation Zapatista Front, but we did not forget our academic work. I was a part-time working mother because after my separation Jesús and Jorge Eduardo lived from Monday to Friday with me and spent weekends with their father. This arrangement allowed me during the weekends to participate more in the work of non-governmental organizations and to devote myself to graduate study along with a group of national and international teachers and classmates, whom I still see and work with in civil society and public service or as independent educators.

By the end of my graduate work, I frequented La Querencia, a cultural bar, and a gathering place for *onegeneros*,[2] where we met for drinks and to listen to music or poetry. La Querencia was the meeting place for Zapatista polls or referendums. My last day of graduate study, August 31, 1996, I met Sinú Romo Reza, with whom I have since shared my personal and professional life.

Meeting Sinú signaled an important change in my life. In personal terms, he became a part-time father while I was working on my master's degree. In professional terms, we decided to publish materials that included a newsletter called *Apuros*. We also published papers by our national and international guests at the summer courses and workshops, such as Abraham Magendzo, Peter McLaren, Michael Apple, Marcela Lagarde, Sylvia Schmelkes, Silvia Conde, and Paco Cascón.

During this period, the right to a peaceful coexistence and the fulfilling of basic needs became the central topic of our educational undertakings. We were influenced by feminist studies, critical

---

[2] The popular name for those that belonged to non-governmental organizations (abbreviated in Spanish as ONG).

theory, and a country "unmasked" by those who took away our faces and our names. In addition, we focused on skills that would enable us to exercise power.

From 1998 to 2003, I worked on a master's degree in educational research with the support of Sinú, who helped me take care of my children. Gabriela Barba and I focused our thesis on how gender manifested itself in schools.

One of the problems of coexistence and power sharing in which I was (and still am) able to put theory and methodologies into practice was the construction or reconstruction of our family life. I am very proud of our family life because it has been widened and enriched in such a way that all its members – not without headaches, separations, reformulations, and all that daily life implies – could arrive at compromises they could live with and equally balanced responsibilities.

Future Plans Between the University and the Education for Peace Collective (2003-2012)

The Human Rights Commission of the Federal District (2003-2009)

In 2002, Emilio Álvarez Icaza sought the presidency of the Human Rights Commission of the Federal District, Mexico City (CDHDF) and won from a pool of more than a hundred candidates. That same year he began work on structural reforms to create a Department of Education. He invited me to join them because he knew of our work and he had participated twice in our courses and workshops. Although I was chosen to head the department, I declined because of issues related to my family's reconstruction process, which I have mentioned above. Nevertheless, I asked Emilio to invite me to be an external consultant, a post I held for seven years. This role allowed us to document and reformulate the experience of the Education for Human Rights Program, adapting and using it as a frame of reference for the Commission's strategy on education.

This period made it possible for our work as educators for peace and human rights to have power imbalances and balances as a starting point, with the ultimate goal being a united coexistence and concern for the "self," the "other," and the "us" as a middle ground. The program began at the university, but it was continually enriched by the synergy between the Human Rights Commission and other governmental departments working in Mexico City. This allowed us to advocate for non-violent resolution of conflicts through the development of books for citizenship and ethics education and the training of public servants, policemen, and, of course, teachers.

During this period Cecilia Loría, head of the National Institute for Social Development (INDESOL), had obtained a special budget to deal with the multiple murders of women in Ciudad Juárez. To do this, we established a civil association, and in 2004, we created the Education for Peace Collective, A.C., widening our sphere of influence. With the help of INDESOL, both as part of the University and as a civil association, we were in charge of graduate studies for the Strengthening of Civil Society Organizations. We published seven editions of *Espacios Educativos*, an academic review that came out four times a year, and we joined organizations in Ciudad Juárez to help in the reconstruction of the social fabric in order to confront both cultural and structural violence. Meanwhile, the magazine *Espacios Educativos* was chosen as a successful example that enabled its distribution by mail of a thousand copies around the country, both to schools and social organizations.

Encouraged by Emilio and presented as a Human Rights Commission proposal making use of my original ties to the arts, we designed a space for the interactive education of human rights. This space did not see the light of day, but it served as a point of reference in classrooms and workshops established by the end of his administration in September 2009.

In 2007, thanks to an initiative by Cecilia Loría in what would become her last project and now is part of the Department for Public Education, I was invited to participate in the Federal program Construye T (a play on words in Spanish that means "build yourself"). We are still in charge of its coordination in the state of Aguascalientes through the Education for Human Rights Program of the UAA, and in the state of Michoacán, through the Education for Peace Collective, A.C. Collective, established in Pátzcuaro in 2007. The program Construye T has allowed us to work with students at the high school level to reduce the school drop-out rate and promote the development of basic skills as they address the problems they face in their increasingly violent environments.

Consultancy to the Government of the State of Aguascalientes (2005-2010)

Thanks to the educational strategy of the Human Rights Commission, we were able to publish a model of skills and competencies for conflict resolution with McGraw Hill. The State of Aguascalientes purchased the program to provide support for their teachers. The book was also used as the conceptual and methodological framework for the Program for Values at the Education Institute of Aguascalientes. For five years, workshops, manuals, and research were organized in a cooperative effort between the IEA (Instituto de Educación de Aguascalientes), the Women's Institute of Aguascalientes, the EPDH Program of the UAA, and CEPAZ. Thus, the scant resources assigned to education on values, human rights, and gender equality were multiplied.

However, in spite of the program's influence and prestige both at the state and national levels, the University did not include it in its budget. This was done even though the program represented a very small part of the university's overall budget and was primarily developed through external funding. This budget cut weakened us from both an administrative and political standpoint. It was also surprising given a national environment in which human rights had attained a level of constitutional importance. Currently, and in spite of the widespread social violence documented in studies undertaken in districts all around the country, the program is still unsupported by the University.

The Education for Peace Collective (2009-2012)

Near the end of Emilio's time at the Human Rights Commission, I was invited by Clara Jusidman to assess the levels of social violence in the metropolitan area of Aguascalientes. This assignment gave us the opportunity to work in several districts around the country on crime prevention by means of assessment, municipal planning, work with gangs, and training of civil servants, as well as tours inside cities to develop a safe-city strategy that among other programs included non-violence toward women. I do not quite know what the future of the program is, whether it will continue or whether I will work independently. What I do know is that we have had such direct positive influence and impact in the creation of public policies, especially at district levels, that we can expand our educational horizons both with hard facts and with the application of qualitative programs in the short, mid, and long term, and not just in schools or organizations.

Today, CEPAZ has revisited previous experiences and has opened its doors to a program for educational tourism, with twelve workshops of education for peace: *Los 12 del 12*. This process for social reconstruction will help to quell fear in the state of Michoacán that has mainly resulted from the violence among organized crime gangs and from the equally violent policies put in place by the federal government to deal with organized crime. Thanks to a project that calls for an interactive education space that was planned by Emilio Álvarez Icaza in 2009, after sixteen months of hard work, CEPAZ presented a proposal for a tasteful museum exhibition to the government of Iztapalapa (a political demarcation in Mexico City) in April 2012, in particular to Clara Brugada and the Museo de las Culturas of Iztapalapa. The project employed a cross-curricular notion of human rights and respect for cultural diversity. Headed by Tinitus and Martha Papadimitriou, this was a project of the highest quality, even though it was accomplished with a much reduced budget.

This recounting of my activities and projects serves to highlight a widespread social need to recover the meaning and confidence that will allow for a more humane life and coexistence in both private and public life, especially considering the vicious violence that continues to expand in the twenty-first century.

I am an educator for peace and human rights. I am not good at anything else so, wherever I am called to, I will use the best of us as a collective to develop the ability to live and coexist with dignity.

I am thankful for all those people who have been essential for my development and being, for those who are still close to me, those that have gone, and those who remain in spite of time and distance.

BIBLIOGRAPHY

Human Rights Commission (2004). *Marco conceptual educativo de la CDHDF* (Educational Conceptual Framework). Human Rights Commission. Mexico City.

Engaging People through Human Rights Education
Jefferson R. Plantilla (Philippines, Japan)

> **Jefferson R. Plantilla** currently works as the Chief Researcher at the Asia-Pacific Human Rights Information Center (HURIGHTS OSAKA), where he has been involved in regional human rights education, research, and publication. Previously, he was the first Coordinator of the Bangkok-based Asian Regional Resource Center for Human Rights Education (ARRC). Starting with his work at the Structural Alternative Legal Assistance for the Grassroots (SALAG) in the Philippines (1985-1992), he has been involved in the preparation of a number of publications related to human rights education, including directories of institutions, material collection, research reports, teaching/training materials, publications on human rights education experiences, and newsletters. He has also written articles on human rights education and been involved in organizing workshops sponsored by other institutions in Asia, as well as invited as resource person or facilitator.
>
>

I grew up in a small Philippine town located at the foot of two mountains - Mount Banahaw and Mount San Cristobal. During *semana santa* (Holy Week) people trek to Mount Banahaw for a religious pilgrimage. Our town has many spiritual healers, mostly women, who combine Christian beliefs with indigenous rituals in healing the sick from the town as well as from afar.

During the 1960s, people in the town were largely divided between two dominant political parties. Families were either with the Partido Liberal or with the Partido Nacionalista. Our family supported the Partido Nacionalista.

The 1970s started without much difference from the previous decade until martial rule was declared. I learned about it from my father who came home, his face visibly worried, to tell my mother that martial law would be declared. I thought he was worried about the future under a never-before-experienced martial rule. That was one day before the government announced that martial law had indeed been declared. September 23, 1972,[1] was not a normal day. The radio and television were not broadcasting, and the newspaper did not arrive. When television programming returned, it showed the then President, Ferdinand E. Marcos, telling the whole nation that the martial rule that had been declared was not a military takeover. From that time onward, public announcements were made straight from the executive house, Malacañang, about presidential decrees, orders, and issuances. For several days, the town was eerily quiet. Almost no one dared speak about martial law or the government except in whispered tones. One old medical doctor in our neighborhood did not bother to hide his feelings about the situation. He always spoke loudly as he walked on the street, while his old neighbors smiled at him.

In school we started to sing a new national song and swear an additional pledge of commitment to the country. Mass media repeatedly broadcasted a slogan: *Sa Ikauunlad ng Bayan, Disiplina ang Kailangan* (For the Progress of the Nation, Discipline is Necessary). Young men lined up at the barbershops for a haircut because the government banned long hair. Long knives (*itak*) used in farming were considered deadly weapons; people hid them when going to their farms. There was a curfew at night. And the police seemed to have become stricter.

The circulation of information was restricted. The media evolved from a boisterous and free press to one that exercised "freedom of the praise." Every media person was totally free to praise the government. Courageous writers who dared write articles critical of the government got invitation for a so-called "talk" in military camps, as several courageous women writers experienced. There was also "envelopmental" instead of developmental journalism, one that thrived on corrupting the media people. Several years into martial law, a newspaper critical of the government came out, but it had very limited circulation – mainly in Metro Manila. I know of only one newsletter produced by a church-based media center that was circulating carefully presented critical issues of the day. This newsletter was sent free to government officials, including my father, among other recipients. I suppose one could read much between the lines of the statements in this newsletter.

September 1972 was supposed to be the start of the rebirth of the country, towards a New Society.

I grew up in that town, 150 kilometers away from Manila, till I was ready for college in the late 1970s.

The Beginning?

Because my father was both a lawyer and also a judge in a neighboring municipal court, many different types of people sought him for advice. As a little boy, I was a silent *miron* (bystander) listening to what they were discussing. Our small house was open to those who sought legal advice, and I got used to welcoming people into our modest living room.

---

[1] A report from a Philippine government website corrects the popular understanding that the then President Ferdinand E. Marcos proclaimed martial law in the Philippines on September 21, 1972. The report states that the televised proclamation of martial law was made on September 23, 1972. See "Declaration of Martial Law," *Official Gazette*, in www.gov.ph/featured/declaration-of-martial-law/.

In secondary school I was a member of a group that taught catechism to primary school students in the *barrios* (now formally called *barangays*). In 1977, I went to Manila to attend a prestigious private university for college and law school. While in college I joined a couple of small student organizations, including an immersion program that required me to stay in a rural community for about a week. There I learned about the different aspects of life of the people in this community.

I decided to enter law school after college, but before law school classes began in 1981, I joined a two-day seminar on "alternative profession." The seminar dealt with issues that confronted Philippine society at that time and the need to respond through alternative profession (one that serves society) and alternative lifestyle (non-materialistic, non-consumerist, non-violent, pro-environment). In law school I got involved in the Legal Aid Office, was elected as Vice-President of the Student Council for one term, joined a new student organization instead of any of the old fraternities, attended a seminar on "alternative law," and with a fellow law student did my first field research on laws on the urban poor. These initial involvements eventually and unconsciously became stepping-stones to my involvement as a young law graduate (and soon after as a young lawyer) in the so-called alternative legal practice.

When I became a lawyer in 1986, I could have joined a law firm in the country's business district, but I joined a non-governmental organization (NGO) instead and found myself going back to places similar to where I grew up. I was visiting sugarcane farmers, fisherfolk, and Indigenous Peoples in different rural areas. I once found myself in the midst of a vast sugarcane field and a question came out from nowhere: "What am I doing here?" I never got to answer it, but the question did not come to mind again.

Learning from the Field

The people I met in my work fascinated me. I admired their wisdom. One leader of a farmer's group said: *Hindi natin dapat iasa sa mga taong busog ang paglutas ng problema nating mga gutom.* (We should not entrust to people with full stomach the resolution of problems of us who are hungry). I sensed the strong belief in empowerment in this statement, of standing on their own feet despite the difficult situations they face.

I also learned that despite outward displays of respect, lawyers like me were not spared suspicions. People would comment that I would probably become a politician later on since I started to be "known" by communities. While that seemed to be a compliment on my work, I also saw it as a suspicion that I might have been harboring a secret, selfish desire to gain a powerful public office with the "service" I was providing to people as my political investment.

Once in an Indigenous Peoples' community, I overheard a young person asking whether or not they should sign the papers I brought that would register with the government their indigenous community as a corporate entity. He was not sure if I should be trusted. The socio-religious worker of the place responded by saying that they could sign the documents because I would not deceive them. While I should rightly be upset by the stance of that young indigenous person, I realized that I should leave to him and his community their freedom to decide and that I should work hard to earn their respect. Being a lawyer from Manila was not enough to deserve respect. And who was I to require from them blind faith in what I did?

I also learned that my role was not to push people to act but to help them think of the options before them and to make them conscious enough of the consequences involved in each option. I never insisted that I knew better than they and thus could decide on their behalf. Instead I emphasized that they had to be responsible for their decisions. I reminded them that what was at stake was their necks not mine. It is morally wrong to force people to decide on a certain path that can potentially bring greater problems to them and that they cannot run away from. If they wanted that path, they deserved to be properly reminded of the potential adverse consequence.

I also learned to be critical of people and their search for help. We did not want a dole-out type of legal service. Alternative law practice subscribes to the view that the people in general and the sectors served, as the primary force for social transformation, must be empowered to be able to play this role. We wanted to enable people to be with us as partners, and in most cases non-formal legal education was needed to realize this partnership. We wanted them to solve their own problems as much as possible. But, unfortunately, sometimes a small legal victory was enough to make some of them stay away from any further involvement in the community – leaving me distraught at the wasted efforts to empower them or at least change their perspectives.

On a number of occasions I, as a lawyer, would be expected to present all the solutions possible. But instead I would always ask them to think about solutions and explain that I would support them in the process. They would say, "Attorney, we do not know anything. You are a lawyer, you know more. Tell us what to do." Many years later, I learned that Paolo Freire experienced exactly the same situation in his educational activities in the 1960s.

Indeed, a "super hero" who rescues people from their suffering is a fantasy.

Human Rights Education

My first human rights education activity was in late 1985. I was asked by an NGO to discuss the Universal Declaration of Human Rights (UDHR) before a group of fisherfolk. The activity was held in a fishing village at night, the time most available to the fisherfolk who normally went out to fish in the evening. I was confident that my knowledge of law would be more than sufficient to help me make the fisherfolk understand the UDHR. I was eloquent and clear in my discussions about civil and political rights and other rights in the UDHR, which were not much different from what we had in the 1973 Philippine Constitution. After my rather lengthy discussion, the fisherfolk started to ask me questions. And soon my eloquence started to wane. They asked about their fishing grounds: how would their access to these resources be protected? What rights would be available to fisherfolk? I could not directly respond. I could not find an appropriate provision on their questions in the UDHR.

I could not simply retort using the workers' rights provisions. I realized that the UDHR, adopted thirty-seven years earlier, was largely framed in the context of an industrial society. There was no mention about natural resources such as forestry, agrarian, and aquatic resources upon which many people's livelihood depended.

In my subsequent work, the issues I faced were those related to natural resources that adversely affected Indigenous Peoples, poor farmers, and subsistence fisherfolk. We relied much on the existing domestic laws as we both educated and litigated on those issues and the pertinent legislations.

Every court case I handled had an educational component ranging from discussing with the people involved each step of the court process to having a special seminar for them on the cases and the related larger issues, providing paralegal training to some members of the community or group involved in order to mobilize them to support the case (e.g., getting witnesses, obtaining documents, drafting statements, filing documents in court, and following up on certain matters).

I was involved in implementing a legal education program based on the alternative law approach. The program aimed at empowering people with the knowledge of the law, legal procedures, mechanisms, and skills. It aimed at demystifying the law and turning it into a resource for the poor. In the Philippine context, this approach supported the reported policy of a former Philippine President, Ramon Magsaysay, who espoused the idea that those who have less in life should have more in law.

I admit that it was not easy to discuss human rights regarding local issues. This was particularly true in the case of economic and social issues. The presentation of general principles, such as the international human rights standards, in local community education activities must not appear as a strained effort.

Fortunately, sometime in 1986, I came to know the United Nations Declaration on the Right to Development, which gave me a better way of linking human rights to the issues of fisherfolk, Indigenous Peoples, farmers, and even urban poor. Around 1987 I had been using the Declaration as a starting point in legal education activities, emphasizing its provisions that inter-relate all human rights and those that speak of right to natural resources and social and economic development in general.

Approach to Education

While in college, I got into a debate with a person who was recruiting me to join an underground political movement. I did not know why I was targeted for recruitment into such a movement except that I probably looked poor in a university where the country's children of the rich and the powerful went. I went to that university because of financial aid, since my family could not afford to send me there. I argued against the idea of political vanguardism. I used the image of a fly on the head of the *carabao* (water buffalo) to stress my point. Staying on the head and feeling the strength of this relatively big animal, the fly began to think that it was the carabao! I questioned the claims of political movements that they represented the "masses."

I was probably sensitive to any effort at ideological generalization of situations and righteous assumptions about the needs of other people. If this sensitivity was the concept of respect for others, then I was probably subscribing to it.

Back in high school I had attended sessions that prepared us for our catechism classes for primary school students. In these sessions I felt no compulsion to accept the ideas being expressed. I was given time to absorb them in a nice, quiet way. Inside the classroom I appreciated the time when the teacher was part of a circle in discussing the lessons with the students. I did not see the higher status of the teacher; I felt instead a sense of equality.

I learned from a fellow law student the word "facipulation," which combines "facilitation" with "manipulation." In facipulation there is an ostensive free exchange of ideas and opinion but only on the surface. Underneath it a sophisticated manipulation of the process occurs at the same time in order to ensure that the session leads to a predetermined conclusion. Political education and campaign activities have used facipulation to get support.

I have experienced the beauty of an honest subscription to an inclusive process of information and opinion exchange. I have seen how this process brings genuine learning to and from all participants.

In sum, I favor an educational approach that begins and ends with genuine respect for each other. Lacking this, only forms of top-down teaching and learning occur.

The Institutions

I joined the Structural Alternative Legal Assistance for the Grassroots, better known as SALAG, in December 1985.

Litigation, education, and law reform formed the core of SALAG's program. And it focused on communities or groups of farmers, fisherfolk, and Indigenous Peoples in different rural areas. Travelling by bus, ferry boat, and small plane, I handled cases in courts in different provinces.

SALAG started the Alternative Law School (ALS), whose students were members of the so-called people's organizations (POs) and staff of NGOs that worked with grassroots communities. It focused on specific issues relating to farmers, Indigenous Peoples, fisherfolk, and urban poor. It had a specific program on human rights discussed in relation to these marginalized groups. An essential feature of the education program was the critical review of laws and legal mechanisms from the perspective of the marginalized groups and also of human rights. Part of the educational exercise was the drawing up of law reform measures by the participants based on their analysis of the laws and legal mechanisms. This exercise not only enriched their knowledge of the law, but also enhanced their critical views of the issues.

But SALAG's regular educational program was paralegal training. It was held in the communities of the marginalized groups, with each training tailored to the needs and situation of the community involved. Often the training was held in collaboration with a political organization (PO) or NGO. This strategy helped maintain the training over a longer period of time, making possible training for several sets of participants in the same community and covering different levels (from basic to advance) of knowledge and skill.

Paralegal training in my case did not stand alone; it was always part of other activities. While I litigated, I also educated. While I advocated or lobbied for legal and policy reform, I also educated. Paralegal training became a requirement for the parties being supported in court cases. In handling cases I required the assistance of paralegals to help me gather information, documents, and even witnesses; prepare statements of witnesses; file documents in court or administrative quasi-judicial bodies; follow up on pleadings filed with the courts; and other activities. I thought of the value of the paralegals beyond the cases being handled. Given their commitments to their communities, the paralegals embodied the very concept of people's empowerment. Paralegal training was not a two- to three-day program, but a continuing process of learning by doing. The training participants learned while serving their own communities.

In late 1991 I was informed of a plan to establish a regional (Asian) resource center for human rights education. The idea originated from Amnesty International and was proposed to the Asian Cultural Forum on Development (ACFOD). With funding from the Amnesty International Norway (through its Operasjon Dagsverk), the Asian Regional Resource Center for Human Rights Education (ARRC) was opened in May 1992 in Bangkok. As its first Coordinator, I drew up a program based on the original idea from Amnesty International. But I, and also ACFOD, wanted the ARRC to reflect more the ideas and needs in the Asian region and thus several activities were held that facilitated consultation with representatives of NGOs from various countries in the region on what ARRC should do to serve the perceived needs. The suggestions from the consultations shaped to a large extent the work of ARRC in its first three years.

After ending my work at ARRC, I went to work for the Asia-Pacific Human Rights Information Center (HURIGHTS OSAKA) based in Osaka, Japan. HURIGHTS OSAKA is a local institution with a regional program. It was established mainly through the efforts of the Osaka anti-discrimination movement, but also with the support of both city and prefectural governments. This local government support for HURIGHTS OSAKA made me propose a regional human rights education program that focused on the formal education system. I developed projects under this program that essentially followed the pattern of work I used in ARRC.

Broader Context

Human rights work is a multifaceted endeavor that requires different talents, perspectives, forums, and mechanisms. There is no singular solution to human rights issues, just as there exists no single way to facilitate human rights realization. It poses a problem to me when some human rights workers claim to have the exclusive privilege of knowing what to do to address human rights issues.

There are so many concerns that require attention, in different forms and means.

I remember leaving a massive demonstration in Manila in the mid-1980s and seeing how normal life was just a few blocks away from the place where a huge number of people sang songs and shouted demands for change. People in the neighborhood did not seem even to know that a huge demonstration was happening and that the following day it would be featured in the alternative media,[2] international media included, and bannered as a show of force of the Filipino people demanding change.

I thought that it would not really be possible to get every person tuned in to the same view on what to do to address societal problems. The society was too big, too complex, and too disorganized to be wholly involved. Thus the only feasible way was to seek diverse solutions to diverse problems. And it would be more appropriate to seek focused interventions, not only because of inadequate resources, but also because that was the most natural way of changing things. People Power in the Philippines solved some problems, but left many more untouched. People empowerment did not mean that people would always have the same perspective as that of their facilitators or organizers. *"EDSA Tres"* happened in Manila because people mostly from the urban poor communities took to the streets in protest. It happened not only because of a big campaign, but also because the participants saw "injustice" after *"EDSA Dos"* and could not bear to stand in silence. Many social development workers in poor urban communities asked: Where did we fail with these people? Why did these poor, oppressed people throw support to a deposed President who had been popularly known as guilty of crimes against the country as a whole?[3]

The mind and the situation of people are indeed complex.

---

[2] During the martial law era, the non-mainstream media was called "mosquito press" because while it was small in terms of reach it caused irritating "bites" to the government.

[3] The first so-called People Power (with hundreds of thousands of people out on a highway called EDSA) was waged against then President Ferdinand E. Marcos in 1986. The second People Power was in 2001 against then President Joseph Ejercito. It was also known as *EDSA Dos*. Not too long after a new government was inaugurated, and former President Ejercito was arrested for corruption charges, thousands of people in the urban poor communities of Metro Manila expressed anger at the way things happened. They went out in the vicinity of EDSA and fought battle with the police when they attempted to go to Malacañang. When they were asked why they supported the deposed President Ejercito, they said that they believed he was not treated fairly.

I have learned long ago that human rights education is not just for human rights educators. In the same way that I saw society as a huge unwieldy entity, I saw human rights education as a vast, largely undefined field. So many initiatives and people did human rights education in their own ways and would never claim that their initiatives were human rights education. Neither would they necessarily claim to be human rights educators.

I have learned many years ago not to limit myself to the few who were vocal in calling themselves human rights workers or defenders, and instead seek out those who were doing their "non-human rights" work without much publicity.

I have learned that in order to promote human rights education, I should take the paths that most people would not associate with human rights. I realized that gems of experiences have not yet been fully dug out from the depths of these "untrodden" paths.

These thoughts guide my current way of promoting human rights education in the Asia and Pacific region. And I am also always looking for answers to questions about lasting impact of human rights education in the little corners of society.

In view of the "problem" associated with human rights in our region, especially some people's image of human rights work as a mere cover for political design to grab power in whatever form, and also the supposed cultural arguments against human rights, I have had to broaden my perspective about what makes an education activity human rights education.

I also have realized the need for serious documentation of all forms of human rights education done by a variety of people and institutions regarding different issues and communities. Thus, for the past twenty-five years, I have been documenting human rights education experiences in various ways. I started documenting our limited experience in SALAG in the 1980s, and that extended to the regional type of documentation through ARRC in early 1990s and then HURIGHTS OSAKA from 1995 till the present.

Ironically, documenting these very interesting experiences is a lonely job. Similar to my experience while I was in SALAG, I found most human rights educators would not sit down and write and analyze what they do. To some extent, the same is true of institutions. Thus I patiently and persistently coax them to start with their little documentation. I never fail to offer help in developing it into a fuller report that captures to some extent the meaningful work they do. Not a few of them expressed appreciation afterward at being "forced" to write the report. Similar to what I learned as a young lawyer, when little bits of information are put together as one piece, a new perspective arises that allows for more or less objective analysis of what one has achieved or failed to do.

Since joining ARRC in early 1990s, I have learned about the need to report the good practices in human rights education to others in the region. I know the strong demand in our region for information on programs, materials, and pedagogies in human rights education. Although the use of English language limits dissemination coverage to a large extent, it is still necessary to start with. Eventually people may try to translate the information into languages that local practitioners use. The only requirement is the availability of information in proper form and with decent level of completeness.

Since I joined SALAG, I have learned the need for collaborative efforts. A collaborative approach stretches limited resources, creates a sense of ownership among the many people involved, and develops better information that can be shared with others. I know how efficient "experts" are and how high the quality of the materials they develop is. But to me their materials lack soul because they do not capture the different ideas and experiences of different people.

Finally, I learned about the richness of the experiences in our region. I believe that there are so many experiences waiting for me to discover. Despite the decades of searching for and documenting them, I would not be able to find most of them.

And thus the lonely job of human rights education documentation in our region goes on, year after year.

As a reward, I learn very much from the experiences of people and groups hardly known in the human rights circle. I have the privilege of celebrating the diversity of their human rights education perspectives, approaches, methods, and materials. When I was a young law practitioner, such reward was known as "psychic income."

Concluding remarks

My mother is a silent worker. She sets her mind on something and works hard on it without fanfare till completion. I must have inherited from her the same work ethic. Once the task is set, I work to complete it as much as I can. I do not want to make noise about my work.

Silent work is a natural requirement when one sets out to do something that requires patience, persistence, and trust over a long period of time. Buildings are constructed by adding little parts one after another in an almost monotonous fashion. And construction workers do the task like little ants building an anthill – in a quiet and continuing manner. The same is true with the kind of human rights education I am doing now.

The development of my human rights education perspective is rooted in my local experiences. I agree with the view that what is local is global. I believe that what happens in a little local corner happens also in so many other little local corners around the globe. This is the reason for my search for local human rights education experiences. I simply find them meaningful and satisfying.

BIBLIOGRAPHY

ARRC, *A Survey of On-going Human Rights Education in Asia-Pacific* (Bangkok: Asian Regional Resource Center for Human Rights Education, 1995).

AARC, *ARRC Resource Material Collection on Human Rights Education*, (Asian Regional Resource Center for Human Rights Education, Bangkok, 1994).

Aspiras, Jose V., editor, *Law as Weapon* (Makati: PROCESS, 1992).

Claude, Richard Pierre, *Educating for Human Rights: The Philippines and Beyond* (Quezon City: University of the Philippines Press, 1996).

Committee of Alternative Law Groups and Structural Alternative Legal Assistance for the Grassroots, *Proceedings: Alternative/Developmental Law Workshop II* (Makati: Structural Alternative Legal Assistance for the Grassroots, 1992).

Dias, Clarence J., *Initiating Human Rights Education at the Grassroots – Asian Experiences* (Bangkok: Asian Cultural Forum on Development, Initiating, 1992).

Freire, Paolo, *Pedagogy of the Oppressed* (New York: Continuum, 1984).

HURIGHTS OSAKA, *Schools, Human Rights and Society – Report of the 1998 Workshops on Human Rights Education in Schools* (Osaka: Asia-Pacific Human Rights Information Center, 1999).

Plantilla Jefferson R., "A Glimpse at Alternative Lawyering in the Philippines," *Beyond Law*, vol. 2, no. 4, March 1992, 17-27. Available at http://ilsa.org.co:81/node/279.

Plantilla Jefferson R, "Philippine Paralegalism: A SALAG Experience," in *Sourcebook on Alternative Lawyering* (Makati: Structural Alternative Legal Assistance for the Grassroots, 1992).

Plantilla Jefferson R, "Elusive Promise: Transitional Justice in the Philippines," *Human Rights Dialogue*, 1.8 (Spring 1997). Available at http://www.carnegiecouncil.org/publications/archive/dialogue/1_08/articles/553.html.

Plantilla Jefferson R, editor, *Educational Policies and Human Rights Awareness – Japan, India, the Philippines and Sri Lanka* (Delhi: Academic Excellence, 2008).

Plantilla Jefferson R and Sebasti L. Raj, SJ, editors, *Human Rights in Asian Cultures: Continuity and Change* (Delhi/Osaka: HURIGHTS OSAKA, 1997).

Social Development Index and BATAS (Sentro ng Batas Pang-tao), *Career Paths in Alternative Law: Toward a More Just and Humane Society*, pamphlet (Quezon City: Social Development Index and BATAS, undated).

Silliman, G. Sidney and Lela Garner Noble, *Organizing for Democracy: NGOs, Civil Society, and the Philippine State* (Honolulu: University of Hawaii Press, 1998).

Structural Alternative Legal Assistance for the Grassroots, *Understanding Human Rights* (Makati: Structural Alternative Legal Assistance for the Grassroots, 1989).

Structural Alternative Legal Assistance for the Grassroots, *Human Rights and the Grassroots* (Makati: Structural Alternative Legal Assistance for the Grassroots, 1989).

Education: Justice, Freedom, Non-violence, Pastries, and Boleros

Aura Helena Ramos (Brazil)

> **Aura Helena Ramos** has a Ph.D. in education and is a professor at the State University of Río de Janerio, Brazil. She is part of the Curriculum Group in Research, Training and Education for Human Rights at that university. Since 1999 she has coordinated research projects and human rights education activities in the public elementary schools of Baixada Fluminense, a part of the metropolitan area of Río de Janeiro.

> To remember is not to live again, but to make anew.
> It is reflection, understanding today from what was,
> It is feeling, reappearance of what has been done and is gone, not merely repetition.
>
> Marilena Chauí, 1994

I am proud to have been chosen as part of this team of human rights educators. Coming from such an important figure in the field as Abraham Magendzo, it is an invitation that humbles me and for which I am grateful!

As I begin to write, I confess my curiosity at reading other accounts that like mine will be recorded and published in this volume. The apparently naïve question posed by Abraham Magenzdo is a challenge not because of the plurality of answers, but because of the questions it poses. What do we each want to answer? Will everybody understand the question in the same way? What will each one of us understand by the terms "education" and "human rights"? How will each one interpret these terms to create something we can call human rights education? Will we all have the same idea of what human rights and education are? What did it mean to work on human rights education, twenty, thirty, or forty years ago, even if we accept the hypothesis that we were then exactly who we are now?

Having stated my concerns, I wish to say that all I can write are answers to only one of the many perceptions I have of myself. It is a perception based on the present, influenced by the person I am today. Since this is not really an academic text, I will not question or try to understand what has happened. I am only a narrator in this text. In the narrative there will surely be an intention, which I believe responds to the human wish to encourage other people to join us in what we do and in what we believe in. I will, however, leave all interpretations and questions to the reader, who will interpret the text to understand whatever he or she wishes (I suspect this was Magendzo's original intention when he requested these essays).

This prologue helps me state that I reject the idea that it is possible to satisfy our understanding on the basis of one singular point of view, that there is only one answer that encompasses all truth. Although I have seen this belief contradicted many times, it continues to support my trust in politics and in the many struggles to defend what I understand to be human rights.

The "why" or "how" I became a human rights educator is interlaced with many histories: of the world, of our Latin America, of my country, and of my personal life during the last fifty-seven years. Since this is not an autobiography, I will limit myself to writing about experiences that have kept me going or that have upset me, encouraged me, made me angry, and moved me to look towards the world of the school and work to make it better. This has to do with how I have become an educator. It also makes sense to speak about how I believe the idea of doing things differently from the way they have been done is both our responsibility as individuals and a power we possess as a collectivity. All this has kept me close to issues related to human rights. I believe this opportunity to tell my story will help me understand the process that has made me a human rights educator and researcher. From here on out, I will rely on what I remember that is pertinent to this process.

Sketches of a Story

I am a teacher. When and where did I become a teacher? I do not know. Ever since I can remember, every step of my life has affected that choice and my professional identity as an educator, which is still under construction.

I was not born a teacher, but the facts are that I was born in this country, I have lived through a coup d'état, I have danced to the Beatles, and I have lived under a dictatorship and its liberalization with fear and the cry of war. I have lived through the clandestine reconstruction of the Brazilian National Student Union after the 1964 coup d'état and the period under General Médici, which was one of the most violent of the military dictatorship. I have also lived through the ABC strikes in Sao Paulo[1] and through the struggle for amnesty. I had peers such as Figueiredo, Tancredo, Collor de Melo, and Lula; such as Chico Buarque, Irmã Dulce, Roberto Marinho, and Paulo Freire; as well as Archbishop Mauro Morelli, who played such an important part in the defense of democracy and the denunciation of political violations during the Military Period. Much more than any academic

---

[1] The ABC region, an industrial area in Greater Sao Paulo, was the birthplace of the labor union movement that fought against dictatorship in the 70s and 80s. In the late 1970s, Brazilian industrial workers conducted a series of strikes calling for higher wages. This was the first time Brazilian workers had organized on a wide scale in defiance of the military dictatorship.

background or training, all this has made me a teacher and defined my political commitment to education.

But I got to where I am now by an unlikely road. During my first years at school I was the worst student any classroom could possibly have. In fact, I was not a student. I could not even understand that place (school), where everything seemed strange to me and did not have anything to do with what I wanted or thought I needed. I was convinced this feeling was mutual, for the people there did not understand my life and found no educational potential in me. If this had happened today, they would probably say that I came from a broken home that had no values. This was why the teachers gave up on teaching me anything (I was a waste of time) and also why I could not make friends with other children, who had probably been warned off by their strict families, who did not want them to associate with someone like me who was born in such lowly circumstances and had evidently had such a bad upbringing. The point was that I considered school to be an unpleasant place, useless, and extremely hostile, and I avoided it as much as possible. How? Cutting school as often as I could. So I got bad grades and was always on the verge of being suspended, all of which just served to justify their expectations for my future: I would be a nobody.

These are the principal memories of my first years at school. I came from a bad family, and I would not adapt to school. This offered me a bleak future. It is amazing how, even today, children whose family does not conform to ideas about how a family "should be" are thought to have a damaged future. I must admit that my family really was quite different from the socially accepted model of family that was valued by the school in the early years of the sixties.

My mother came from a middle-class family. Her father was a military man; her mother was a doctor. They made her leave her home when she became pregnant at twenty-one by her boyfriend, a young man doing his military service, who had no money to his name and espoused leftist ideas. Even worse, he collaborated on *Voz Operária* (*The Workers' Voice*), a newspaper of the Brazilian Communist Party (PCB). They got married, lived together in a room of a *"casa de cómodos,"* [2] and had two children. I was the youngest. These were my parents. They shared a great hope for the future and an irrepressible joy in life. She was a woman made of desire, improvisation, and commitment to life and a great believer in freedom. He was an upright and loyal man with an incredibly practical point of view that he put to use in the service of his humble but untamed spirit. They separated when I was six, and my mother moved us to an apartment in Urca, Río de Janeiro.

The fact that my mother was a single woman seemed to threaten all the families on the street where we lived. Not only did she not have a husband, she worked outside the home, wore pants, smoked cigarettes, attended college, and worse yet, was a Communist. The truth is she was single but not "alone." A group of young men used to visit our house; they would pass the day eating what they cooked, singing to the tune of a guitar they always carried with them, and talking avidly and at great length about things I hardly understood but felt were extremely important, though they might be

---

[2] A popular residence that consists of a big house where different families live, each in a single room.

too complicated for many. Their ideas were inspired by news from the Soviet Union, a faraway place with a happy population where there was no misery, hunger, rich, or poor; everyone was equal. Their idea, which I also adopted as my own, was to make Brazil take the same road. In order to do this, we had to fight the government and to convince anyone we could that this was a just and necessary struggle. That was all my seven-year-old self managed to comprehend.

Clearly, my origins and family environment were very different from what was acceptable at school, an institution to which I could not adapt and which I voluntarily avoided. I can't understand how I managed to finish elementary school. The only plausible hypothesis is that with so few friends and a daily routine so different from that of other children, I spent a lot of time reading everything I could find: a habit my mother promoted by spending the little money she had to buy books she considered educational, and in those times that meant every book written by Monteiro Lobato.[3] She was an avid reader herself and proud of the bookshelf that took up the whole living room wall.

In addition, my father was a great storyteller who enjoyed reading and telling stories, some of which he admitted to having made up to encourage us to fall asleep. Other stories he told as if they were true, including many details to make them believable though they were really the product of his imagination. People would often joke that aliens had abducted him on a deserted highway when he was traveling through the northeastern part of the country.

Around 1962 my mother began to work a few days a week as a dactylographer (someone who studies finger prints as a means of identification) for the head of the União Nacional dos Estudantes (National Union of Students, or UNE), a job she undertook at night because during the day she held a governmental post and also studied literature at the university. Since she did not want to leave me alone at home, she frequently took me with her. For me this was something spectacular because instead of sleeping on the sofa that she carefully placed near her desk, I would run away to see the "workshops" and rehearsals of the actors of the Centro Popular de Cultura (Popular Center of Culture, or CPC), an organization linked to the UNE. CPC had been created in 1961 in Río de Janeiro by a group of left wing intellectuals with the goal of creating and promoting "popular and revolutionary art."[4]

I loved being among adults, and those who worked there were extremely interesting. My mother would joyfully recall that I once told her I loved her friends at the UNE because they did not ask me things like: "What year are you in at school?" or "Do you like studying?" or "Is the *tía* nice?"[5] (No!) I remember their asking my opinion about everything. Sometimes they agreed with me, other times they did not, but they seemed to like the fact that I had an opinion on anything they mentioned. Except for some specific issues, I do not remember understanding anything they said

---

[3] One of Brazil's most influential writers, best known for a series of educational but entertaining children's books.
[4] For more information on this organization, please visit: pt.wikipedia.org/wiki/Centro_Popular_de_Cultura
[5] *Tía* (aunt) is how, even today, children call their teachers. This tradition was questioned by Paulo Freire in his book *Professora sim, tia não! (Teacher Yes, Aunt No!)*.

among themselves. I do not recall that I followed their stories or understood the heated debates they had on politics, art, love, and revolution. What impressed me, enchanted me, and influenced me was the atmosphere of camaraderie, of straightforwardness, and of freedom and understanding. You could "breathe free" when you were among them.

When I wonder how I was able actually to finish school, I can see now that my mother was a big influence through her love for reading. So was the curiosity that my father's stories had nurtured in all of us, as well as the company of adults who enjoyed conversation and who talked to me. Such a "different" life enabled me to develop strong writing and interpretation skills that most of the children my age did not have. Maybe this was what convinced my teachers that I had somehow learned something, and thus, although I didn't deserve it, they would promote me to the next grade.

My experience at school was neither positive nor insignificant in my professional or academic development. I did feel I was different from the other children, which was not nice. Not being able to learn most of what was taught at school made me feel inferior. My present work is not a defense of the idea that "life is a better school" but a reflection on how I managed to survive school in spite of everything. I want to understand how my feelings towards schooling took shape because when I chose to dedicate my life to education, I chose to spend the rest of my life in exactly the place I had fled from during my childhood! This shows that the unexpected can happen, or in other words, that bad things can get worse, but on the other hand, they can sometimes get better.

In the midst of economic difficulties at the end of 1963, we had to abandon the house where we were living because the rent was too high for my mother. We packed all our furniture and possessions in boxes and stored them in a room at the UNE building until my mother could find another place to live. Meanwhile, my mother stayed with a sister one day and with a friend another. My brother and I were accepted into a boarding school, which I later learned had been paid for by friends in the PCB.

We had visited a lot of schools until my mother decided which one was best and enrolled us, but it was hell itself. My brother and I would live there from Monday to Friday. I do not recall ever having lived in such difficult circumstances and for so long. We spent each day in silence, doing nothing, all our gestures controlled by a supervisor who watched us closely as if we were a grenade about to explode. In my case, she was right, for I hated her. I found a way to frustrate her sadistic instincts by not giving her any reason to punish me, although she sometimes did anyway just to teach me what could happen if I ever released the feelings she could sense were brewing inside me. I had never been in such a position before. My mother was proud of giving us what she called a modern education, based on dialogue and guided by child psychology; ideas she took from a book by a certain Mira y López.[6]

---

[6] Emilio Mira y Lopez (1896-1964) is considered the most outstanding psychiatrist and psychologist of the Spanish-speaking world in the 20th century. He believed in the need to teach morality and ethics to children and the profound importance of education in contributing to the construction of a better society.

All I wanted to do in boarding school was become invisible. The only moment we were not under the direct care of that woman was when we went to the classroom, that is, during school time. Something happened that I consider of great importance in my experience and for my choice of profession. The classroom became my oasis, my refuge. A young, serious, delicate, friendly woman came into my life; she did not accept my negligence, lack of interest, and almost mute behavior. She was my teacher. Seeing I would not come to the front, she allowed me to sit in the last rows of the class, but she took to sitting frequently at my side, making the whole group turn and look back at her (at us!) while she read or explained a lesson. I do not know how it happened, but from one day to the next I actually had notes in my notebook. I loved not only the praise I received, but also the feeling of being part of the group! That made me stronger and reinforced my self-esteem, something that was like a survival kit in a place that seemed to be created with the sole purpose of subduing and humiliating us. School, reduced to the classroom, became my favorite place in the world. That teacher was named Mariza, and if I had any drawing skill, I would still be able to draw her face from memory. It is obvious that emotional connections had a lot to do with how she won me over, but I was still impressed by how curriculum contents became interesting and made sense to me. I even studied mathematics, and it felt great to solve problems!

My brother and I were at that institution from December 1963 to December 1964, living with my family only during the weekends. The only exception was Wednesday, April 1, 1964, when my mother unexpectedly appeared and after a heated discussion with the principal, took us by the hand, out to the street, and onto a bus. It was the coup d'état. The Army had taken over the city, and buses were not running regularly. As we passed in front of the UNE building, I saw that it was surrounded by policemen. I could still see black smoke rising out from it. My mother lowered her head and closed her eyes tightly; then she said, "Don't look!" Even today I do not know exactly what happened. Some say the troops had set fire to the building to make those inside surrender and come out. My mother said that those inside were responsible for the fire because before fleeing by a side entrance, they had tried to destroy any document that could reveal the main members of the resistance and their plans. The truth was that everything disappeared: dreams, freedom, youth, and what few possessions my family had, which had been stored inside until we had our new home. Anxious, I asked my mother, "And now what do we do?" She answered, "We are going to start all over again." She might have been thinking about the revolution, but I was worried about my bed, my toys, the kitchen things, the table. But I believe there were other layers to her answer!

I was right in believing what she said because in December at the closing celebration of the school year, I received a gold medal from my teacher as a reward for all my hard work. Then I left the boarding school auditorium without looking back or saying goodbye to anybody, never to return again. True to her word, my mother took us home for good. She had rented a loft with one bedroom and a living room in a small villa in Cascadura. There was absolutely nothing inside the house. We cleaned it thoroughly with soap and water, we cooked pasta with sausage on a small alcohol stove, covered the whole floor with sheets and blankets that we had brought from our boarding school, and the four of us fell asleep in the room: my mother, my brother, a teenage cousin who had arrived from Acre and had no place to live (my mother took her in, of course!), and me. It was the first and most unforgettable night of the best year of all my childhood, which was coming to an end.

Our house stood on an isolated road in a poor neighborhood on the outskirts of the city. There were two factories (one made furniture and another suitcases), an abandoned lot occupied by very poor people who had improvised some fragile, unhygienic shacks, and a school where I was enrolled. Unfortunately, I was not able to establish the same connection with this new school I had had with the class in the boarding school. Once again I felt weird and displaced in school. I hardly saw my mother during the week because we lived far from where she worked and she had to spend a lot of time commuting. The teachers at school could not accept the fact that she was not able to attend meetings, and my schoolmates stayed away from me, a girl who wandered about the streets. But I was not lonely. Every afternoon I made coffee and took it to the furniture factory for my friends who worked there. It was a large warehouse with long benches where they cut fabrics, sewed cushions, and nailed wooden frames to create sofas and chairs, which I thought were beautiful! So that I would not hurt myself with the nails that covered the floor, they made a pair of clogs with wooden soles and a blue leather strap exactly my size, just like those they wore to protect themselves. Whenever I arrived, Mr. Martinho would point to my shoes, which he kept under his work table, and I felt so happy under his care. One woman, Doña Ofélia, the seamstress, hardly talked, but she laughed all the time. I loved being there, talking to them and watching them work. They were very welcoming and a bit paternal. They would scold me when they thought I had been hanging out for too long on the street. They would ask if I had eaten, and they said that I was very clever and had to study but that I should not forget to bring them their coffee in the afternoons because it was delicious. They did not mind the fact that my mother was separated from her husband or that she had to work all day: that was life.

It was 1965 and I was ten years old. For the next forty-seven years surely many important things have happened to make me become a human rights educator. During my teens I was somewhat of a hippie, but during high school I joined some social movements that struggled to put an end to the dictatorship and rebuild the rule of law.

Background and First Years in Education

In 1977, I began my studies in the History Department to become certified as a first and second grade teacher. I chose history because it required skills I had mastered, reading and writing, and because it had a lot to do with political issues, in which I was very interested at the time. Above all, it was a career dedicated to education. When people asked me then if I was going to be a historian, I would immediately answer, "I will be a history teacher." In college I was a member of the Brazilian Communist Party and as such participated in the student movement. Among other things, I was part of the process of rebuilding the UNE, which had become clandestine after the military coup d'état.

A year before I graduated, I taught in a private school that transitioned students from preschool to second grade along with taking a course on teacher training among other things. The principal was a history teacher who had been forced to retire by the military dictatorship and decided to invest the family's resources in the creation of SOBEC, the Society for Brazilian Education and Culture. Here he worked with his wife and children, and he hired a group of students and recently graduated teachers with left wing ideas: a real Brancaleone Army.[7] The pay was low, but we could do anything we wanted. I was able to put into practice my "political-educational ideas" and realized how weak, inconsistent, or irrelevant some of them were in the context of teaching low-income children. Three years later, I had to leave this group because I had graduated and was accepted for a teaching position in public schools, a position I held for ten years.

I was personally able to testify to the alarming consequences of the government's policy of neglecting public schooling. The inadequate training received by teachers, the dismantling of many public schools, and the destruction of the minimum requirements that ensured a quality education were just some of the issues that began to emerge from the schools and enter the speeches of members of all political parties. However, rather than being overwhelmed by a sense of frustration and impotence, I was emboldened by what I identified as a gap in my educational background.[8] I decided in 1984 to get a master's degree in education, hoping that I would be able to find the answers to the questions and challenges posed by my experience as a teacher.

It did not take me long to see that the answers were not to be found in academic studies and that the problems facing the schools required more than well-trained and well-meaning teachers. At that time I met Vera Candau, who was not only my teacher in two education courses, but also the head of my dissertation on the topic of school discipline. This dissertation became the seed that enabled me to focus on school violence and human rights. But aside from being my thesis director, something she in some way still remains, Vera has been an inspiration – professionally, ethically, politically, and in human terms. She has been an essential and decisive reference in my work as an educator and researcher on education. Thanks to her influence, when I was a college professor in 1999, I joined the activities of the Movement of Human Rights Educators and began my journey as a researcher in this area.

The Present (and the Spirits of the Past)

I believe there is no need to go further to address the question posed by Magendzo for this volume. I feel that what I have said up to now is sufficient for me to attempt to conclude this essay.

"To educate requires an understanding that education is a way to intervene in the world." (Freire, 1997)

---

[7] A term for a "bunch of misfits"; derived from *L'armata Brancaleone,* an Italian comedy from 1966.
[8] As can be inferred, the idea that problems in school have to do with lack of training and commitment by the educators has since then been widely believed and affected the image the educators have of themselves as professionals.

Moved by the words of Paulo Freire and by the sensitivity and competence of two essential teachers in my life, Mariza and Vera Candau, I have been able to understand that education is a way of intervening in the world and in the school itself. So like them, I became an educator, turning myself into a human rights educator. But above all, this was due to a disastrous school experience (which denied me the development of other possibilities) and significant childhood experiences with romantic communists and solidarity workers. All of which I owe to my mother, a tireless and just woman who loved freedom, denied any type of violence, read, baked pastries, and sang boleros all day.

> Precisely at the time when men seem keen on transforming themselves and reality, in creating something that has never existed, exactly in those periods of revolutionary crisis, they anxiously call upon the spirits of the past, taking over their names, their war cries and clothing, to show themselves in that borrowed costume.
>
> Karl Marx

BIBLIOGRAPHY

Chauí, Marilena (1994). "Presentación: Os trabalhos da memória." In *BOSI, Ecléa. Memória e sociedade: lembranças de velhos*. São Paulo: Companhia das Letras.

Freire, Paulo (1997). *Pedagogia da Autonomia: saberes necessários à prática educativa*. Rio de Janeiro: Paz e Terra.

Marx, Karl (2011). *O 18 Brumário de Luís Bonaparte: A discreta farsa da burguesia*. São Paulo: Boitempo. (Edición original de 1852).

Letters to Abraham: My Roots as a Human Rights Educator

Kristi Rudelius-Palmer (USA)

Kristi Rudelius-Palmer became co-director of the Human Rights Center at the University of Minnesota in 1989. She is an adjunct associate professor of law and, as director of the Humphrey Fellowship Program at the University of Minnesota Law School, she serves as advisor for 12 international Fulbright Humphrey Law & Human Rights Fellows each year. She has designed and taught human rights courses at the university, primary and secondary school, and community levels, and assisted more than 600 students and community leaders to have internships, fellowships, and professional affiliations with human rights organizations in the United States and in more than 100 countries around the world. She has collaborated with hundreds of human rights activists and educators on creating innovative programs and models of human rights teaching and training in classrooms and communities throughout Minnesota and the United States as well as in Africa, Asia, Europe, North and Latin America, and the Middle East. She also edits and publishes the Human Rights Resource Center's Human Rights Education Series and has written numerous articles on human rights education and training.

August 16, 2012
Flying from Minneapolis to Denver

Dear Abraham,

You have posed a great challenge to me. I love listening to others' stories and reflections, but I find your request for me to share my own personal narrative and journey of becoming a human rights educator exciting, humbling, and daunting. I have found the only way to be able to accomplish your request is to write personal letters to you, which are taking me back to my youth as well. Your question provides an opportunity to combine our stories into one common web of life's purpose and practice and gives a beacon of hope and light for our children and the next generations.

I deeply believe in what you have described: "There are no narratives that are more valuable than others; all should be equally appreciated because they each represent humanity."[1] If there is one characteristic that I have always embodied, it is listening to other people's stories. As a human rights educator and activist, one of my most transformative learnings was recognizing that deeply listening to another's story of trauma and suffering is essential. Sometimes the needed action is just truly hearing someone's troubles and pain. Although this response is counter-intuitive for me, I believe that just listening is important to restore the human spirit. Through listening I also rediscover my own tears and have learned that tears are not a sign of weakness, but rather a source of strength and a connection of hearts.

To illustrate my last point, I want to share my greatest time of burnout. It was 1998, the year we were all working hard to honor, celebrate, and educate on the fiftieth anniversary of the Universal Declaration of Human Rights. My colleagues and I were implementing Human Rights USA, a national initiative to educate students and community leaders about their human rights and responsibilities. However, during this same year more than six of my colleagues and friends lost their fathers, and my own "second-father" figure died of cancer. In June, I realized another deep loss and my own vulnerability when a colleague, friend, and human rights worker was murdered brutally while working overseas for an NGO.

During this period, I wasn't sure whether I could listen to any more painful stories or facilitate opportunities for social justice. Then out of the blue Jim O., someone I hardly knew, called to ask if I remembered a question that I had posed to him when we first met a year earlier. I hadn't remembered. He said, "You asked me what I thought was the connection between spirit/spirituality and human rights." He was calling to invite me to join a series of dialogue circles he had organized, bringing together spiritual and human rights leaders to discuss just this question.

These dialogues provided an important synthesis for me. The pivotal moment came during a guided meditation when I started crying and clearly understood that to be an effective human rights educator and advisor, I must deeply listen to everyone's story. Even if I shed tears and did not immediately recommend ways to take action on the injustice, it was okay. Before I had been afraid that leaving my heart completely open would cause me to become ineffective, but I now realize that opening my heart, ears, and eyes fully is essential. This revelation was reenergizing. Since this point, I definitely cry more, and I'm not afraid to show my deep connections with others' pain and suffering. I discovered that one's spirit and human rights are integrally connected.

As I write this, I am realizing for the first time that my life quest is to find hope amid despair and discover and uncover light in the dark. I am not the beacon, but rather I strive to be the

---

[1] A quote from Abraham Magendzo's letter to authors inviting them to share their stories as human rights educators.

catalyst for others, and myself, to reach for the stars and leave the world a better place. I will write again soon!

Love,
Kristi

August 17, 2012
Sitting by the St. Vrain River in Lyons, Colorado

Dear Abraham,

I am currently at the Rocky Mountain Folks Festival in Lyons, Colorado. This place reenergizes me in my life's purpose of human rights and education. I try to reach deep into the spirit and natural world around me every day to see if I am on the "right path," making a difference by and through human rights education. Because we never truly know the impact of our work, we must hold onto the little things that indicate we do make positive change. In reality, I guess that I go deep within to find my innate motivation and inspiration.

I grew up in Golden Valley, Minnesota, which borders Minneapolis. Special places there opened the world to me as child, in particular a "hideout" in the woods across from my home that I discovered around the age of three. I continued to visit this special place throughout high school and college and have since brought my children there. This space allowed me to talk to the animals, trees, bees, and higher power. Whether this spiritual source is defined as the natural environment or as the Great Creator or God, I truly felt connected to the energy of that place and the spirit world. I was able to go to this space in the woods and wonder about life's purpose and why I was brought into the world. I would run there to cry, pray, laugh, and sing.

My deep connection to the land and my becoming a human rights educator intersected dramatically in 1992. On the five-hundredth anniversary of Christopher Columbus' "discovery of America," I realized that I must educate myself and others on the truth of Columbus' conquest of the lands of Indigenous Peoples, who had been here thousands of years prior to his arrival. In 1992, I worked with numerous community leaders, coordinated by the University of Minnesota Human Rights Resource Center, to launch a Mock Trial of Christopher Columbus held in Minnesota's St. Paul Capitol rotunda. While most of the United States was celebrating the five-hundredth anniversary of Columbus' "discovering" America, Indigenous leaders and human rights activists shared a common vision of trying to unearth the truth about what really happened in 1492. This experience made me realize that for me human rights education was an essential process in continuing to uncover truth and promote community healing through creative participatory processes and reflections about acknowledging human rights violations and discriminatory practices in USA history. Strangely enough, I recognized the myths that were continuing to be taught through our educational system, which devalued, dishonored, and dehumanized the Indigenous Peoples of the land called the United States of America. I felt a moral urgency to set the record straight.

I have always felt very connected to the natural world. To this day, when I need to find balance and get my energy level up, I will go for a walk in the woods or sit in the forest or near water. The outside natural world allows me to "get grounded" and reconnect with my life's purpose, hope, and faith. The land and its ancestors seem to help me find purpose in speaking truth to power. As I travel, I also search the skies for an eagle flying overhead. The eagle miraculously appears, which reassures me that I am heading down the right path connected with higher spirits.

Love,
Kristi

August 31, 2012
Sitting on the Shores of Lake Pokegama in Grand Rapids, Minnesota

Dear Abraham,

Why am I a human rights educator? Your inquiry has me trying to weave together different life experiences that may begin to answer this question.

Education as a cornerstone for life was drilled into me from infancy by my family. I was the child of two educators, one a college professor and the other an elementary school teacher and nursery school director. My grandmother, aunt, and cousins were teachers, too. Even my three older siblings taught me, the youngest in the family, that education was important, and they pushed me to do my best as I tried to keep up with them. My sister Kathy, who is five years older, had me dividing five digit numbers by five digit numbers at the age of five. This appreciation of education as transformation was constantly reinforced. I was also motivated to participate and to never miss out on learning something new. I loved learning.

During kindergarten I had my first conflict with authority. My friend Dolly and I loved sitting in the back of the bus to school, but when we arrived at school, we were always the last ones off the bus as we walked down the aisle talking together. The principal saw us from his window and thought we were taking too much time, and decided to teach us a lesson. He made us sit in the front of the bus the rest of the school year. This small act of punishment changed my life. I felt that this treatment was unfair. He should have just asked us to stop being so slow or even asked us how we could solve the problem. Instead, he chose an act of punishment that seemed tragic to my five-year-old being. I later became friends with my former principal and realized that he was not an evil man. At the same time, I realized at a very deep level that such small acts have life-long impacts.

As I found my voice to stand up for others, I recognize that I have always held an innate drive for justice and fairness. I want people to treat each other with respect and to tear down any barriers or systems that do not work to that end. Whether it was gender equality, racial equality, or the simple nature of treating someone who acts or looks differently without disrespect or discrimination, I needed to move equality for all in a positive direction: forward.

I was and am still horrified when people cut each other down or discriminate against another. My parents have told me that I was the only one of their children whose teacher called them in for a special conference. My fourth grade teacher said, "I think Kristi believes that I have favorite students in my class." My parents said, "Well, do you?" She, of course, had to admit that she did. Oddly enough, I was one of the "favorites," and didn't like it. I thought that it was unfair. On one occasion, I told the teacher that another student was feeling sick and needed to go to the nurse. My teacher said that the student must speak for herself. Unfortunately, because my friend was shy and not one of the "teacher's pets," she would not speak to her. I recognized early the power of the teacher in empowering or deflating a student's self-confidence.

This same fourth grade teacher also helped to bring the classroom out into the community. She opened the classroom to having a friend's grandparents, who were deaf, share their personal stories, and my friend served as a sign interpreter. This experience gave me a window into a new culture that I treasured. I feel very fortunate that I also was encouraged to see the classroom outside of the walls of the school. When one classmate, who was adopted, was being sworn in as a new US citizen, the entire class was able to go down to the Minneapolis Government Center for his citizenship ceremony. Having amazing teachers and librarians made learning about new cultures exciting and fun.

Anti-Semitism and the horrors of the Holocaust were very real to me, as four survivors lived in my neighborhood with permanent numbers burned into their flesh. Their stories impacted my worldview. I began facilitating prejudice-reduction workshops through the "A World of Difference" Program of the Anti-Defamation League. The experience of discovering my white privilege and creating learning environments for others to uncover their own unconscious perpetuations of institutional racism, oppression, and discrimination was not only invigorating, but allowed me to feel like I could make a difference and leave the world a more respectful, just, and equitable space for future generations.

When I was thirteen, a boy in our small school community committed suicide. Later that same year one of my friend's sisters, a former homecoming queen, also committed suicide. Both of these experiences hit me hard. I remember wondering whether my own life was important or whether if I died, would anyone notice or care. I realized in my teenage years how challenging identity issues are and how up and down hormones can take you. An important tool for me during this period was the pen. I always had been encouraged to write in a diary, and ever since I can recall, I have kept one. I also wrote poems to process my sadness and joy. In the same way, this opportunity to write you a letter with pen to paper initially has opened my heart and allowed memories to flow.

The notion that someone can feel so lonely and isolated without friends or family scares me. This idea along with the unkind, degrading words both kids and adults can use toward each other makes me continue being a human rights educator. I guess that I *hope* in some small way that I am able to uplift someone to find *hope* and reconcile the acts and feelings of being less than human and less than someone else.

As my own children will say, "Mom always tells us that if someone has said something mean or hurtful, it isn't about us at all. Instead, it is about the name-caller's own insecurities and hurt." I have tried to teach my children to understand why the person may be in pain and consequently trying to bring down someone else. I do know one thing for certain: Everyone is good at heart!

Even those individuals or leaders, who have killed, raped, or stolen, have "good" in them. Human rights education provides a vehicle for understanding and forgiveness as well as an opportunity to chart a course for oneself and others so the abuse, oppression, brutality, or discrimination will not happen again. It gives us hope and the will to create an environment for our children's children and seven generations to come[2] in which everyone is treated with human dignity, equality, non-discrimination, and "justice for all." In this land of hope, everyone will also take responsibility for his or her actions and have the skills and abilities to intervene to resolve conflicts and restore faith in the human spirit, acting and being good at heart.

Love Always,
Kristi

September 30, 2012
At home in St. Louis Park, Minnesota

Dear Abraham,

Each of my letters to date has tried to explain why I am a human rights educator. Yet, each letter appears to be only one snapshot rather than a panoramic view. My last letter explained my belief in "the power of education to end injustice." I will now describe "the power of human rights to name injustice."

In primary and secondary school, I was a Brownie and a Girl Scout, learning the value of community service and caring for the environment. Church Sunday School also reinforced the importance of treating others as you want others to treat you. I served on the Respect, Relations, and Responsibility Committee in high school and the Social Concerns Committee in college. I facilitated decision groups for individuals recently released on parole from prison and mentored a single mother of two young children struggling to become economically self-sufficient after being incarcerated.

Although I always remember working for equality and justice, I first connected my passion and work to "human rights" in the summer of 1985 at the age of twenty when I visited a Dutch friend in the Netherlands. I knew that I wanted to work internationally and assumed that international business may be the only option. However, my Dutch friend's father observed that I was cross-culturally sensitive and recommended that I consider human rights work. He talked about the work

---

[2] Seven generations is a reference to the core principle used by Indigenouse Peoples (from whom I learned) describing a long-term vision for humanity and sustainability.

of Amnesty International and Green Peace. I became intrigued by the idea of working in the field of human rights.

My next wake-up call for human rights was seeing racial discrimination in France. I naively spent the year saying that racial discrimination was minimal in the USA and was shocked by the overt discrimination I witnessed against North Africans, who were officially French citizens. Being overseas allowed me to take off my "rose-colored glasses" and view the USA from different perspectives. For example, while I was in France, the USA bombed Libya, yet I was surprised to learn that friends at home did not even hear about the bombing.

When I returned to the USA, I went first to a family reunion in North Carolina. There for the first time in my life, I heard a derogatory racial slur, which was especially shocking since it was from a cousin my own age. A heated discussion about racial equality in the USA ensued with the result that I became labeled as the "Communist cousin." Oddly enough, my views at the time were not really political, but rather a reflection of my deeply held belief that all people were born free and equal and should be treated as such. I can surely say that my return home was an enormous culture shock, for I came face-to-face with racism alive and well in the USA.

When I returned to Lawrence University, I started an Amnesty International campus group and accepted an earlier invitation to join the Black Organization of Students (B.O.S.). I am still really thankful and honored that the group voted to have me as a member. As a result, I learned more about racial discrimination during my last year in college in 1986-87 than I ever could have imagined. Some White friends felt threatened by my joining B.O.S., especially when one B.O.S. member of the group wrote a very controversial article on racism. He argued that as a privileged group all Whites were racist since they held the economic, social, and political power to subjugate non-Whites in the USA, whether they individually exercised that power or not due to the systemic nature of racism in society. I had numerous debates about this article with my White friends, whose hostile response shocked me. These emotionally draining confrontations provided me with a tiny lens into the daily discrimination faced by non-Whites in the USA. I also realized the multiple layers that racism exhibited and personally had to reconcile whether to maintain friendships with individuals who still held racist points of view. What would my role be in helping to change another's perspective to be more aware of their biases and discriminatory actions? How could I remain non-judgmental and uphold my own ethical principles of respect and equality?

My senior year in college also launched my political organizing work. We held rallies to encourage my university to divest from South Africa in order to end Apartheid. We also tried to educate students about the Contra Wars in Nicaragua and brought to campus a former CIA agent who had become a critic of US government policies after serving the agency for thirteen years in the Congo Crisis, the Vietnam War, and the Angolan War of Independence. These experiences reminded me to think critically about what I am learning through the media and to recognize there are many sides to every story.

After graduating in 1987, I went on a four-month study trek through the Soviet Union and Eastern Europe. I was able to interview individuals who participated in the US-Soviet Peace March from Leningrad (now St. Petersburg) to Moscow. I later interned with Article 19, a London agency working on freedom of expression issues. This experience gave me a wonderful opportunity to edit Article 19's first publication on the human rights conditions related to freedom of expression and censorship issues in fifty countries.

When I returned to the USA, I wrestled with whether I was pursuing the correct path. When my grandfather asked me why I seemed down, I explained my struggle with being called an "idealist." He then said to me, "Kristi, I am an idealist. Once you stop being an idealist, you might as well stop living. You have to hope that the world can get better." My grandfather's words continue to keep me on the path of human rights education. He helped me to lift my head up and embrace "idealism" and "hope" for a better tomorrow. I knew that I had my feet on the ground and saw the realities of injustice, but I needed to work to improve this reality and push for justice for all.

My work with Amnesty International, USA and its Human Rights Education Steering Committee helped me solidify the importance of human rights education. At the annual AI meeting in Chicago a former prisoner of conscience warned everyone not to hold him up as a hero because he was human and would make mistakes, but he hoped he would never degrade another human being or pass on the abuse that he faced. His challenge highlights the goals of human rights educators. Human Rights Education can prevent human rights violations by teaching individuals about their rights and empowering them to take action to protect them. It also has a place after violations have occurred to help heal victims, perpetrators, bystanders, and interveners through faith and hope for a better tomorrow that can prevent these same violations from occurring again. Human Rights Education is essential for everyone to move from despair and darkness to hope and light. More concretely, Human Rights Education provides the vision and process for achieving a culture in which human rights and responsibilities are core principles in practice.

Peace and Justice for all,
Kristi

April 1, 2013
Foxboro, Massachusetts

Dear Abraham,

For the past three decades, I have had the privilege to participate in and witness the evolution of Human Rights Education in Minnesota, in my region of the country, in the United States, and around the world. Across the globe during this time period, community leaders have worked hard to develop and share effective practices of Human Rights Education norms, pedagogies, methods, healings, collaborations, reflections, evaluations, innovations, and personal stories.

In my role as the Human Rights Center's co-director at the University of Minnesota since 1989, I have worked with amazing community partners and colleagues around the globe in formal and non-formal training and professional development. We have launched initiatives such as the Partners in Human Rights Education Program[3], the North American Partners in Human Rights Education[4], Amnesty International's Human Rights Education Steering Committee[5] and *The Fourth R* newsletter[6], the Human Rights Library[7], Human Rights USA and the Human Rights Resource Center[8], the *Human Rights Education Series*[9], the National Training of Trainers (TOT) for Human Rights Education[10], the Global Human Rights Education listserv[11], the Global Human Rights Education Resource Center Alliance and Workshop Partnerships[12], *This is My Home: A Human Rights Education Experience*[13], the Human Rights and Peace Store[14], Equitas' International Human Rights Training Program[15], and now Human Rights Educators USA[16].

I feel amazingly lucky and honored to have collaborated with human rights educators from Minnesota to Mongolia. International Fulbright Humphrey Fellows[17] and countless other educators, who have been my teachers and put their lives on the line by lifting up their voices for justice, freedom, and peace in the world, continue to feed my soul. I thank you for your inspiration! Measuring the true impact of Human Rights Education is a forever dream. The simple stories and dialogues that we have shared make my heart continue to beat hard for Human Rights Education as a tool for change and a collective energy source to light the world in the depths of darkness.

My personal quest to measure the "real" impact of human rights education and training began in 1992 with the creation of a new program called Partners in Human Rights Education. I had been approached by two lawyers, Brad Lehrman and Dwight Oglesby, who were interested in teaching students in primary and secondary schools about human rights. I had been working with teachers on integrating human rights into their curriculum, so I was definitely excited by their interest. During this experience, I learned the power of community leaders to help students learn how to become agents of change in their school and larger communities. I saw the benefit of community leaders' partnering with teachers to teach students about their human rights and responsibilities. In

---

[3] http://www1.umn.edu/humanrts/education/pihre/ and http://www1.umn.edu/humanrts/edumat/HREEval.shtm
[4] http://www1.umn.edu/humanrts/education/partners.htm
[5] www.amnestyusa.org/resources/educators
[6] http://www1.umn.edu/humanrts/edumat/fourthr.shtm
[7] www.umn.edu/humanrts
[8] www.hrusa.org
[9] http://www1.umn.edu/humanrts/edumat/hreduseries/default.shtm
[10] www.hrusa.org/advocacy/tot.shtml
[11] http://Archive.hrea.org/lists/hr-education/
[12] http://www.hrusa.org/workshops/HREWorkshops/globalresourcecenters.htm and www.hrusa.org/workshops/HREWorkshops
[13] www.thisismyhome.org
[14] www.humanrightsandpeacestore.org
[15] https://equitas.org/en/what-we-do//human-rights-defenders-and-educators/ihrtp/
[16] www.hreusa.net
[17] https://www.humphreyfellowship.org

addition, I saw the power of bringing students outside of the classroom into the larger community by integrating community action projects that address real social justice issues with ideas for resolutions.

This Partners in Human Rights Education Program was founded on the basis that everyone should *know, value,* and *act for* human rights, which corresponds to cognitive, attitudinal, and behavioral learning. Through the years, I have realized that human rights education helps individuals *connect, heal, and reflect* on past human rights injustices to honor both one's personal dignity as well as that of others. These elements restore peace and hope in our relationships and communities by seeking truth and reconciliation. Finally, I have recognized that to build on each other's learning in human rights education, we must *communicate, celebrate,* and *inspire* others by modeling human rights education in practice.

I learned a great deal from observing Jane Elliott's teaching practices. Ms. Elliott was a teacher in Iowa, who wanted to educate her White primary school students about differences and discrimination. She decided to conduct an experience often called "The Blue Eyes & Brown Eyes" lesson.[18] She set up a simulation to have the students with blue eyes be given special privileges denied students with brown eyes. The next day, she changed the roles. The lack of civility between students when this power differential was put in place was remarkable, with emotions flying high. Ms. Elliott in these simulations, which were videotaped for others to see the reactions, made me realize the power of teaching methodologies in furthering a respect for human rights of all peoples, regardless of eye or skin color, gender, class, sexual orientation, etc. *This is My Home: A Human Rights Education Experience* curriculum[19] strives to integrate a scoped and sequenced, primary through secondary lessons, and a holistic process model to assist communities in this transformational learning. We have continued to improve human rights education tools to end bullying and create the next generation of change agents.

While teaching parenting classes to men in prison, I realized that everyone is good even when they violated norms of society. More than 90% of these individuals had been survivors of physical, sexual, or emotional abuse. They were now fathers, who wanted to treat their children with respect and stop the cycle of violence. Hence, they wanted to learn new skills of disciplining their children to replace the abusive punitive treatment that they had learned. The mothers on the outside were so excited by the class that they asked to start a parenting class for mothers. We simultaneously started self-esteem classes for offenders. All of these members of a family network wanted to learn healthy ways of treating each other with dignity and encouragement.

I also learned the power of mediation and talking circles in human rights education. These practices allow individuals to deeply listen to each other's stories. Most recently, I have been in a circle within

---

[18] www.janeelliott.com

[19] This is My Home (www.thisimyhome.org) was launched in 2004 as a joint initiative of the Minnesota Department of Human Rights and the University of Minnesota Human Rights Resource Center. The project reached over 5000 educators in Minnesota, and thousands of others in the United States and other countries.

a correctional facility in Minnesota with international leaders witnessing offenders and victims' families sharing their experiences of suffering, remorse, and need to reconcile their traumas. Although these circles will not bring back a murdered loved-one, they do provide a way to move forward and try to find a sense of purpose and hope again in life for both the victim's family and the offender. Offenders also need to heal as well, recognizing the impacts of their actions while also moving on to help others not go down the same violent path.

My deeply held belief is that no one can ever truly know the impact of human rights education initiatives. Every individual whose life has been touched is changed in some small way. Relationships twist and turn, but if we can create opportunities for individuals and communities to learn more about human rights and hold themselves responsible for their own actions, then we are validating the power of human rights education and creating safer, healthier communities in which all members can thrive. I hope that as a human rights educator I can uphold the meaning and practice of peace, justice, and equality and help those lives I touch find purpose and meaning. I challenge all human rights educators to continue to hold ourselves accountable for our own behavior and to work to uphold the dignity of human rights within our own organizations.

I will leave you with one personal story. A faculty member from a Minneapolis college asked me to speak at her class. She wanted me to talk about my recent experience training on HRE and Conflict Resolution in Russia and get her students inspired about human rights work. She said, "Kristi, I need to share with you something. One of my students, Joe, last year changed his life because of your presentation. He dropped out of the military, and he became a human rights and peace activist working against the war." Now, in reality, I'm sure that there were other impacts in his life, but this student had identified the connection between my presentation and his new phase in life. Who knows if Joe will continue in this work? All I know is this connection has provided me with energy to continue as a human rights educator and given me a glimmer of personal proof of the power of HRE to ignite and empower others. If I can touch one life in a positive way, the world is really changed forever. Of course, my conscience keeps me in balance saying, "Kristi, look at what the United States government is doing in the name of human rights." I breathe deeply and reach to my heart and say to myself, "I have to keep my dream, ideals, and hope alive. Maybe, my true journey in this work is to keep my learning, values, and actions holding up the principles of dignity, peace, equality, and justice."

Your Forever Partner in Human Rights Education,
Kristi

A Multicolored Fabric: My Life in Human Rights Education
Susana Sacavino (Argentina, Brazil)

Susana Beatriz Sacavino has a bachelor's degree in political science from the Catholic University of Córdoba, Argentina. She also has a master's degree in juridical sciences from the Institute of International Relations and a Ph.D. in Education from the Pontifical Catholic University of Río de Janeiro (PUC-Rio). She is Director of the Revista Latinoamericana Novamerica (Latin American Magazine of Novamerica) and the NGO of the same name. She is also Coordinator of the Observatory of Human Rights Education in Focus (www.observatorioedhemfoco.com.br). She is Associate Researcher of the Study Group on Education and Cultures (GECEC) of the Department of Education of PUC-Río. She is a member of the Latin American Network of Education for Peace and Human Rights, promoted by the Latin American Council of Adult Education (CEAAL). She is consultant and advisor on socio-educational projects both for Brazil and Latin America. Her main areas of work are human rights education; education, citizenship, and democracy; human rights and intercultural professional development for educators; and the prevention of school violence and bullying. She has authored several books and essays for academic reviews, as well as educational materials.

I learned to knit as a child. My mother taught me how to hold the needles and how to make my first stitches. From then on I threw myself into the daily adventure of knitting, which is similar to life itself. I did not like copying patterns from the magazines. What I enjoyed most was the adventure of inventing stitches, mixing different colors and textures of yarns, imagining shapes, and creating garments.

In the province of Córdoba, Argentina, where I was born and raised, it was common practice to gather with the family after dinner, drinking *mate* and talking while the women knitted. It was a gathering of generations, for it included grandfathers, grandmothers, uncles, aunts, and kids of all ages. It was an opportunity to share daily life and to listen to the family. It was an opportunity that strengthened our roots and helped us give meaning to our lives, though we might not have been too conscious of this at the time.

There, in the bosom of my family, I began knitting the fabric of what today is my engagement in human rights education. I knitted the threads and colors of the agricultural and fishing cooperative movement, which my father strongly believed in and dedicated his life to, as well as the harsh environment of the Argentinean interior. In this part of the country, the land and cows were extremely productive. It was common to save up for one's own family, but also to distribute, share, and connect with others, values that were regarded as "countercultural." To this fabric of my personal history my maternal grandfather added another thread, that of being part of the Peronista (Justicialista) Party. He was a man whose main concerns were social justice and the defense of the rights of the workers.

The feminine threads and colors of my mother and grandmother completed this "pattern" of my story. My mother was always open to any opportunity to defend the poor. In the sixties, my paternal grandmother was a strong advocate and sponsor of public education and local schools. She worked for what we now understand as the right to quality public education. In this environment begins the knitted pattern of my life that would lead me to education and human rights.

My Interest in the Subject: New Stitches and Patterns

My interest in this subject and in its research, practical work, and even advocacy, are closely linked to the story of my life and the discovery of my citizenship as a door to human rights practice. It is, of course, a knitted pattern still under construction and shaped by time and place.

Because I had a great interest in humanitarian issues, my first choice of study at the university was medicine. After my first year, however, my humanitarian interests took a new and different turn, and I transferred to political science. I wanted a career that would allow me to work on social issues that would enable the development of a more just and democratic society. I began my university life at Córdoba, Argentina, in 1976, in the same year of the military coup that began the terrible experience of dictatorship in Argentina. This experience would mark the destiny of the country and its society. Those were violent years of urban guerrillas, persecutions, silence, distrust, fear, torture, disappearances, and suppression of liberties and rights. Years of repression, terror, and control shaped by the Doctrine of National Security.

Political science was not an easy subject in such a context, where anything that did not fall within the system was considered hostile, immediately became a threat, and had to disappear. Authoritarianism and repression also affected academic life, making the attainment of knowledge a difficult task. The right to learn this was now a right that was severely limited. Anything or anyone suspected of having a link with the left, Marxism, Socialism, or Communism was censored and in some cases eliminated.

Time passed, and in the midst of pressures and achievements, I managed to graduate. The dictatorship came to an end in 1983, and the process of re-democratizing the country began. In 1985, I had the opportunity to go to Brazil for graduate studies at the Institute of International Relations at Pontifical Catholic University-Río de Janiero. The process of re-democratization was also beginning in Brazil after twenty years of dictatorship. I chose this program because it was the only one interested in and open to a Latin American perspective. My dissertation was entitled *Democracia y Política Externa: la diplomacia Argentina en la ONU (1983-1987)* (*Democracy and Foreign Policy: Argentinian Diplomacy at the UN, 1983-1987*) (Sacavino, 1989). It covered the post-war period of the *Islas Malvinas* (Falkland Islands) conflict, as well as the negotiations with Great Britain conducted under the auspices of the United Nations.

My experience at college and with Brazilian culture was overwhelming. It was a rich source of development, freedom, and the discovery of rights unknown to me. It was my first opportunity to have access to information and knowledge that was censored in Argentina. It enriched the way I viewed my profession and widened my education, not just academically, but also in a human-existential way. New colors and inspiration took over my knitting and created more beautiful, interesting, and defiant patterns.

My graduate studies did not only widen my knowledge in political science and international relations, but also allowed me to concentrate further on research and develop a taste for the adventure of producing knowledge. I received a scholarship from Conselho Nacional de Pesquisa (the National Research Council) and Conselho Nacional de la Capes (Council for the Improvement of Higher Education), two national institutions in Brazil that sponsor and fund research and graduate studies in the country.

These academic discoveries did not only widen my horizons, but also allowed me to affirm the value of citizenship and social participation for the common good. At the same time, I was concerned with the extreme inequalities of my new country, Brazil. These inequalities suggested a limited space for the practice of citizenship for the majority of the people. The fact that I was a foreigner with a scholarship from the Brazilian government in a world where most citizens did not have access to university education also worried me.

In Brazil I discovered that a society that offered a life worth living to the majority of its people was the result of the participation and collaboration of different actors. From this perspective, government is as important as civil society, including all its different social components.

When I finished my studies, my life changed course. There were new yarns, threads and colors that took over my knitting when I decided to stay and live in Brazil. I wanted to work in support of social groups that were excluded, subordinated, and denied citizenship. I wished to collaborate in the affirmation of democracy and the difficult process of building and expanding social and political citizenship.

My interests and wishes became possible through a collective program that came about by collaborating with other workers in human and social fields and the creation of a nongovernmental organization (NGO). At the beginning of the nineties, some Brazilian NGOs acquired great visibility after years of repression; others were born in the re-democratizing process of the country. They were all establishing and asserting themselves as an important and strategic platform for the creation of social actors.

So it was that in 1991 I took over the executive coordination of the NGO Novamerica, whose mission we stated as follows:

- Promoting the development of democracy as a way of life and participation in civil society.
- Working for the development of a Latin American consciousness and an ethic of solidarity.
- Stimulating the acknowledgment and appreciation of diverse cultures both at a national and global level by means of educational and cultural processes, with the goal of training self-multiplying social agents, especially those belonging to popular or excluded groups, as well as the training of educators (www.novamerica.org.br).

From the very beginning we created the Programa de Derechos Humanos, Educación y Ciudadanía (Program on Human Rights, Education, and Citizenship), which focuses principally on education in and for human rights in schools. Although many institutions were working in non-formal education, formal schooling was the least developed sector in Brazil at that time.

Since then I have continued to develop my work in the area of education in and for human rights and citizenship. This has given me the opportunity to gain experience and professional training. The focus of my work was on formal education, specifically for teachers of public schools in the different districts of the state of Río de Janeiro, and other Brazilian states, as well as some Latin American countries. In the area of non-formal education I trained social activists from popular settings belonging to different social movements.

The activities promoted by the NGO Novamerica are diverse: research, organization, formative processes, creation of educational materials and diverse publications, and involvement with other civil society institutions and movements. Beyond these, my main objective and interest have to do with social transformation as well as the creation of a counter-hegemonic social project, where democracy is not limited to the act of voting but becomes a daily practice in all spheres of life. I am also interested in developing and working on practices that serve to develop a human rights culture: a culture that is capable of transforming present-day democracies, taking into consideration the interrelation, integrality, indivisibility, and interdependence of all rights. Such a human rights culture would also take into consideration the different societal arenas ranging from the civil, political, and economic to the social and cultural.

My work with Novamerica as well as my professional experience has enabled me to participate with diverse groups. I have worked both at a national and international level especially with groups whose work is related to education in and for human rights.

On a personal level, the creation of educational processes for the development of citizenship of individuals and social actors allowed me once again to question my own citizenship, since my political rights as a foreign national were somewhat limited. The fact that I was a resident of Brazil, my intercultural coexistence and my personal identification with Brazilian socio-cultural context made me request Brazilian citizenship, which I obtained in 1999. This furthered my opportunities and possibilities, and thus new colors decorated my knitting project and enabled me to embrace both Brazilian and Argentinian characteristics in this new global world.

At this time Novamerica began promoting the Movimiento de Educadores en Derechos Humanos (Movement of Human Rights Educators, or MEDH) to provide citizenship training for public school teachers. Conceived as a civil society initiative, MEDH was a focal point to enable the development of education in action. It aimed to create a collective individual who would work for collective citizenship and democracy as a way of life. We regarded education as an internal process that results from accumulated life experiences, and believed it to be essential for instilling a collective rather than a purely individual notion of citizenship.

The topic of education in and for human rights in the processes of re-democratization has not only deeply influenced my view on life and my professional activities, but it has always encouraged me intellectually and refined my practices in different ways. In order to specialize this perspective, I worked towards a Ph.D. in education at PUC-Río de Janeiro from 2004 to 2008. My research was a case study of Chile and Brazil focusing on the development of education in and for human rights in the re-democratization processes. I firmly believe that access to human rights knowledge and the possibility of disseminating it is an important right that needs development in education. This thesis was later published as a book in my two languages, Portuguese and Spanish (Sacavino, 2012).

In recent years, I have been especially interested in issues that have to do with justice, overcoming inequalities, democratization of opportunities, and their effect on the open acknowledgment of different cultural groups. In this sense, the issue of human rights widens – usually it is taken to mean the civil and political rights of the individual – and focuses on the importance of collective, cultural, and ecological rights. This reality highlights the fact that in multicultural and multiethnic societies, the fight for the acknowledgment of diverse identities shows that cultural injustice is the other face of distributive justice, especially when we consider that the development of democracy implies that rights to equality must be articulated with the right to be different. From this perspective, intercultural education seems like a valid political way to create the conditions and spaces where these rights can be realized in the real world. It is also a challenge for education in and for human rights.

After completing my Ph.D., a new door opened that allowed me to participate and work on these subjects as associate researcher in the Study Group on the Education and Cultures (GECEC) of the Department of Education of PUC-Río.[1] Here I am involved in the following research projects:

---

[1] This Study Group was coordinated by Professor Vera Maria Candau.

Educación en Derechos Humanos en América Latina y Brasil: génesis histórica y realidad actual (Human Rights Education in Latin America and Brazil: Historical Development and Contemporary Reality) and Interculturalidad y Educación en América Latina, y Brasil: saberes, actores y búsquedas (Intercultural Education in Latin America and Brazil; Knowledge, Subjects, and Searches).

During the last decade my knitting has been colored by more threads that have given me the opportunity to work as international advisor for the Movimiento Socioeducativo Educar en Tiempos Difíciles (Socio-educational Movement for Educating in Challenging Times),[2] which encourages different development levels in twelve Latin American countries. Its main goal is to bring together women, youth, and adults who through their work are conscious of the persistent inequality, discrimination, and exclusion in our societies. They are interested in creating alternatives that encourage justice, equality, solidarity, and active citizenship by means of social action education. The main focus of our activities has to do with putting into practice the right to a quality education that will promote equality, fairness, and the acknowledgment of diversity, social justice, and human rights in the South American continent, a humanizing and transforming alternative to the dominating tendencies in our societies.

The Knitting Continues, Expands, Never-ending ...

My grandmother's advocacy in favor of education for my native town in the province of Córdoba received public acknowledgment in the nineties when a new elementary school was named after her. Since then whenever I visit my family, I am moved when I see my grandmother's name reproduced on students' shirts as they walk through the town. It makes me recall the original family knitting project. It has now expanded to include different faces, stories, and colors of individuals who now have access to education and as social actors are building their citizenship. Education in and for human rights is also growing, though slowly, and in some places it forms a bigger part of public policies and local laws. We still have, however, many challenges to face…

Yes, the knitting goes on, it gets bigger, it never ends … so does my road to education in and for human rights.

BIBLIOGRAPHY

Sacavino, S. (1989). *Democracia y Política Externa: la diplomacia Argentina en la ONU (1983-1987)*. Disertación de Maestría. Departamento de Ciencias Jurídicas, PUC-Río.

Sacavino, S. (2012). *Democracia y educación en derechos humanos en América Latina*. Bogotá: Ediciones Desde Abajo. (2009. *Democracia e Educação em Direitos Humanos na América Latina*. Petrópolis: DP et Alli).

---

[2] See www.msebrasil.org (in Portuguese) or www.msebrasil.org/carta_txt.htm (in Spanish).

Teaching against Forgetting

Cosette Thompson (France, USA)

Cosette Thompson is an international consultant in human rights and organizational development. She was born and raised in France and earned her doctorate in Comparative Literature at the University of La Sorbonne. After a decade of teaching, she dedicated herself to working for Amnesty International USA as an organizer, educator, and Regional Director. She has worked for a decade as a consultant for the London-based International Secretariat of Amnesty International. She resides in Arizona, USA.

Spain, Greece, Portugal – all prime tourist destinations for many European families and world travelers. When I left France in 1976 at the age of thirty, I had not visited any of these neighboring countries. Why? All of them represented for me some of the worst forms of post-war dictatorships that I was aware of; my conscience would not allow me to cross those borders and spend vacations where so much cruelty and fear were a part of daily life. Many of us who grew up in the immediate post-war era would not risk witnessing more atrocities or indirectly supporting (through tourism revenues) repressive regimes.

For those of us who lived in urban areas and for those of us who became college students, there were many opportunities to meet political refugees from those countries, but also from "the other side" of Europe where the so-called communist dictatorships were using similar forms of persecution. The political contexts were significantly different, but the stories of torture and repression were the same – relentless suffering, divided families, silenced dissidents, fear of neighbors and colleagues. And the same questions were raised by survivors, witnesses, and bystanders alike: after the lessons and memories of the World War II, how can we let this happen? How can drastically opposed ideologies lead to the same human rights abuses? Can this cycle of violence ever be broken? Can new forms of truly transformative awareness-raising and civic education be invented? Can we still learn from history? Can we teach against forgetting?

These questions, as a leitmotiv of my personal and professional life, have in many ways informed some of my beliefs, choices, and decisions; they stemmed from a wide range of events, circumstances, and encounters that led to and influenced thirty years of human rights work often focused on education. But which were the main driving forces behind this commitment to human rights education? As I see it, the main risk is what I would call "retrospective determinism," that is to say the temptation to reconstruct *a posteriori* causality chains and "influence" links; the challenge, therefore, is not to let the analytical or reflective approach add a layer of significance to circumstances and experiences that seem to fit perfectly in the pattern of past events but may not qualify as "proximate cause."

Interestingly enough, whether we seek to identify "motivations" or "influences" we are, etymologically speaking, on the same quest for what "moved" us into action (including "emotions"), and for experiences which, tributary-like, flowed into the main channel of our professional life.

I would like to start my personal account with the chronological "flow" of events that led to my initial professional involvement in human rights education. I grew up in a family of educators who, by the time I was born, completely assumed that teaching was one of the noblest vocations; when I turned fourteen, I was put on a path that would allow me to become an elementary school teacher (I was a girl, so my career path was obvious). A decision had to be made about which "track" I would follow during my high school years; my English and math teachers had a fight – and the advocate for languages and literature path won. That decision, more than any other taken for me or by me, may have been the single most determining factor at the root of my professional life.

My developing skills in the study of foreign languages meant that I would have to become a high school teacher since none of them were taught at the elementary level. My remarkably supportive teachers/advocates convinced my parents to let me shift to an Ecole Normale Superieure track that would give me a full scholarship to get the best teaching credentials available at the time in France. More than anything else, I wanted to obtain a degree to teach English; unfortunately, when I took the competitive entrance exam, I got a much better grade in French and that single "incident" meant that I had no choice but to pursue a BA in French. Luckily for me the Ecole Normale Superieure was in Paris and many of our courses were taken at La Sorbonne. Still determined to study foreign literatures, I got the idea of choosing comparative literature as the best available compromise for my MA and doctoral studies. The latter required me to study a third foreign language (in addition to English and Italian).

The year was 1969. As a result of the student protests that had shaken the traditional university the previous summer, several inter-disciplinary choices became available to doctoral students and started attracting comparative literature specialists from all parts of the world. That year was also the beginning of an era that brought to La Sorbonne many foreign students fleeing political persecution; among them were Romanian students enrolled in the same research field that I had just selected. Not only did they give me the idea of choosing Romanian as my third language, but they also gradually exposed me to the reasons why they fled their home country and to the atrocities committed under the Ceausescu dictatorship, which culminated while we were fellow students.

This series of events led to multiple summer trips to Romania during which I attempted to help my new friends obtain political asylum in France for themselves and their relatives. During this process I had my first direct experience with the pain and dilemmas of living under a dictatorship. I had to take extreme precautions so that my friends would not be arrested for "having contacts with foreigners" (hence the added motivation to learn their language). I learned that the best way we could have safe conversations was to swim out to sea. There, I learned, I could not be seen or heard by the neighbors, or even worse the mailman. When one day I asked one of my friends, "Whom around you do you fear most?" The answer I got was "My seven-year old son." The idea was that at that age his son would probably and innocently answer any questions that "neighbors" might ask about his family's beliefs and activities, which would eventually cause the arrest and likely torture of his parents. And then I realized that the fear of torture and torture itself were probably the worst forms of human suffering that I would ever encounter.

After teaching a few years in France, I received an unexpected invitation to teach French language and literature in San Francisco. After a few months, although fully enjoying my new California life, I started missing some aspects of my European culture and at the recommendation of a few new friends, I decided to explore the offerings of the so called "most European" city in the United States. I had just left an Irish boyfriend behind and nostalgically decided to look for one of the famous San Francisco Irish pubs; from the first one I passed came out the wonderful sounds of traditional Irish music. As I walked in, I was asked to pay an admission fee – a most unusual request for such an establishment! As it turned out, the pub was hosting a benefit for Amnesty International, an organization known to me because my mother was a contributing member. The honored guest of this fundraising event was Kay Boyle, a well-known San Francisco-based writer, professor, and human rights activist. Before the end of the evening Kay had convinced me that I should join the Amnesty International chapter that she had founded and hosted twice a month. She added that they especially needed to recruit teachers because we had to "spread the word" about human rights violations around the world.

The year was 1977 and Amnesty International was awarded the Nobel Peace Prize. In San Francisco, the organization, founded only sixteen years before, started attracting many new activists and funders. After I left my teaching job, I started volunteering at the regional Amnesty office and organizing a few local events to promote the organization's worldwide campaign on the abolition of torture. Because I had several years of experience as a teacher, I was asked to develop the first high school teaching guide devoted to the issue of political torture. This was at first an enormous challenge: a new type of project for me, a new initiative for the organization, and a new endeavor in the field of education. How to even begin? Luckily for me I discovered a documentary that had just been made based on the practice of torture under the recent Greek military dictatorship, an issue that I became familiar with during my student years in France. Its main message addressed one of the issues that horrified me most about the practice of torture: how easy it is to create a torturer. Even your neighbor's son (the title of the film), given the right circumstances and training, could become one. And then I realized that raising awareness about the "banality of evil" would probably be one of the most significant challenges that I would ever encounter.

As I was about to complete this teaching guide, the Director of the Amnesty Western Regional Office where I was conducting some of my research fell ill, as a result of which I was asked to "step in" to manage some of his projects. This temporary assignment led to a permanent human rights post that I kept for over twenty years. At the time I started on this new path, Amnesty USA did not have a human rights education program; it soon became clear to me that the best way of capitalizing on my personal and professional experience acquired in Europe was going to be the development of such a program as a perfect bridge between my two careers.

Summarizing in this way how I became – one step, one challenge, and one adventure at a time - a human rights education "specialist" allows me not to lose track of the fact that regardless of how I look back on this sequence of events, happenstance and serendipity had a major role to play. But they might not have led to the same choices or decisions, and to the same level of involvement and commitment in the absence of equally important contributing factors.

When I was asked to write this essay my first thought was to try and make a list of the political situations and events (prior to the beginning of my involvement in human rights education) that I could vividly remember as contributing to my gradual awareness of and interest in human rights. A self-imposed rule was to only list what immediately came to mind, without any attempt to filter, analyze, or censor what would surface.

As soon as the exercise was completed, I started checking the exact dates of the events on my list: all of them started, culminated, or ended within the 1967-1976 decade: the dictatorships of the military junta in Greece and of Ceausescu in Romania, General Pinochet's coup d'état, the death of Franco and Mao, the Northern Ireland "troubles," the 1968 student uprisings and invasion of Czechoslovakia, the beginning of the Argentine "Dirty War," the Soweto uprising, the last wars of independence in Africa, and the forceful relocation of the Chagos Islanders out of Diego Garcia.

All of these events either received wide media coverage in France, where I was living at the time, or affected me (through personal circumstances or connections) at a deeper intellectual or emotional level than many other political developments of that era. Then I realized that the 1967-1976 decade corresponded exactly with the academic period of my life, first as a student and then as faculty. My field of research had nothing to do with human rights, but everything to do with solidarity (Paris in general, and La Sorbonne in particular, as I mentioned, were a destination of choice for political exiles from many parts of the world), critical thinking, and artistic expression: all three became tools and values that no doubt guided my future choices and priorities.

Overlying these personal and political events are a multitude of influences that gradually convinced me that teaching about human rights had to include the nurturing of empathy and personal experiences that would transform the act of learning into a commitment to understanding, reflecting, and acting.

Throughout the first decade of my involvement in human rights education, several remarkable films and works of literature greatly contributed to the raising of my own awareness and informed my ability to explore different contexts of political violence, to try to grasp how "ordinary" people become unrepentant perpetrators, and how other "ordinary" people cannot only survive extreme forms of suffering, but display such fortitude that our own social justice engagement becomes almost inescapable. Among these landmark works are the already mentioned documentary *Your Neighbor's Son* (1976) based on research by Greek psychologist Mika Fatouros; *Calling the Ghosts* (1996), another documentary by directors Mandy Jacobson and Karmen Jelincic on rape survivors in Bosnia-Herzegovina; and *Closet Land* (1991), a "fictional" rendition of the use of torture to coerce confessions.

Most memorable in my mind as well are the powerful testimonies, poetry and short fiction of women writers such as Margaret Atwood (*Two-Headed Poems*, 1978), Alicia Partnoy (*The Little School*, 1986), Marjorie Agosin (*Circles of Madness*, 1995, and *An Absence of Shadows*, 1998), Carolyn Forche (*Against Forgetting: 20th Century Poetry of Witness*, 1983), and Irina Ratushinskaya (*Beyond the Limit*, 1987).

Without the often shattering discovery of those testimonies and creative works, I may have been a different "moral being" and educator, and I may not have acquired the tools and found the voices to communicate about the sacredness of our basic human rights. As I write this essay I realize even more the immeasurable impact of words, images, and encounters that exposed me to human suffering resulting from the *abuse* of those rights. But how do such empathetic responses lead us to pedagogical engagement and advocacy focusing on the genesis, relevance, and promotion of universal rights themselves? During my career with Amnesty International I often wondered about the best way to move from denouncing and shaming to building a culture of human rights, and from "just" motivating to transforming. Reflecting on my own experience and at the path that led me from witnessing to educating, I can only say that the deep understanding of human rights, of their connections, their protection mechanisms, and their "real life" application increasingly became the foundation of my pedagogical commitment. Here again I believe that I greatly benefited from the convergence of a whole set of circumstances and events that – directly or not – steered me in that direction as my own interest and specialty in human rights was developing: the United States ratification of major international treaties (Genocide, Torture, and Civil & Political Rights); the various anniversaries marking the adoption of the UDHR (1988 and 1998); the awarding of the Nobel Peace Prize to several prominent human rights figures (Sean MacBride, Andrei Sakharov, Adolfo Perez Esquivel, Lech Walesa, Desmond Tutu, Elie Wiesel, and Aung San Suu Kyi); the setting up of truth and reconciliation commissions; and of course, the creation of innumerable organizations promoting an ever-increasing number of rights. These developments, documents, and narratives gradually provided us with the language and framework necessary to the articulation of the fundamental values underpinning human rights and their legitimate relevance to any form of moral and civic education. But would those circumstances, experiences, and learnings have triggered and sustained my involvement without the extraordinary tales of civil courage that I grew up with in a region of France known for its resistance to the Nazi oppression? In his profoundly important *Moral History of the Twentieth Century* (2001), British scholar Jonathan Glover, writes about the French town of Le Chambon (near my ancestors' birthplace), which gave refuge to many Jews during World War II: "The capacity to resist is not only a matter of individual psychology, but also of a shared moral culture."[1] The same could be said of the capacity to teach against forgetting.

---

[1] Glover, J. (1999). *Humanity: A Moral History of the Twentieth Century*. London: J. Cape.

Shadow
Felisa Tibbitts (USA)

> **Felisa Tibbitts** is the founder and Senior Advisor of Human Rights Education Associates (HREA, www.hrea.org), which she directed from 1999-2010. She established the Human Rights in Education Program at the Carr Center for Human Rights Policy at the Harvard Kennedy School of Government (2012-2013) and has taught human rights education in numerous institutions, including the Harvard Graduate School of Education, Teachers College at Columbia University, the UN University for Peace, and the University of Lucerne (Switzerland). She has worked with numerous government and international agencies in developing curricula and policies that support the integration of human rights into teaching and training, including the Office of the UN High Commissioner for Human Rights, UNICEF, UNESCO, UNDP, OSCE, the Council of Europe, the Organization of American States, and numerous NGOs such as Amnesty International. Dr. Tibbitts has engaged in adult trainings in over twenty countries, serves on numerous advisory committees, and has published articles, book chapters, and manuals addressing such topics as human rights education in schools and the empowerment model of human rights education.

I.

In my youth
I gravitated towards the darkness.
With my small flashlight at night
I read books on Hiroshima
and nuclear holocaust.
I visited Dachau and Birkenau
walked along the Berlin Wall
interviewed the Klan Titan
in a New Orleans diner.

Such encounters
made me strong and fearless
but they did not help me
to recognize evil.
Because once I got close
the East Berlin guard on the watchtower
looked human to me.
We recognized each other
in our skin.

II.

If I cannot with confidence
predict how evil will come about
I know that such intentions are never far away.
And so I think
not of future evil, or darkness or death
but only of now.

Over time I have become convinced
that a single gesture
an affirmation
a kiss
a kind look
can heal and comfort
make someone strong.
So I take this perspective.

III.

Now the years left are less
than the years spent.
The part of me that searched
out darkness now understands
that this shadow has always
been my company.
We take a quiet tea together
hunched over my kitchen table
knowing a great deal
about the other.

Personal Narrative in Three Acts
José Tuvilla Rayo (Spain)

José Tuvilla Rayo is an educator, writer, and researcher for peace in Andalusia, Spain. He is very dedicated to the promotion of human rights and democratic values in school. He has been included by UNESCO in the World Directory of Peace Research and Training Institutions as a world specialist in education for Peace. He is a founding member of the permanent Education for Peace Seminar of the Asociación Pro Derechos Humanos de España (Asociation For Human Rights in Spain). He is also a member of the International Steering Committee for the World Association for the School as an Instrument of Peace and a member of the education team of the International Center for Training in Education on Human Rights and Peace (CIFEDHOP) in Geneva. He is currently Education Inspector of the Education Council of Andalusia. In 2005 he received the Merit Prize for Education in Andalusia. He has authored many papers and books on human rights, school life, and education for peace, as well as poems and studies on literary matters. He writes the blog *Cultura de paz y Educación* (http://tuvilla.blogspot.com).

It is not an easy task to define how, why, and what are the personal reasons that have encouraged me to commit myself to human rights education for more than three decades. It is not easy because ideological, moral, and religious reasons, as well as intellectual motivations, comprise the unique life experience that inspired diverse literary and educational activities at different times and in various circumstances. This essential, vital experience and this unfinished journey has shaped my personality, as well as my unique way of looking at and envisioning the world. It has also defined my position in this world.

I can safely say, without fear of being wrong as I recall Galeano,[1] that working for Education for Peace and human rights is the horizon which encourages me to take the path in search of utopia. It

---

[1] Eduardo Hughes Galeano is a Uruguayan journalist, writer and novelist. His best-known works are *Las venas abiertas de América Latina* (*The Open Veins of Latin America*) and *Memoria del fuego* (*Memory of Fire*).

has also afforded me the privilege of knowing how to chart a prodigious adventure, both personal and collective. It compels me to wish that, through education, we can learn what we are capable of doing. Education enables us to be active and responsible citizens and to be a part of a society whose main feature is a shared identity based on values that inspire human dignity. Education gives us strength and power. It offers us the ability to transform realities through commitment and enables us to be involved in the welfare of the most vulnerable and needy. What other purpose could education have, besides this ideal? As Eleanor Roosevelt once wrote, "Giving love is giving education itself." This is what Freire[2] means when he writes that educating is an act of love, as well as an act of courage. From this perspective, education is the greatest and noblest of missions. Throughout the years it makes us feel the miracle of a tiny seed that once attached itself to a heartbeat and that now has been transformed into a tall, strong, dense, and indestructible tree.

I confess it is not easy for me to describe with the required humility and passion the motivations and reasons that encouraged me, and still do, to dream and work in search of a better world. To imagine a school, close by or far away, small or big, filled with honest and luminous beings. Civic spaces where we can all, without exception, imagine and build a free, educated, participatory, and egalitarian society, banishing injustice and violence. A school capable of teaching us to defeat selfishness, to resolve conflicts by means of dialogue, and to trust in the ability of all human beings to create peace, the essence of human rights: first as a feeling, then reflecting upon it, and lastly planting and harvesting it.

Time for Silence: I Ask for Peace and the Opportunity to Speak[3]

In spite of my efforts, a dense mist obscures my memories. Every time I start, I give up because all I can manage to identify are certain childhood events with strong feelings. These were experiences that shaped who I am and left an indelible mark on my memory. So I have decided to start at the beginning: I was born at the end of the fifties in Guadix, a city in the south of Spain, to a family of railway workers. My grandfather was a railway man and so was my father. I was born nineteen years after the end of the Civil War (1936-1939), and two years after the dictator, Francisco Franco, visited my native town. I can't recall any conversations in my home about the "victorious general" or about the sad and bloody events of that fratricidal war. Those were times of silence, a vivid, decoded silence. The dictatorship had enforced its terrible gag, allowing only the peace and the words of the victorious. Years later, I learned that in my street had once stood *la Casa del Pueblo* (the House of the People), the union headquarters. I also learned that my city remained faithful to the Republic until March 29, 1939, when it was occupied by Franco's troops, signaling the immediate beginning of repression. My maternal grandfather, a miner, was taken prisoner to the makeshift concentration camp at the San Torcuato sugar refinery, though he was later freed.

---

[2] Paulo Reglus Neves Freire (1921-1997) was a Brazilian educator and philosopher who was a leading advocate of critical pedagogy. His most influential work is *Pedagogy of the Oppressed*.
[3] I refer to two Spanish works from the postwar period: *Tiempo de Silencio*, a novel by Luis Martín-Santos, published in 1962 with twenty censured pages, and *Pido la Paz y la Palabra* by the poet Blas de Otero, who sang to democracy for forty years.

Like many others, my native city was marked by the difficult postwar years, when Spain remained chained to a kind of archaic society. The accelerated social change that according to historians began with the sixties would not be felt until much later. From my childhood I remember my mother's tears when she said goodbye to her only brother, my Uncle Pepe, when he left for Germany. He was one of the two million Spanish citizens who were massively displaced from their rural surroundings to the cities and to Western Europe. Even though emigration had certain positive results, such as lowering the unemployment rate, it also caused a great uprooting; and it increased the differences between the rich and poor in the different Spanish regions. Among them Andalusia was one of the regions in a state of great decline.

In Guadix those differences were notable, and in my street, San Marcos, which was the border that divided the city and the neighborhood of *las cuevas* (the caves), it meant the difference between wealth and extreme poverty. I have written the following about this sitiuation:

> From La Escalera hill, the city seemed like a forbidden, sealed place. It appeared unwelcoming and incapable of love, like a walled paradise that made us tremble. We had conquered, we who were simply neighborhood boys and poor through no fault of our own. We conquered the streets, trees, fountains, towers, the air that was warming, that signified our deepest wishes that would never come true. We would walk happily down from San Marcos with our eyes stinging from the quiet feeling of discovery. The air smelled like newly harvested wheat. At sunset, with a certain air of indifference, we pretended to be gods who steadfastly walked the streets as if the world was being created with every step we took, and with it the city, ignored by rocks and arches until we learned about the clouds of accumulated history (Tuvilla, 2010).

I vividly recall the faces of the gypsies: dirty, barefoot, almost naked, who on their way back to their caves from the welfare lunch room would look into the lower window of our house. I can also remember the broken-down bodies of their mothers loudly knocking at the door to ask for a hand-out, their wicker baskets tied to their waists, and my mother handing out what she had in the cupboard: dried fava beans for a stew, chickpeas, some potatoes, a bit of bacon. We certainly were not rich, but never as truly poor as they were.

I belong to the generation of powdered milk, a food distributed during recess in the "National Schools" from 1955 to 1963, thanks to humanitarian aid from the United States, in exchange for allowing them to establish their military, air, and naval bases on our territory. The teachers would heat water in enormous pots, stir in the powdered milk that they took out of big sacks, and then pour the milk into those yellowish plastic cups. Some children, though not me, would add a bit of sugar and some Cola-Cao (a popular powered chocolate at that time) to make it more drinkable. I belong to the generation of mended pants, of prayers, of "to spare the rod is to spoil the child," of extreme discipline.

School was clearly discriminatory, segregated according to sex and social status. It mirrored an imposed way of life, regulated according to the National Movement Principles that were extoled in the Spanish nation "... as seal of honor the obedience to the law of God, according to the doctrine of the Holy Catholic, Apostolic and Roman Church, the only true faith, inseparable from the national conscience and which will serve as inspiration for its legislation."[4] National-Catholicism was the identifying national symbol of Spain after the war. Once cleansed of all Republican teachers, school was one of the institutions in charge of the ideological education of new generations.

Two events in school undoubtedly marked my personality. Writing these lines, I now believe that they unconsciously inspired me to ask for "peace and a word." The Catholic religion teacher, an ecclesiastical authority of the cathedral and dioceses of Guadix, had a particular methodology that was in keeping with the educational traditions of the time. This method consisted of reviewing the catechism with us in a circle. We would be ordered to recite the catechism from best to worst student, so that the student who answered correctly was made to take a place among those that did not know the answer, while at the same time hitting each of them in the head. For many years I had to bear the punches of my classmates, for though I almost always knew the answer, I remembered God's commandments summarized in two: "Love God above all things and love thy neighbor as thy self." Nevertheless, one day I decided to answer the priest's questions correctly, and I informed my classmates of my plan in advance. That was what I did, and from the lowest place I passed to the first place, pretending to hit my classmates while repeating, "Love God above all things and thy neighbor as thy self." But, once I was discovered, I was again sent to the last place, thus becoming the laughing stock of the class and receiving a hard blow from the teacher. Whenever I recall this event I think of the First Article of the Universal Declaration of Human Rights: "All men are born free and equal in dignity and rights, they are endowed with reason and conscience and should act towards one another in a spirit of brotherhood."

On December 14, 1966, close to my ninth birthday, a national referendum took place in Spain for the approval of the Organic Law of the State. Along with seven other basic laws, this law represented the process of institutionalization of the Franco regime under the slogan, "A guarantee for peace, a guarantee for the future." Some weeks before that date, we made banners in school from different materials with a big "YES" in favor of the law. For a long time I stood there in silence watching what we were doing. Then I turned to the teacher, quoting a section of the 1945 Referendum Law (which pretended to show that universal suffrage was guaranteed in Spain) and suggesting that we could add a banner with a "NO," to show the diversity of opinions in the town and thus to guarantee that the law itself was implemented. The teacher shook me and shouted, "We have a Red in our midst!" I would not learn what that meant until later because once I mentioned the incident at home, my father answered me with a flat tone, "Keep your mouth shut and obey!" And that is exactly what I did for a long time.

---

[4] Without consulting the courts, in 1958, Franco passed the *Ley de Principios del Movimiento Nacional*, as a warning that the old Falangist ideas remained intact.

Time for Hope: "Freedom, without Hate, Freedom"[5]

At the beginning of the seventies, we moved to the seaside city of El Puerto de Santa María, where I was overtaken by a great desire to become a writer. I had been told that to become one, I had to read a lot. Fascinated, I dedicated hours to reading everything I got my hands on. In this town I began to breathe the fresh air that would bring a political transition in Spain. I was in high school, and my teachers at the institute taught me, not without taking precautions, their political ideas and dreams for democracy. By then, I was writing my first verses: "With words we ask for peace and justice/ towns shout to the wind and to the tyrant." Those were times of hope. Sonorous protest songs repeatedly proclaimed by young people filled the city streets with their lyrics full of promises. In the port city of the exiled poet Rafael Alberti, I got to know the accent and heartbeat of the verses of the *Generación del 27* (Generation of 27).[6] Little by little I forgot the silence I had been subjected to, timidly expressing my desire for freedom. Out of my personal context I also expressed my pain for a world that I wanted to improve through my first verses. I wrote, "From the word to the world there is only desire."

With the death of Franco, Spain began a period of long-awaited change with the establishment of the monarchy, the liberation of political prisoners, and the legalization of political parties, and amnesty. I vividly recall walking home with my twin brother and parents from my school, which was also a polling station, all deeply moved after voting in favor of the Law for Political Reform. A decade had passed since the last referendum, which also had been held during December, but in spite of the cold we felt happily comforted.

During those years, poetry seemed ideal for expressing my protest against events for which I could not find justification. These events included the militancy of my father, a worker on the national railroad network, to challenge a collective agreement in January 1976; the war in Vietnam; hunger; and poverty. "This love hurts, this love I have saved here/ in the border of autumn and grass." Little by little, an uncontrollable and confessed desire to work for a just and peaceful society emerged. It was a spirit of determination that has remained intact throughout the years and defines my poetry: "the materialization of the constant desire for freedom," for the discovery of an unjust and violent world, as Teresa Vásquez (1981) wrote in the prologue of my first book of poems, and "the deeply felt hope" that human beings will create peace, as stated by Juan José Ceba (1991). Now, in another time and historical context, these convictions remain unchanged, as I wrote in a poem of my unpublished work *Don de la ternura* (*The Gift of Tenderness*):

---

[5] Name of the song of the group Jarcha from Andalusia, used during the inauguration of the newspaper *Diario 16*, in 1976. A few days later its distribution was prohibited due to its content in defense of democracy. It became a popular hymn during the Transition. On YouTube: www.youtube.com/watch?v=NrROdpJb4Ek&feature=youtu.be

[6] The Generation of '27 (Spanish: *Generación del 27*) was an influential group of poets that arose in Spanish literary circles between 1923 and 1927, essentially out of a shared desire to experience and work with avant-garde forms of art and poetry.

> Light warms the defeated body,
> A body lying yoked to the road.
> It arrived seven days ago and awaits the precise hour
> When silence abounds, falls
> And breaks the ice that holds
> A long and wintery suspicion.
> Then, in this tiny space in time,
> In this useless period when all comes to a stop,
> Where forgetfulness abides
> And takes over all,
> And everything keeps still,
> The long frontiers seem like a fine
> And determined line that crosses.
> With luck we will be on the other side at midnight,
> Knocking at the fog's door,
> And someone, sleepless, will hear the voice, broken
> Tenderly human, that asks for help.

Some time later, we would live in Almería, and with its light my dream of becoming a writer would come true in a small flat located above the Gutenberg Press, on the other side of the Plaza Vieja, where we, the editors of the *Revista Andarax de Artes y Letras*, would meet to review galleys, read articles and collaborations, organize the mail we received, answer subscriptions, and write.[7] My unfathomable love for books and unsatisfied desire for a world of solidary grew, and the young student of education that I was, then became a man. It was 1978; we Spaniards now had a constitution that which proclaimed popular sovereignty and democracy, interpreting articles relative to basic rights and freedoms according to the Universal Declaration of Human Rights.

My participation as writer and literary critic allowed me to meet the poet and Belgian pacifist Albert Chantraine, with whom I established a good relationship. I translated some of his poems into Spanish. Albert would regularly send me newspaper clippings of his poems and texts from Liege, Belgium. Through his letters I had two educational experiences that influenced my professional life. I am referring to the "Non-Violence and Peace School Day," proposed by the Spaniard Lorenzo Vidal, an education supervisor; and the proposals made in Switzerland by the World Association for School as an Instrument of Peace (EIP) funded by Jacques Mühlethaler[8] and sponsored by Piaget.

---

[7] The magazine *Andarax* was published for the first time in April 1978 and closed with number 27 in 1983. It was a vital element for art and literature in the publishing world of Almería and Andalusia, during difficult cultural times when democracy had recently been established.

[8] The World Association for School as an Instrument of Peace (EIP) was funded in 1967 by Jacques Mühlethaler, who in 1946 had already realized the danger of books as mediums of nationalistic and discriminatory ideologies, as well as the importance of schools working for humanity in the whole world. With this idea in mind in 1959 he visited schools on all the continents, meeting intellectuals and politicians, promoting that their educational systems should have as an aim tolerance, solidarity, and the ideals of equality among people. With more than a quarter of a century dedicated

They gave me great joy because they embodied all my dreams: word and poetry at the service of the people and my vocational passion for school as a transformation tool towards a more just society. The principles of civic education proposed by EIP were, and continue to be, an inspiration for my thoughts and activities, especially the first: "School must be at the service of humanity."

As a future elementary teacher, I wanted to know the promoters of both of these educational initiatives with whom I now shared a sincere friendship and a deep admiration. The magazine *Andarax* was in charge of disseminating information about the rights of children and the activities of EIP,[9] an association I joined in 1979. Since then I have actively dedicated my life to promoting the ideals of this non-governmental organization, to exchanging information with organizations from all over Spain, with some Francophone institutions, and with regional and international organizations, in addition to a long process of self-development in the sphere of education and human rights. This task took me hours of hard work and a considerable part of the salary that I then earned as teacher in a private school close to where I lived.

Later, in 1981, I received my first teaching administrative position in a small school in an agricultural town of Almería. Every Monday at daybreak after a long and solitary walk through a dusty path, I would arrive at the boarding house where I was staying. I arrived with dreams and the cold clinging to my bones, but I was incredibly happy. I was in charge of thirty-six children. In spite of the number and variety in age, my classes seemed to pass quickly, and I wished for the next day to arrive, to give myself to teaching with all the affection and gratitude I could offer, because each child was, every morning, a new gift:

> Fruit of my hours, children, apprentices of man;
> My soul awakens with your mad laughter.
> Innocent fireflies spelling syllables,
> Inventors of image, magicians of dream.
> ...
> School elves, jumble of larks, winged
> Bodied of willows, bees of my marrow:
> May turns sweet with your games,
> With your songs that are birds of blood." (Tuvilla, 1982)

There during the afternoons in that little town, inside my modest, narrow room that was more like a prison cell, I would spend hours preparing for my college exams in philosophy and the science of education. I wanted one day to become an education supervisor. I would also revise and edit the galleys of my first book of poems, *Ritual de la Palabra* (*The Ritual of the Word*), which I had written as a young

---

to the promotion of peace through education, with human rights as its essence, in 1978 EIP gathered educators and researchers of the University of Geneva with the object of adapting the Universal Declaration of Human Rights of the United Nations to a more popular language, comprehensible for elementary students.

[9] To celebrate the 20th anniversary of the United Nations Declaration of the Rights of the Child, the magazine published a leaflet: *Pizarra de Papel*, the title of my proposal. My first article was on the role of school aimed at peace and human rights, and it was published in 1980, during a session for promoting educational experience in EIP.

man. This book, which was well received by the local press, was published a few days before February 23, 1981, which became known as "23F." It is remembered because that was the day when some military commanders tried to carry out a failed coup d'état. This episode became famous for the assault on the House of Representatives during a voting session to elect the candidate of the *Unión de Centro Democrático* (Union of the Democratic Center, or UCD, a center-right political party at the time) to the presidency of the government. That incident was closely tied with other events of the transition period, a time of permanent tension that included economic crisis, terrorist attacks by the Basque separatist group ETA (Euskadi Ta Askatasuna), difficulties in the territorial organization of the state, and resistance from certain sectors of the army who did not accept a democratic system. It was witnessed live on television by all the citizens. I was among them. I had gone downstairs for dinner when the owner of my boarding house stopped me for some gossip, as was her custom. I listened in a polite silence, but I remember that when turning to look at the television, I saw that the voting was interrupted and a great number of shots could be heard inside Parliament. I felt that it was the end of our fragile democracy and with it all of my expectations. Desperate, I tried to phone my family, but the operator told me nervously that it was impossible for no lines were available. I was nervous in the following hours and unable to sleep, fearful for many members of the family, even though around 1:15 in the morning I had heard the King rejecting the coup in a live broadcast. In the morning around ten, close to my birthday, the members of Parliament left the Congress unscathed, and by noon everything was happily over.

I can recall the joy of the entire faculty gathered in the schoolyard. I can also see the transparent looks and smiles of my students, who hugged me after class. That afternoon I wrote my poem "Magos del sueño" (Wizards of Sleep).

And on my birthday I once again promised myself, in that small and humble room of that unpretentious boarding house, that I would continue on the road I had chosen for myself decades before.

Time for Harvest, Remembrance, and Crisis

Vibración de la ceniza (*Quivering Ashes*) is the title of my second book of poems, which was published in 1982 with a dedication to my then recently born son. A book that strengthened my commitment to peace and education:

> Maybe tomorrow peace will be taught in schools
> ...
> But today it is time to awaken to life
> To stop gagging our truths,
> To clean up, to take off those fake veils
> And to shout, shout, shout.

One could say that in that book, in part, I express more clearly what, day by day, year by year, would be my emphatic commitment and hopeful testimony for a new future in the hands of new generations:

> Earth, you are made to shout out
> The fear that nestles inside us,
> The time for peace,
> The blood that is the fruit,
> The drams of ancient men.

That book was also for me a strange catharsis and the definitive abandonment of literature as a tool of social activism. From that moment on, I focused all my strength on developing actions (in both militant and educational activism) with the aim of promoting human rights in school (information), on teaching the faculty educational methods to bring about a personal and collective democracy (teaching), and lastly and simultaneously, on opening opportunities for human rights and basic freedoms (research and practice).

Going over reports I sent to the EIP in Switzerland about the countless activities developed during one decade (1980-1990), I am astonished at both the activities and the difficulties I faced. It was time of sowing, of incessant correspondence, and of hasty activities for the promotion of materials that in some cases had been typed and reproduced with resources taken from our family income. My passion for making this school a place for living and building democracy was becoming obsessive. Now, as I write, I remember with sadness the time taken away from my wife and children. Though I spent hours with them, hours of tenderness and caresses, hours of deep listening and hours spent on the care they needed, I knew then, as I know now, that I was committed to the cause, to a task that could not be delayed because, as the Spanish philosopher Ortega y Gasset (1938) said, "One cannot ignore that, if war is something that is done, peace is also something one has to do, to manufacture...."

As a conscientious objector to military service – a conviction born from thinly veiled childhood experiences, experiences of a moral and ideological origin based on non-violence principles – I understood there was no time for pauses, that it was time for a collective effort, for joining: "all hands in a call for a kiss; /... Hands should bind together like rivers, / And to stand up firm to the sky like sprigs" (Tuvilla, 1982). It was time for sowing and the land had to be carefully prepared. But if you talked about peace, you were taken for a missionary, and if you talked about the defense of rights, you were taken for a leftist. I was neither.

On July 1983, I gave my first and most important presentation at the summer school of the University of Granada. I was barely twenty-four; my voice shook in front of a public made up of three hundred professors. I embraced courage, and after an analysis of the problems faced by education, I spoke passionately about the need to teach human rights as a basis for a peaceful world. A few claps concluded my presentation. Later when somebody told me that even though he agreed with me, he doubted that it would be possible to put in practice my educational proposals, or even that the country was ready for them, I felt desolate. It was true: we were not ready for that great task; we had not been trained for it, and it was difficult to get rid of the indoctrination we had been subjected to by the dictatorship. Totally convinced of that difficulty, I was more eager than ever to take my experiences into the classroom and to convince my peers of the urgency of this project. By then I had contacted UNESCO and some NGOs and had the support of other institutions. We created a permanent working seminar after my proposal to create a Department of International Understanding was accepted at the public college of Alhama in Almería. Later, in 1985, the socialist government then in power passed the Organic Law of the Right to Education, which included among its aims "education for peace, cooperation, and solidarity among people." Everything was easier in that setting, going to national and international conferences and seminars, especially in Switzerland, creating educational and promotional materials, as well as researching a basic bibliography on human rights. In 1986, I became part of the permanent "Education for Peace Seminar" (Sudupaz), which was sponsored by Asociación Pro Derechos Humanos de España (the Human Rights Association of Spain, or APDHE).[10] Made up of faculty and activists from all over the country, this seminar published important educational materials that received several prizes. It also introduced in Spain the campaign "Against Violent and Sexist Toys," which since then takes place during Christmas. Some educators for peace also gathered at the first national congress of the Basque Country. The next year the college of Alhama in Almería was acknowledged as an Associated School of UNESCO, and *Derechos humanos: Guión didáctico (Human Rights: An Educational Guide)* [11] was distributed in all the educational centers of the Spanish and Latin American associated schools. Later my activity would increase with the fortieth anniversary of the Universal Declaration of Human Rights, and the tenth anniversary of the Spanish Constitution: bibliographic and photography exhibitions, a radio program, training courses, an interview in the autonomous television channel, editing of educational materials, and writing of press articles were some of my many activities at the time.

At the end of the eighties, I was transferred to Morón de la Frontera, a town in Seville Province known, among other things, for a North American air base. Leaving our native region was hard for my family. Nevertheless I have to say that it was a bit less difficult for me, for I was excited about the proposal made by Amnesty International to develop an agreement signed by the Council for Education and Science of the Junta of Andalucía. My new destination was the public school Juan Antonio Carrillo Salcedo, which was not highly esteemed by the *Moronense;* its students came from the poorest neighborhood of the city with a high rate of violence and school failure. The school's participation as an Associated School of UNESCO was a way of dignifying both the neighborhood and the educational community.

My proposal was well received by the faculty, considering that in the framework of the agreement with Amnesty International, the Andalusian government had published my work *Human Rights: A Proposal of Education for Peace* based on the Convention on the Rights of the Child, which was distributed to almost six thousand educational centers in Andalusia, to the centers of educational

---

[10] Created in 1976, APDHE was the first Spanish organization to promote human rights, which I joined at the end of the seventies. I was part of Sedupaz from 1986 to 1992. Sedupaz made it possible for the APDHE to receive the Prizes Emilia Pardo Bazán in 1990 from the Ministry of Education and Science, and Messengers for Peace, from the United Nations for "an important contribution in favor of peace." For more information, please visit: www.apdhe.org

[11] Tuvilla Rayo, José, ed. *Derechos humanos: Guión didáctico.* Almeria, Spain Diputación Provincial de Almeria, 1987.

resources and teacher training, and to both national and international libraries and official institutions. In the Preface, dated November 20, 1989, the anniversary of the Children's Convention, I wrote:

> The need for education for peace and human rights in school is pressing for two reasons: the continuous violations of the most basic human rights and the content of the principles included in the UDHR that are the founding stone of any educational system.

I admit that my success, more than making me momentarily happy, did not make me feel important; it made my responsibility heavier. It is now that I feel a certain dizziness, and I congratulate myself for my inner strength during those days because I did not see any value in my actions other than an interest in solving the uncertain future of my students in a city that rejected them. The happiness of publishing that book ended in August 1990 with the first Gulf War (1990-1991) and Spain's involvement in it. The inhabitants of Morón de la Frontera knew very well the moment of "D Hour," when the American B-52 warplanes took off from the base. Every day we heard the buzzing of their motors as they overflew our homes, and we heard about the American victims through the information leaked from the base by local workers, among them the father of my neighbor. More than ever, it was necessary to reaffirm the value of peace in schools.[12] My feeling of helplessness was such that I again wrote a long poem filled with my emotions:

> And you get darker among the shadows
> Of others that like you, cry hungry and desperate
> As terrible hounds with their fearsome length,
> Toward the tenderness, total immense tenderness
> That defeated human bodies give off.

Thanks to a request from adult students, during that time the General Direction of Educational Regulation of the Education and Science Council had asked three professors, including me, to create educational material for a program of adult education. That material was our contribution for peace and an argument against any war. Nevertheless we feared for our work because we knew that the socialist government had a clearly ambivalent stand vis-á-vis that international conflict. In light of the fact that I had done most of the work, Pedro Julián, a member of the editing team, called me to ask if I would agree to remove some text. I categorically said, "Of course not!" Luck was on our side because a personnel change inside the General Direction made it possible for the book to be published unchanged, including an illustration that reproduced an anonymous graffiti on a city wall: "Imagine there was a war and nobody came."

---

[12] Fourteen days before the end of the Gulf War, the newspaper *El País* published a long article on education with the title "Tal vez después de la guerra: Crece la demanda de una pedagogía de la paz, hasta ahora irrelevante en las aulas españolas" ("Perhaps after the War: The Demand for Education for Peace Grows") that expressed the opinions of those of us who made up Sedupaz within the APDHE. The article began: "The crews of the B-52 bomber that overfly Morón de la Frontera have seen a gigantic 'paz' (peace) written in the yard of a local school." It was my school.

In September 1991, I returned to Alhama de Almería, my adoptive town, because it was where Nicolás Salmerón Alonso was born, he who in 1873 resigned the Presidency of the Spanish Republic when he refused to sign a death sentence. I took up my academic and development activities again, renewing work groups. I wrote and published several works on education, participated in the Spanish Association of Research for Peace, and coordinated the Andalusian Network of Associated Schools of UNESCO.[13] I was also regional coordinator of education in values and cross-curricular education. I traveled abroad, published several articles in educational magazines as well as four more books. Again I undertook important activities in favor of education for peace and human rights, absolutely convinced that the harvest of peace and democracy is an unfinished task that, like Sisyphus, we have to begin again constantly. On the other hand, I was also sure that in spite of the cross-curricular topics introduced in the educational reform in the nineties, deeper changes needed to be applied in the field of education for peace and human rights.

At the beginning of this century, in view of the social alarm created by the phenomena of school violence and within the framework of the International Decade of a Culture of Peace and Non-Violence for the children of the world, I was invited to work as coordinator for planning and developing the Andalusian Plan of Education for the Culture of Peace and Non-Violence.[14] This plan was officially presented by the President of the Government of Andalusia two days after the terrorist attack on the Twin Towers in New York, and it was put into practice in the context of Spain's later involvement in the war against Iraq with a significant opposition from the citizens, as evidenced by several demonstrations in the streets. During five long years, despite obstacles and an undeserved lack of empathy, I journeyed from one part of Andalusia to the other. I tried to convince skeptics, incorporating synergies, joining forces, and building commitment to improve coexistence in schools. I also incorporated an ecological perspective, which brought added value to the creation of a culture of peace with the participation of agents of social and educational change. Those were five long years of tireless work and painful experiences, but also of great help, unexpected collaborations, and new and close-knit friendships. In spite of it all, if I had not been fully confident, thanks to years of work and commitment for peace and human rights, I would have instantly given up. But I kept on, like a shipwrecked survivor in the middle of the ocean, bouncing among the waves.

This review of past events allows me to greatly value the Andalusian Plan, the first one of its kind in Spain, for its development is an example that can be applied in other places. The Plan has gained strength due to the vitality and commitment of the faculty, other social agents, and the honesty of the educational administration that has made it possible. Culture for peace is a collective work in progress that is a basic principle of the educational system of our Andalusian Community, as is stated in our Statute of Autonomy of Andalucia. This Plan has enabled the creation of new projects and efforts, both to strengthen what has been already achieved and to gain new competencies in an interdependent and sometimes violent world. In brief, I can say that the Andalusian Plan has

---

[13] For further reading I suggest an article from the *Revista Andalucia Educativa*, N° 16, September, 1999, titled: "Hacer de la utopía una esperanza." Visit: josetuvillarayo.es/obras-pedagogicas/recortes-de-prensa/index.html

[14] For the text of this plan visit: http://www.ceipaz.org/images/contenido/Plan Andaluz de Educacion para la Cultura de Paz y Noviolencia_ESP.pdf

made a reality of utopia, as can be seen in the strength of the Andalusian Network of "Schools: Space for Peace,"[15] comprised of more than two thousand educational centers and considered by an educational magazine as "the network of hope." When I received the gold medal of Merit for Education, I confess I did not feel proud. I was confused, for I did not expect any reward further than knowing I was on the right road. I remember that I felt a surge of emotion during a moment of my speech:

> Human beings have traveled to the most hidden and vast places …, they have also analyzed and studied each of the parts of our body until they discovered the code of life. All this is due to our heritage and teaching. But I honestly believe that we have been mistaken in our outlook, in our view of the world, in our way of organizing it. One has to do no more than look quickly at the world to discover the pain of anonymous beings who have lost their sons, daughters, and other family members due to the madness of war. We only have to feel close to the others, our equals, to understand, in other places, that dignity is poorly valued. It is true we still have a long road ahead of us, an adventure with a hidden treasure. … It is not a journey for a few, it is for all; our ship is education, and its oars the participation of a responsible and committed citizenship. This adventure does not depend on discovering frontiers, but on weaving a common culture that will keep us together, wherever we might be. In a beautiful Argentinian children's book I read: "Rights are the clothes of the soul… for any occasion and every moment." This is the treasure of our fortunate journey: identify, defend, and promote human rights, especially those of the weakest among us.

Now, after this recollection, I feel that it is time to start again. We live in a time of crisis, both of the economy and of values. When we believe ourselves to be near the top, new dangers appear; we must be ready, resist, and not submit so much to unreasonableness.

The Andalusian writer Francisco Ayala wrote, "When one writes, one mirrors what one is." This has been my intention.

BIBLIOGRAPHY

Ceba, Juan José (1991). *La selva de los rostros*. Granada: Biblioteca General del Sur.

Ortega y Gasset (1938). *En cuanto al pacifismo*. In *The Nineteeth Century*, julio.

Tuvilla Rayo, José (1982). *Vibración de la Ceniza*. Granada: Colección Dauro.

---

[15] Visit: www.juntadeandalucia.es/educacion/convivencia

Tuvilla Rayo, José (1990). *Derechos Humanos: propuesta de educación para la paz basada en los derechos humanos y del niño*. Sevilla: Consejería de Educación y Ciencia, Junta de Andalucía.

Tuvilla Rayo, José (1992). *Sudhi, el kurdo, abandona la ciudad de Sulaymaniyah huyendo de las bombas de los B-52*, Revista Andarax.

Tuvilla Rayo, José (2010). *De cuando Guadix estaba reciente como el mundo… En: Blog de José Tuvilla Rayo*, http://josetuvillarayo.webcindario.com/miscelanea/accitania/de-cuando-guadix-estaba-reciente-como-el-mundo.html.

Vásquez, Teresa (1981). *Prólogo. En: Ritual de la Palabra*. Editorial Cajal, Almería 1981.

Appreciating Paolo Freire, Antonio Gramsci, and this So-called Life: A Human Rights Educator's Story of Journeying out of Hegemony and Awakening the Conscious Self

Feliece I. Yeban (Philippines)

Feliece I. Yeban is among the pioneers of human rights education. As an academic, she is professor of human rights education at the Philippine Normal University (PNU) and currently the Associate Dean of the Faculty of Behavioral and Social Sciences. As a human rights educator, she has trained educators in integrating human rights into all school subjects and diverse groups such as chiefs of police and the military, government officials, refugees, Asian human rights commissions, former members of Hamas and PLO, and youth and activists from different countries. She has frequently taught at the international human rights education program of Equitas, the Canadian Center for Human Rights Education. As a consultant, she has participated in the drafting of the UN global human rights education agenda as well as advising many governments and NGOs. In 2006 she expanded her practice of human rights to the corporate sector, joining one Canadian mining company to serve as Vice President for Corporate Social Commitments and another to design its community development program using human rights and assets-based approach to development. Her experience bridging business and human rights has made her an advocate of Corporate Social Responsibility (CSR) among mining companies. She helped draft the Philippine Chamber of Mines' national CSR standard for the Philippine Mining Industry. She has since resumed her academic work.

A Confession ...

Unlike most of the Filipino human rights activists and educators I know, my life has not been dramatic. I was never incarcerated or tortured. I do not come from a family of activists. I led a very uneventful life during my youth. In fact, I was on the wrong side of history in 1986.

I started schooling when the then Philippine President Ferdinand E. Marcos declared martial law in 1972. I completed my undergraduate education two months after the People Power Revolution successfully brought down the Marcos dictatorship and eventually restored democracy in the Philippines in February 1986. The machinery of the dictatorship to create the "responsible citizen" needed by the "New Republic" succeeded in making me a "Marcos loyalist."

I am forever indebted to the work of Paolo Freire and Antonio Gramsci. I was a young educator in 1989. After a year of teaching the way I was taught, I felt a sense of irrelevance and meaninglessness. What use would teaching classical western political theories have on my students who belong to the poorer section of society? As a closeted "Marcos loyalist," the inconsistency between the beliefs I had about Marcos and the new information surfacing as a result of having a free press and open discussion, which had been a luxury during the martial law period, was creating in me cognitive dissonance and an ethical dilemma. I was groping for answers. It was obvious that I had to think about what I was thinking. I had to unlearn many of the things I thought were true. It was a moment in my life where I felt there was nothing in between my ears.

Then in the course of my reading for my graduate studies, I stumbled on the work of Paolo Freire and Antonio Gramsci. Their work paved the way for my understanding of my own experience of false consciousness. In Gramsci I learned the concept of hegemony. The authoritarian reality of the Marcos regime successfully created my consent for it by using the school and the controlled media as the machinery that manufactured the ideology supportive of the norms and values of the ruling class. With Freire's powerful description of banking education as a "false consciousness" creating process, I realized that indeed, I did not stand a chance.

My awakening was a cathartic experience. While I was finally reconciling my fissures, I could not help but feel a sense of guilt, shame, and anger that I was on the wrong side of history. I became consumed by the need to "make up" for lost time, for not being able to contribute to society during those dark years. The only way I could redeem my place in history was to give my students the opportunity to critically examine their lived experiences and the content of what they know. I have practiced Freireian pedagogy since then. I teach in a teacher-education university. Our students are would-be teachers. The potential for multiplier effect is so powerful. In Philippine Normal University (PNU) I have located a perfect place to practice my agency.

My Love Affair with Human Rights Education ...

I was formally introduced to human rights in 1991, when I attended a human rights education training seminar organized by Amnesty International Philippines (AI), which was about to develop a human rights education program called Education for Freedom (EFF). The content of the training resonated with me, but I thought that the methodology could still be improved. The experience led me to signing up as an AI member and volunteering in the EFF program. It was the start of my love affair with human rights education.

After the fall of the Marcos regime in 1986, a lot of those who had gone underground to wage a protracted war against the dictatorship "re-surfaced" and continued their activism through non-governmental organizations that had sprouted under the presidency of Corazon Aquino, regarded as the icon of Philippine democracy. The 1986 revolution did not and could not have totally dismantled the state apparatus that was used to sustain the authoritarian regime. Being "new" in the game of political activism and given the context prevailing at that time, it was inevitable that a Marxist orientation dominated my conception of human rights and practice of human rights education. The anti-state model became the lens with which I viewed my work as a human rights educator. I believed that the state continued to be oppressive and that the marginalized and the oppressed sectors should be equipped with the tools to fight for their human rights.

My students and I studied Freire and Gramsci and developed a more process-oriented approach to human rights education. We went to the slum areas of Metro Manila, to the crowded prison cells of the national penitentiary, to the most underserved schools in the country. We trained teachers, activists, and community leaders. Along with other like-minded students and faculty in PNU, we established the Peace and World Order Studies Unit, which later on became the Center for Peace and Human Rights Education. We summarized our experience through a book entitled *Shopping List of Techniques in Teaching Human Rights,* which was published by AI.

The Center for Peace and Human Rights Education did not receive funding from anybody, but it helped organize a national conference to draft the Philippine response to the UN Decade for Human Rights Education. Members of the Center helped the Department of Education write modules integrating human rights in all subjects in basic education. Teachers and principals in the country were trained on human rights and the teaching of human rights.

My human rights education work brought me to the West Bank and Gaza Strip to train former members of Hamas and the Palestinian Liberation Organization (PLO) on human rights as preparation for the turning over of authority of the Occupied Territories from Israel to the PLO. I trained teachers from Liberia on how to teach democracy in schools seven months after the end of the civil war. Together with my Filipino and Burmese friends, we "smuggled" ourselves into refugee camps along Thai-Burma border to train Burmese activists on human rights education. I trained Sri Lankan and Bangladeshi activists on using human rights to promote peace between Tamils and Singhalese and to explore reconciliation of religion and women's rights.

For years I dedicated my time doing human rights education work, training students, teachers, youth, activists, urban poor, peasants, and the marginalized sectors. But it was never enough. I was gradually sensing that the anti-state model seemed incomplete.

In 1997, I was invited by the Aquino Center to help them develop a training course for the chiefs of police in the Philippines. I was initially hesitant to accept the project because my colleagues in the human rights movement would not approve of equipping the "enemies of the people" with the very tool that the oppressed use to protect themselves from the "thugs" of the state. I accepted the project and formed a team of seasoned facilitators. For one year and a half, we travelled around the country training chiefs of police who were young inspectors during the time of the martial law period. We used a more psycho-social approach to human rights. That experience significantly changed the way I view HRE.

Training the police allowed me to peep into the world view of the "oppressors." Unless we look at them as victims themselves of what Freire calls "dehumanizing" situations, we will never be able to fully understand the indignity of human rights violations. They have been as dehumanized as their victims. The transformative promise of human rights can never materialize unless we connect both the oppressors and the oppressed through a dialogue about human rights that will allow them to cultivate a sense of ownership of human rights as human beings with dignity. Human rights ceased in my mind simply as obligations of the state but rather as a common language that allows individuals and communities to engage in a dialogue about their lived experiences. It is the lens that connects people, strengthens relationships, and sustains the process of transformation for better institutions, system, culture, and practices. Oh, yes, for a more purposeful life.

By this time, I had been convinced of the narrow path that my anti-state approach was leading me to. Human rights are not just about the state. It is personal. Ownership is a key to a more meaningful practice.

My experience with the military and the police made me become more open to bringing my human rights education work to the doorsteps of the state bureaucracy – the local government. While human rights is a set of values and is about managing our own personal woundedness, it is equally about designing the bureaucracy to meet the human rights standards. My exposure to local government units led me to realize that it is not enough that the individual values human rights; the system to sustain and strengthen that value has to be put in place. There are factual conditions within the state apparatus that hinder as well as facilitate the delivery of human rights.

There are areas in the country where the state is weak if not invisible. Clearly, the anti-state approach, which presupposes that the state is dominant and all-encompassing, cannot adequately address issues of good governance. We hold the state accountable for human rights, but we need to empower that very state to practice good governance for it to fulfill its human rights obligations.

There are many areas in the Philippines where alternative "governments" exist. There are armed groups and insurgents espousing secession from the Republic or socialist substitutes to the existing market economy. There are ancestral domains run and managed by Indigenous Peoples and ethnic communities. Given this complexity, the Philippine state frequently finds itself impotent to manage the "national commons." Where power is exercised, abuses of human rights become common. The non-state actors are as accountable as the state, especially in the situation where they are the surrogate state. The painful truth is nobody seems to come to the table with clean hands anymore.

In 2007, I embarked on a social experiment. I left my career as an academic specializing in human rights education to join a Canadian mining company as its Vice President for Corporate Social Commitments. I joined a company that had been accused of human rights violations. As I had experienced in 1997, when I accepted the project to develop a human rights education program for the police, I again was vilified by colleagues in the development and human rights movement. I was accused of selling out and abandoning my principles as a human rights educator, but I stood by my decision. I was tired of doing more of the same things. As an educator and a student of society, the dominant social analyses and theories no longer made sense.

My brief stint in the corporate sector was a very enriching experience. Let me share what I have learned:

1. If not properly regulated, mining as an economic activity renders communities vulnerable to human rights abuses both by the company and the government. Most mining areas are located where the government presence is weak; where armed and lawless groups operate; where the rule of law, particularly property rights, is more breached than observed; where communities are among the poorest of the poor; where local government is not as accountable to the people as it should be; where agents of regulating agencies can be bought; where companies are vulnerable to extortion; where both companies and communities have to fend for themselves to decide on the rules of their engagement; and where informal rules are used more often and negotiated rather than what the law requires.

2. If there is a security risk, mining companies will hire security personnel through either public or private security arrangement. Communities would often regard such company action as militarizing their communities. The presence of the company also means entry of "outsiders" and flow of cash into the communities, which radically alters the social, environmental, and economic conditions of host and impact communities. Company rules often run counter to community traditions and customs, which generates conflict.

   All these form the context that gives rise to human rights issues such as displacement, intimidation, discrimination, violation of the right to self-determination, the right to health, freedom to travel, etc.

3. There are good and bad mining companies. There are genuine and false non-government organizations. There are many sectors who pose themselves as mining stakeholders, but more often than not the primary stakeholders – the communities – are caught in the crossfire because too many stakeholders are appropriating unto themselves representation of the communities. I realized all sectors are guilty of "framing" issues. The more effective the framing is, the more likely it will be perceived as the "truth" but not necessarily what the truth actually is.

In June, 2011, I returned to my former university and resumed my career as an academic and as an advocate of human rights. I believe I have come full circle. Now is the time to sit down and reflect on the diversity of my experience.

Praxis: Constructing My View of Philippine Society

I am eternally grateful to Paolo Freire. He taught me praxis. My theory is my practice. My practice is my theory. My human rights education work has greatly influenced my understanding of Philippine society. As a student of society, I would use constructs to guide my practice, but eventually both theory and practice would influence each other as I engage in my internal dialogue.

I see the Philippines as a colonial construct. There would have been no Philippines had we not been colonized by Spain. What we have is an inorganic state that was imposed to put under its umbrella our more than one hundred ethnic communities and lump them all together as Filipinos. We are not a homogenous state but rather a deeply multicultural state whose main challenge is to "engineer" in the minds of the current population the idea of Filipino citizenship, which I would venture to say, is not yet totally successful. The idea of "imagined communities" by Benedict Anderson is very insightful to understand why statehood cannot be imposed on peoples found within the jurisdiction of Philippine territory. I do not, however, subscribe to "balkanizing" the country. It is important to note here the role of the traditional agents engaged in the "social engineering" process of constructing "Filipinoness" – the state and the school system.

The Philippine state, from my view, is suffering from what Alfred McCoy calls "anarchy of families." Historically, the elite of this country have always had access to both political and economic power. From north to south, the government is run by traditional names in Philippine politics that have time and again run roughshod over the country's resources and laws. We both have the old and new "rich" controlling government and its subsidiaries at different periods. It is no wonder then that the state is not felt on the ground. How then can we galvanize support for an entity that is "absent" in the day-to-day business of its people?

The school system is likewise suffering from perpetuating what Antonio Gramsci calls "false consciousness" – that of educating the population in knowledge, values, and skills that promote the interests of the dominant group. Thus, the general population unconsciously subscribes to a worldview or "ideology" that perpetuates the hegemony of the dominant group. The history of the school system in the Philippines is replete with "pacification" goals of either the Church or the colonial masters. Sadly, the western system of education that the eminent education theorist Paolo Freire calls a "banking system" of education has not totally been exorcised from our schools.

The call for governance and education reform is very fundamental to render effective the construction and re-construction of Filipino nationhood. Nationhood is not a given in the Philippine context. Construction and reconstruction of this "ideology" in the minds of Filipinos (referring to all ethnic communities) must proceed "surgically" through multi-layered efforts of different stakeholders whose role is to foster mutual understanding of this "ideology" and forge a "social contract' among us.

My View of the Social Sciences, My View of Human Rights

There are many exciting things happening in the field of social sciences. For instance, the traditional view of history as linear is now being challenged. *Passion and Revolution* by Reynaldo Ileto, *Contracting Colonialism* by Vicente Rafael, and *Pantayong Pananaw* by Zeus Salazar are just a few among the many "new" ways of writing history. These new approaches are telling us that there are many "histories." The challenge then is how to integrate these "new histories" into the work of the classical historians such as Agoncillo, Constantino, de la Costa, etc. and then learn from them. The writing of our history is not yet complete to accommodate the many narratives of people who have been a part of building this nation.

Both anthropology and sociology are blurring the lines that divide them to better approach the complexities of studying Filipino structures, organizations, and cultures. Filipinology and Philippine Studies are emerging fields resulting from merger. Traditionally, sociology in the Philippines is informed by the very western tradition of the structural functionalist and Marxist schools; nevertheless, postmodernism and post-structuralism as a "fad" in the West has in a way forced Filipino sociologists to revisit their practice of doing sociology. Randy David has even challenged Filipino social scientists to rethink our way of doing research in the social sciences. Rather than being hung up in the methodology, he calls for the reorienting of emphasis on recommendations that to him are the real "thesis" of the researcher. The structure-agency debate in the West does not seem to bother most Filipino sociologists and anthropologists. This is probably due to the fact that most of our social scientists are in one way or another involved in the national project of transformation rather than being "neutral" observers.

Psychology is one field whose role in my participating in the national project of transformation needs to be elevated. I am now particularly interested in positive psychology. Martin Seligman calls for a new psychology that studies the strengths and virtues that enable individuals and communities to thrive. The history of the Philippines is a history of struggle. In the recent past, the active involvement of the civil society in creative alternative-making initiatives is telling me that approaching social transformation from a "what's wrong with us" point of view does not account for the many success stories produced by individuals and groups who have exerted effort in transforming Philippine society. I am interested in tweaking my critical approach of understanding society towards a more appreciative approach.

Appreciative inquiry provides a way to explore what is glossed over by a critical approach. It is a process for catalyzing positive change (Cooperrider and Whitney, 2005). It is the study of what gives life to human systems when they are at their best. It dwells more on what worked rather than what did not work. As a method, it starts with the discovery phase, which requires identifying what worked well in people, communities, and organizations. It tries to take stock of success stories rather than problems to be solved. It aims to build upon the best in people, communities, and organizations. This means identifying of and building on the positive core. The discovery phase is followed by the dream phase. It is the phase that explores what the future might be like if the positive core discovered in phase one is optimized. The third is the design phase, which is simply planning how to optimize the positive core. The last phase is called destiny, which is implementing the plan, making the dream a reality.

In this approach rather than talking about what is not there, the focus is on analyzing and expanding what has already worked in the past to facilitate an evolved and better state of affairs that we could call development. A quote from *The Power of Appreciative Inquiry: A Practical Guide to Positive Change* sums up the mindset of this field well: "We are not saying to deny or ignore problems. What we are saying is that if you want to transform a situation, a relationship, an organization, or community, focusing on strengths is much more effective than focusing on problems."[1]

Political science is a field that traditionally has been very statist in its approach to doing social science. There has of late been a renewed interest in this discipline (political science used to be considered as preparatory to a law degree) due to the rise (maybe a re-introduction is better) of new institutionalism. This new orientation proposes that formal organizational structure reflects not only technical demands and resource dependencies, but is also shaped by institutional forces, including rational myths, knowledge legitimated through the educational system, and by the professions, public opinion, and the law. The core idea that organizations are deeply embedded in social and political environments suggests that organizational practices and structures are often either reflections of or responses to rules, beliefs, and conventions built into the wider environment. The insights generated by practitioners of organizational development could very well enhance political science. Whether we view this field from an institutional or behavioral point of view does not spell much difference for me.

The pursuit of good governance is what I perceive should be at the core of this discipline. I am partial to the role of the human rights paradigm because it is an international normative standard and a very clear framework of governance.

A sense of citizenship – commitment to the realization of the aspirations of the state – must be re-invented in the light of the changing and changed context of twenty-first century societies. One phenomenon in today's politics is the increasing difficulty of governments adequately to address economic and social problems. Political power traditionally exercised by governments dominated by a few is now perceived as indicative of bad governance. Governance is now perceived as shared domain of both the government and the citizens. Gone are the days where people are passive recipients of government services. Governments are increasingly recognizing that efficiency and effectiveness of public service is better achieved if the citizens are involved and engaged.

---

[1] Dianah D. Whitney and Amanda Trosten-Bloom. *The Power of Appreciative Inquiry: A Practical Guide to Positive Change.* (Berret-Koehler, San Francisco, CA: 2010).

Government agencies have three corresponding human rights duties: the duty to respect, the duty to protect, and the duty to promote or fulfill human rights. From these emerge several human rights related tasks and functions such as human rights promotion and education. Traditionally, human rights education for citizens means equipping people with the knowledge, values, and skills to demand that their governments respect, protect, and promote their human rights. However, making governments the audience of human rights education means enabling the governance structures to deliver good governance. Good governance has now come to mean people's participation in decision-making, transparency, rule of law, human rights, responsiveness to people's needs, and government accountability. It means the effective management of a country's resources in a manner that is open, transparent, accountable, equitable, and responsive to people's needs. The rule of law, transparency, accountability and effectiveness of public sector management, and an active civil society are all essential components of good governance. Research in political science, I believe, should be around the core theme of governance and as described herein is not only focused on the state but extended to other actors such as individuals and communities as well.

Economics as a field has conventionally been very positivistic. However, I view this discipline's primary role in facilitating understanding of globalization, development, and poverty. These are the themes that are predominant in the developing countries such as the Philippines.

The government flaunts one development plan after another – Philippines 2000, Angat Pinoy, Beat the Odds, to name a few. These are undoubtedly economistic development models. The left, on the other hand, is still debating whether to affirm or reject a development agenda conceptualized in the 1960s. The civil society sector has more varied development projects either driven by funders or by their avowed commitment (Illo, et al, 2002). The business sector is re-inventing itself by claiming more than ever to be socially responsive. Despite these, we are still at a loss as to how to solve poverty, to control the adverse effects and exploit the positive effects of globalization, and to pursue a development agenda that works for majority of the Filipinos. Both the capitalist and socialist blueprints have been proven inadequate in bringing about genuine, holistic, inclusive, and long lasting development.

What all these point to is that economics as it currently stands cannot adequately help us understand globalization, development, and poverty because these are complicated concepts that require knowledge of other disciplines for us to fully comprehend.

In summary, the social sciences are suffering from fragmentation. Each discipline invariably focuses on the different aspects of Philippine society, thus rendering a fractional and bounded view. The challenge to social science practitioners then is how to integrate insights generated by the different fields to enable the social scientists to formulate new research questions whose answers provide a more holistic basis for our action.

My tool around the fragmentation of the social sciences is to tweak my practice around the idea of rights-based development. I am influenced in this stance by Kalaw (1997) who argues for the "construction of a Science of Development that can provide normative and functional integration of economics, ecology, (self), and society and the development of management technologies that look at ecosystems, cultures, ethnicities, community, and evolution as units of analysis and management."

Development is a mindset, a "heart set", and a "work set." As such it requires a set of knowledge, values, and skills that cultivate appropriate thinking, valuing, and doing development. To engage in this project requires a deconstruction, reconstruction, and construction of knowledge, values, and practices at the personal, interpersonal, communal, societal, and global levels. Concretely, this ranges from simple acts (e.g., continuing self-examination; advocating reforms in education, legal, and governance systems; embracing new business philosophy; appropriate science and technology, and simpler but more meaningful lifestyles) to more complicated initiatives (e.g., social forestry, agronomics, transpersonal psychology, complexity studies, biopsychology, biocracy, and other emerging fields) that blur the boundaries dividing the social sciences, natural sciences, and the humanities.

My Social Science Practice as Educating for Human Rights

I am an educator who is engaged in social transformation. The educative process does not only happen in school. Every social engagement I have with individuals or groups is an educative opportunity both for me and for others I encounter. I have the listening ear and inquiring eye of an anthropologist, the social imagination of a sociologist, the predisposition to ask who has the power and who gets what of a political scientist and economist, and the predilection to understand the individual of a psychologist. All these are mindsets and heart sets necessary in the practitioner of a social transformation. There are many ways to contribute to this, but I choose to be in the field of education.

Education is an occasion for us to confront life as we pursue a meaningful existence. Education should equip us with the knowledge to know, comprehend, and act on our social reality using our different disciplines whether it be the natural sciences, social sciences, applied sciences, or folk knowledge. Social transformation means being able to identify, describe, and confront problem areas in our society and in our world, as well as to appreciate positive dimensions of our realities. This means we need education to enable us to navigate and take control of our inner world and our inner selves so we can relate more positively with the outside world. Education is not only for the good of the society, but also for our personal well-being as well. Without personal growth, we won't have enough citizens who have the consciousness required to co-create a healthy society. In all these, I take human rights as my anchor.

The human rights educator must recognize that the practice of transformative education entails the following:

1. Reflecting continuously on the human condition and how education can help construct new social realities.

2. Using human rights as a standard by which the human condition can be measured.
3. Defying conventions and cultural norms when necessary.
4. Constructing new practice and structures that might require taking risks that include the danger of isolation.
5. Being prepared to deal with resistance.
6. Understanding that the process of transformation is the reward itself.
7. Finding the difficult balance between self-actualization on the one hand and selfless social engagement on the other.
8. Taking action to effect the necessary change.

Human rights education to me is a perspective with which I view things. It allows me to connect my different identities as one conscious self, unceasing and untiring in constructing, deconstructing, and reconstructing situations for a life well lived.

BIBLIOGRAPHY

Anderson, Benedict. 1983. *Imagined Communities: Reflections on the Origin and Spread of Nationalism*. Brooklyn NY: Verso Books.

Archer, Margaret. 2000. *The Problem of Agency*. New York NY: Cambridge University Press.

Bautista, Victoria, ed. 2003. *Participatory Governance in Poverty Alleviation*. Manila: National College of Public Administration and Governance, Ateneo de Manila University.

Baviera, Aileen, ed. 2000. *Partners Against Poverty*. Manila: Philippine-China Development Resource Center.

Bell, Daniel. 1976. *The Coming of Post-Industrial Society*. New York: Basic Books.

Burger, Peter and Thomas Luckman. 1966. *The Social Construction of Reality: A Treatise in the Sociology of Knowledge*. Garden City, NY: Doubleday.

Chin, Ai-Li S. 1998. "Future Visions: The Unpublished Papers of Abraham Maslow." *Journal of Organizational and Change Management*, Vol. 11, No. 1, pp. 74-77.

Cooperrider, David L., and Diana Whitney. 2005. *Appreciative Inquiry: A Positive Revolution in Change*. Oakland CA: Berrett-Koehler Publishers, Inc.

Cupchik, Gerald. 2001. "Constructivist Realism: An Ontology That Encompasses Positivist and Constructivist Approaches to the Social Sciences." *Qualitative Social Research*, Vol. 2, No. 1, Article 7.

David, Randolph. 2001. *Reflections on Sociology and Philippine Society*. Quezon City: University of the Philippines, 2001.

Freire, Paolo. 1975. *Pedagogy of the Oppressed*. New York NY: Continuum.

Gramsci, Antonio. 1971. *Selections from the Prison Notebooks*. New York NY: International Publishers.

Hermoso, Reuel, ed. 1994. *Development and Democracy: A People's Agenda*. Manila: Ateneo Center for Social Policy and Public Affairs.

Horgan, John. 1996. *The End of Science. Facing the Limits of Knowledge in the Twilight of the Scientific Age*. Boston MA: Addison-Wesley Publiching Company.

Ileto, Reynaldo. 1979. *Pasyon and Revolution: Popular Movements in the Philippines, 1840-1910*. Quezon City: Ateneo de Manila University Press.

Illo, Jeanne. 2002. *Reforming Technical Cooperation: The Philippine Experience*. Manila: Institute of Philippine Culture, Ateneo de Manila University.

Kalaw, Maximo, 1997. *Exploring the Soul and Society. Papers on Sustainable Development*. Manila: ANVIL Publishing, Inc.

McCoy, Alfred W. 2009. *An Anarchy of Families: State and Family in the Philippines*. Madison, WI: University of Wisconsin Press.

Rafael, Vicente. 1993. *Contracting Colonialism: Translation and Christian Conversion in Tagalog Society Under Early Spanish Rule*. Durham NC: Duke University Press.

Salazar, Zeus A. 1991b. "Ang Pantayong Pananaw Bilang Diskursong Pangkabihasnan." In *Pilipinolohiya: Kasaysayan, Pilosopiya at Pananaliksik*, edited by Violeta V. Bautista and Rogelia Pe-Pua. Manila: Kalikasan Press.

Seligman, M.E.P. 1990. *Learned Optimism*. New York: Knopf. (Reissued by The Free Press, 1998).

Shor, Ira with Paolo Freire. 1987. *Pedagogy for Liberation: Dialogues on Transforming Education*. Santa Barbara CA: Greenwood Publication Group.

Simon, Herbert. 1982. *Models of Bounded Rationality, Volumes 1 and 2*. Cambridge MA: MIT Press.

Stiglitz, Joseph. 2002. *Globalization and Its Discontent*. New York NY: W. W. Norton and Company.

Wallerstein, Immanuel. 1999. *The End of the World as We Know it: Social Science for the 21st Century*. Minneapolis MN: University of Minnesota Press.

Whitney, Diana and Amanda Trosten-Bloom. 2010. *The Power of Appreciative Inquiry: A Practical Guide to Positive Change*. With Foreword by David Cooperrider. 2nd edition. Oakland CA: Berrett-Koehler Publishers, Inc.

Life as an Educator for Human Rights and Peace: A History of Conjunctions and Possibilities

Anita Yudkin (Puerto Rico)

> **Anita Yudkin Suliveres** is a professor in the Department of Foundations of the School of Education at the University of Puerto Rico-Río Piedras. Since 1999 she has held the UNESCO Chair of Education for Peace of the University of Puerto Rico. She teaches courses on the psychological foundations of education and on education for peace. Her professional interests are teacher development, critical qualitative research related to learning, the rights of children, human rights, and the development of a culture of peace. From 1993 to 2001 she was a member of the management team of the Teaching for Freedom Project of Amnesty International-Puerto Rico, where she led the teachers' network. She collaborates on several educational and human rights initiatives in Puerto Rico. She also participates in national, regional, and international networks and conferences on human rights and peace. She has a bachelor's degree in education, and a master's degree and Ph.D. in educational psychology from the University of Michigan.
>
>

The question about my work as an educator for human rights and peace brings me back to people, events, and experiences that make up the present. It also makes me think about the conjunctions and possibilities that have influenced my educational thinking and activities. It is a story located in multiple contexts, which I use as a framework for this text.

Setting My Experience in Context

The most important context is Puerto Rico, an island nation that has not attained its sovereignty. Since 1898, when Spain ceded it at the end of the Spanish-American War, it has had a subordinate military, political, and economic relationship with the United States as an "unincorporated territory," known today as the Free Associated State of Puerto Rico. As such, it has no juridical status in the United Nations; it is not a signatory of international treaties, including the Universal Declaration of Human Rights. One consequence of this colonial status is its isolation and even invisibility in national and international forums, programs, and reports related to human rights.

The purpose of this account is not a detailed review of the historical and political reality of the country. Nevertheless, I find it necessary to outline certain features of this process that are relevant to the times and topics described. I will deal with them in two ways: firstly, as they relate to my school and college background, and secondly, in the light of present reality.

Three ideological tendencies have dominated the electoral and political scene of Puerto Rico in the last sixty years: 1) the *estadolibrismo* (ELA, or commonwealth status) that endorses the continuation or evolution of the present relationship with the United States; 2) the *estadista* sector that favors the incorporation of Puerto Rico as the fifty-first state of the United States; and 3) the *independentismo* that aspires to the independence of Puerto Rico and its creation as an independent nation. Two of these groups, the *estadolibristas* and *estadistas*, who are represented by the two main political parties of the country, have been alternating as governing powers as a consequence of the electoral processes of the last forty years.

During the 1960s and 1970s, as the *estadolibrista* sector evolved and monopolized political power, the parties, organizations, and people who supported independence were subjected to a systematic process of persecution and incarceration, turning them into criminals and thus reducing their number of supporters. Since the late sixties, the *estadista* group grew in supporters and influence as an ideological movement in the country, and their opposition to independence enabled this systematic persecution during the seventies. These included the creation of "files" on people considered "subversive" and the murder of young people linked to the independence movement by political agents of the state. These processes were not unrelated to US police forces, which went so far as to create their own archives on those who they considered dangerous to their interests and to their dominance over Puerto Rican territory.

This was, broadly speaking, the political context in which I spent my school and college years. During this time I became conscious of the ideological and economic differences among those around me. At the same time, I became more perceptive, able to identify these differences and acknowledge my own privileged position. This was the time when I developed a way of thinking and an appreciation for my native land, as well as a profession that would allow me to work for my country.

Act I. Brief Family Portrait

I want to start this account by mentioning the influence that my father had over me from very early on. My father, William Yudkin, an American Jew whom my grandmother referred to as her "Puerto Rican son," moved to Puerto Rico with my mother so that she could give birth to me. From the time he arrived, he worked as a professor of political science, and his circle of friends included well-known intellectuals both Puerto Rican and foreign. He was in favor of independence and worked with several like-minded groups. Above all, my father was a lover of people and of nature. He enjoyed taking walks and talking to everyone, everywhere. I loved going out with him. From him I learned to interact in diverse social scenes and with people of different economic levels. I learned to be a careful observer, to listen patiently, and to enjoy the life, stories, and anecdotes of different people. I got to know Puerto Rico by taking my father's hand, going out on Sundays, singing loudly out of tune, and laughing at ourselves. He was angered by the manipulation and abuse of power by politicians. I will never forget his face when in the nineties he picked up his file from the Puerto Rican police. Extremely serious and dismayed, he told me, "But none of this is true. This is full of lies."

My mother, named Isabel like my grandmother, is a woman who has never avoided taking action or making a decision just because she is female. Both of them were women who were quite ahead of their times in terms of their attitudes, behavior, and professional work. My mother was a social worker who was always deeply interested in my studies. She encouraged me and gave me enough freedom to explore what I was interested in and to study what I liked. Her work, support, and tenacity enabled me to study in the best schools and university of the country. This I did without ever feeling any kind of pressure to compete or to concentrate only on my studies. I was able to explore several subjects until I chose education. From her I acquired a sense of responsibility that I consider necessary to be an educator, especially for human rights and peace: the responsibility to oneself and to others to do one's best, fully aware of the consequences of our actions.

Act II. Early Experiences

As a teacher of future educators, I want to highlight the importance of early experiences in one's development. They are a framework that makes us look, interpret, and participate in the world to which childhood belongs. These experiences can enhance or limit a student's possibilities and development.

My experiences as a student of the Eugenio María de Hostos School, established and led by Isabelita Freire,[1] made it possible to be in the world and to be in the world with others. This, I understood decades later, was an educational approach similar to what today we would consider human rights education. Each and every child was important for Isabelita. She listened to us, drew with us, read us her poetry, and encouraged us to write. She guided us in the process of appreciating nature and getting to know our native land in order to love it, at a time when this was not done and considered subversive. We enjoyed the freedom of playing and creating, we learned to be responsible, we created our own personal and collective identity, and we were confident enough to raise our voices in cases of injustice. And yes, we learned the lessons required of any school, but this is not what those of us lucky enough to be her students remember as important.

---

[1] Isabel Freire de Matos was a well-known educator, writer of books for children, and promotor of the Puerto Rican culture and nation.

Isabelita wrote *La escuela elemental puertorriqueña* (*The Puerto Rican Elementary School*), which I read as a college teacher. This book compiles essential elements of her work as an educator. First, Isabelita argues that the colonial reality of the country led to an educational system "that demands a double loyalty and creates a divided conscience." In addition, it is a system that "has never had the authority to create a curriculum that teaches the notion of a free native land to its children and helps them develop as citizens responsible for creating their own destiny." (Freire de Matos, 1997, 14 and 31). In opposition to this, Isabelita developed her idea of what Puerto Rican education should be. She asserted that children begin their self-development from very early on and that it is the government's responsibility to make available the effective education they need. She describes the basic elementary school topics that we should aspire to as educators: "First, children should know and interpret their homeland in order to love it"; then they can move to the international level, to be part of it and to develop feelings of solidarity toward their neighbors under the slogan "Homeland and Universe." Another main idea she proposes is "the comprehensive and integrated development of the individual in its different spheres: physical, mental, social, and moral," for the child's self-respect and growth. She suggests that it is urgent to "guide him/her towards essential life values, such as truth, justice, honesty, sense of solidarity, and the concept of freedom." She highlights the importance of developing skills in the vernacular, not only for the psychological well-being of the child, but also for the development of thinking and feeling skills, as well as for the creative work of childhood.

Those of us who had the experience of being her students actually lived that education. Isabelita was an educator for human rights and peace when it was not yet called that. She instilled in each student the notion of being a subject of rights, many years before that concept was used. She instilled in me feelings, knowledge, and actions that have supported my personal development and professional learning for life. Decades later, I started to teach human rights formally in the Teaching for Freedom project at the Puerto Rican section of Amnesty International, which I will go into with more detail later on. Isabelita and her daughter, Marisol Matos Paoli, collaborated on this project and greatly enriched our educational experience. Isabelita shared with us an aphorism: "A child who enjoys her rights integrates peace with freedom." Thank you, Isabelita.

Act III. Developing New Ways of Seeing, Understanding, and Interpreting the World

I attended graduate school in the United States, and thanks to a scholarship for "minority students," I received my Ph.D. from the University of Michigan. Though it is a conservative institution, especially the School of Education, by the eighties its faculty and students had developed alternative work that allowed me to look, understand, and interpret the world from a critical perspective consistent with human rights. This formative process led me to accept the intellectual responsibility of what I studied, to consider how and for what does one study, and to take a stand about the stories I should tell. I read Paulo Freire for the first time in college. Concentrating on doing well in my studies and influenced by the competitive nature of the educational process, I read Freire from a distance, from "up north." I found him interesting, and I even recall a class debate on his writing. Somehow he required me to examine educational issues from a Latin American perspective.

Nevertheless, I did not understand at the time that *Pedagogy of the Oppressed* (Freire, 1970) described the educational process in which I myself was immersed, nor did I understand its importance for my future development as a teacher or how significant it would be for my work in education.

Later as a graduate student, I reread Freire and met him personally. His books and lectures on the relationship between politics and education, reading the world and reading the word, the act of knowing, and the link between reflection and action made me perceive a potential for transforming the educational process. They opened my mind and reaffirmed my commitment to dedicate myself completely to this field. His presence fascinated me. How could someone so well recognized, so strong in his words, so firm in his convictions, be so sweet and generous in his relationships?

At this time, I experienced a convergence both in my teaching and research with other critical thinkers and educators, from the learning processes seen from the perspective of the student, from phenomenology, and from the clash of paradigms in social science research and education between positivism and critical theory. Working with two wonderful teachers, the American Loren Barritt and the South African Valerie Polakow, I gradually took off the blinders that had limited and obscured my studies and my understanding of education, educators, and those being educated. In class we read and held group discussions on the texts of philosophers like Michael Polanyi, Edmund Husserl, Richard Rorty, Jurgen Habermas, Hans-Georg Gadamer, Maxine Greene, and Michel Foucalt; anthropologists like Clifford Geertz and Studs Terkel; writers like Robert Coles and Alice Walker; and educators from all over the world like Paulo Freire, Henry Giroux, Patricia Carini, Jonathan Kozol, Ton Beekman, and Vivian Gussin Paley. Among these books I want to highlight *Children of Crisis*, by Robert Coles (1997) because of its influential ideas on how to envision, think about, and tell people's stories. So through theory and descriptions of human nature, I developed ways of envisioning, understanding, and interpreting human beings – especially in childhood – both in their development and as active subjects of the educational process. I recall these authors as I write now, without referring to any bibliography; I simply remember them. I remember them because they opened and enlightened my being as an educator.

Act IV. Childhood and War

During my college years I gradually became part of a group of Latin American friends from whom I learned about the lived and shared history of our America. Students and teachers from different countries under dictatorships in the south of the continent, others who had suffered civil wars and armed conflicts in Central America, were my colleagues in this personal and professional development process. Among them, I met my first husband, who was from El Salvador. In 1986, we married and moved to El Salvador in the middle of the civil war between the state and the Frente Farabundo Martí de Liberación Nacional (Farabundo Martí Liberation Front: FMLN).

During this critical political and personal juncture, I had to work on my Ph.D. thesis. I decided to return to the question posed by Valerie Polakow in her book *Whose Stories Do We Tell?* (1985). I decided to do a critical ethnographic study of the schooling experience of children displaced during the armed conflict (Yudkin, 1993). The objective was to understand their stories and influence their education through this learning process. My first contact was the Jesuit priest and sociologist Segundo Montes, who was documenting the displacement and refugee process of the Salvadoran population. He was a supportive academic whose work reflected the ethical perspective of a lifetime commitment. His writings, like those of other Jesuits such as Ignacio Martín Baró and Ignacio Ellacuría, created a path for me to read, study, and write from a position of commitment and hope similar to what I had read in Freire.

One of the saddest and most painful moments of my life was seeing, from the distant television screen in the United States, those priests murdered by the Salvadoran army in 1989. That night I walked and walked, repeating a verse by the Cuban composer and singer Pablo Milanés: "I will step again on the once bloodied streets of Santiago and in a beautiful liberated plaza I will stop to cry for those that are not here anymore." At that time and with the image in that song, my feelings, thoughts, and convictions agreed that it was imperative to be a part of the struggle for a better and more just world, a world where the life and dignity of all people is at the center of a common goal from education to all the spaces in which we act.

For my Ph.D. dissertation I visited three schools created for children displaced by the armed conflict. They were a refuge but also a place under observation and threat, for the government armed forces considered those institutions and the people in them to be FMLN sympathizers. My school life for a year and a half with those children and teachers was a learning experience like no other: learning about childhood, education, and the impact of war on both.

Although I could not know it then, over time I realized that this experience had established the bases of my understanding of human rights and peace and their relationship with education. One of the topics I analyzed was the silence about children's lives, their schools, and their communities. This silence was also the silence lived in San Salvador: silence about war and the death of thousands of people, most of them killed by the military and paramilitary forces controlled by the government of El Salvador. While the horrors of the war were being silenced and hidden, I was receiving books and publications that documented them. I received the book *Weakness and Deceit: U.S. Policy and El Salvador* (1984), by Raymond Bonner, a reporter from the *New York Times*. I opened the book right in the middle, where there were dozens of photographs. I read the stories and was shocked by their content and style. I recall a story about how, after student and labor leaders had been ambushed, their blood was washed off the public plaza with hoses. Later, the heads of the military gave a press conference where they assured that nothing had happened. I thought: Nothing happened here? From that moment I knew how important it was to know the non-official history of our Latin American peoples. I also began to understand the problem of the impunity of those in power and to acknowledge the courage and vulnerability of those fighting for justice.

It was in this context that for the first time I learned about human rights and read reports by Amnesty International on violations in El Salvador. I also had access to UNICEF documents on childhood and education and the need to protect children during armed conflicts. For the first time

I tried to understand the connection between human rights, education, and violence. I learned of the existence of international organizations that denounced the violations and defended those rights.

Act V. Educating for Freedom

In 1993, once I had finished my Ph.D. and returned to my country, I started to work as a faculty member in the Department of Education of the University of Puerto Rico. A few months later, my colleague and friend Nellie Zambrana invited me to work on children's rights. She said: "Join us, it has a lot to do with your work; it's a human rights project." That was how I entered the Teaching for Freedom Project of the Puerto Rico section of Amnesty International (PEL/AI), where I worked for more than ten years. Through this project I learned about human rights and children's human rights; at the same time I taught and worked to promote and defend them. Thanks to this project, a group of educators including Anaida Pascual, Nellie Zambrana, Luis Rivera Pagán, María de Lourdes Ferrer, Leticia López, Rocío Costa, José Raúl Cepeda, and Carlos Muñiz shared the process of learning and educating children, youth, parents, and educators about human rights. This was in several formal and informal settings. We prepared conferences, workshops, seminars, festivals, and materials for identifying and promoting human rights, specifically those of children and youth. A common and collective project like this is special because it is more than the sum of its parts; it means a space and time of support and enrichment that develops into a life experience.

In this process of educating for freedom, responsibility, and human rights, I met first through their writings and then personally several Latin American educators, pioneers in this area, who worked both regionally and in their own countries. I read works by Abraham Magendzo, Nélida Céspedes, Rosa María Mujica, Ana María Rodino, and Gloria Ramírez, among others. Some of these works I use today in my college classes, inspiring critical thought and questions in my students that will help them as future educators. Outstanding among these are Abraham Magendzo's *Bases de una concepción pedagógica para educar en y para los Derechos Humanos* (*Foundations of a Pedagogical Approach to Human Rights Education*, 1993) and *Modelo problematizador para la Educación en Derechos Humanos* (*A Problem-based Model for Human Rights Education*, 2006); and Nélida Céspedes' *La escuela y los derechos de las niñas y los niños* (*The School and the Rights of the Children*, 1997). How important to have met them on this road!

The Teaching for Freedom Project (1992-2001) connected us with human rights education and its development both regionally and internationally. Sponsored by the Norwegian section of Amnesty International, the project was part of a human rights education initiative in Asia, Africa, Latin America, and the Caribbean. For Puerto Rico and for us personally, it was an unusual experience that inspired us to leave our insularity and examine ourselves from other perspectives and possibilities. Several of us had the opportunity to attend conferences in countries in the region. We exchanged and obtained educational materials and publications, enough to make a collection of more than two hundred volumes. We worked beyond the limits when we educated and worked for the defense and promotion of the rights of Puerto Rican children since our country is not a signatory of any human rights treaties, including the UN Convention on the Rights of the Child. We also had practical learning opportunities on the importance of forging alliances between organizations and individuals with the idea of promoting a shared educational agenda.

Act VI. From Educating in and for Human Rights to Educating for Peace

From the very beginning of the Teaching for Freedom Project, we linked the subject of children's rights and human rights education with issues of violence that we face in our country. The physical violence and mistreatment faced by our children and youth, especially those belonging to the most vulnerable groups, was our subject of study, concern, and work. We also worked with *Violencia en el sistema educativo* (*Systemic Violence in Education: Promise Broken*, Ross and Watkinson, 1997), proposing educational programs, curriculums, and opportunities for the promotion of learning and experiencing human rights in schools (Yudkin, Zambrana and Pascual, 2002). We deepened our understanding and included in our activities the aphorism by Isabelita, being very clear about the fact that education for human rights is at the same time a way of reducing violence, promoting freedom, and strengthening peace.

In 1996, the University of Puerto Rico received an invitation from the General Director of UNESCO, Federico Mayor Zaragoza, to become a part of the UNITWIN Network Program, an initiative of the Higher Education Division of that international organization. As a result of the cooperation between both institutions, the UNESCO chair of Education for Peace was established. My colleague and friend Anaida Pascual Morán, whose Ph.D. work focused on a curriculum for peace, was its first coordinator. As a participant of the Teaching for Freedom Project, I was invited to be a member of a group of coordinators to organize a workshop-seminar for educators. A year later when Anaida left the University for her sabbatical, I took over the coordination of this important university project.

From the moment I became the part of this project, my aim was to learn about the basis, theory, and practice of educating for peace. My learning curve was very steep since I was also in charge of organizing important academic activities both in the university and in the country. I found and received important works by educators for peace, particularly from Spain and Latin America. Several became essential for my activities: the book *Educar para la paz: Una propuesta possible* from the Seminar for Education for Peace of Madrid (1994), and the Galician writer Xesús Jares's *Educación para la paz* (1999) and *Educación y Derechos Humanos* (2000). Jares's critical perspective on education for human rights and peace strengthened my knowledge and opened up more possibilities for my educational work. His thinking continues to influence mine. Educating for peace is education for human rights from a wider point of view that calls into question any kind of violence and enables activities in favor of justice, freedom, and solidarity. At the same time, I studied other subjects related to peace, like demilitarization and disarmament, conflict resolution, multiculturalism, and a plurality of views about differences. I got to know the writings of John Lederach, Vincent Fisas, and Betty Reardon, among others.

In later years I have also read and met educators for human rights and peace, some critical, who have influenced me. Although all are valuable, they are too many to name. Nevertheless, a significant learning opportunity came from the interdisciplinary group of educators and students that make up the organizing committee of the UNESCO Chair. How can I explain all that I have learned from José Luis (Pinchi) Méndez? A student in Paris during May 1968, he is a sociologist, the former dean of the Department of Social Sciences, and an observer and analyst of the political and social reality of our country like few others. Or what I learned from Luis Rivera Pagán? A theologian, militant for human rights, and a dissident. They both honored us with their presence at the seminal conference of the UNESCO Chair in Education for Peace, which was later published. I mention them both as examples, without diminishing what other colleagues have shared with us in communications, natural sciences, law, counseling, and education. We have learned to follow the true path of interdisciplinary work in education for human rights and peace. In our team work, we have focused on the responsibility of our university towards important issues facing the country, enabling us to view important global topics and their relation with local work ("glocal"). In this sense, I want to highlight some important joint efforts and activities: demilitarization, human rights, and peace in the island of Vieques; overcoming a culture of violence and war, including the war in Iraq; promotion of co-existence from a human rights perspective; the link between human rights, science, and sustainability; and understanding and participating in university conflicts.

Two events deserve special attention due to their influence on us as educators. First, the experience from 1999 to 2003 in the island of Vieques: in 1999, an American bomber plane dropped a bomb and "accidentally" killed David Sanes, who was born on the island. This event attracted the attention of the whole country and later of the world to the reality that the Puerto Rican inhabitants of Vieques had to face. After sixty years of the US Marines using their land for military practice, the island and Puerto Rican inhabitants said "Enough," unleashing a series of protests and events that ended with the Marines leaving the island in 2003. It is very difficult if not impossible to emphasize in a few lines the importance of this non-violent civil action and victory for human rights and the peace it has brought to the island. I want to emphasize that this process underlines the interrelation between local and global events. Issues like demilitarization, sustainable development, civil disobedience, and other protest activities and interventions for human rights and peace grew in importance, especially for our work as educators.

The second event has to do with the experience gained from the proposals and activities undertaken by the student movement in the University of Puerto Rico from 2010 to 2011. In these recent events, students took multiple actions, including two strikes in defense of education and student participation; they opened the eyes of the whole country to the lack of democracy and justice that had resulted from adverse government policies. The use of force by the State Police against the students served as an example of government disdain for certain sectors of the population they considered to be adversarial, or even disposable. Without diminishing the controversies and conflicts involved or condoning the violent events in which many students were involved, the students' heroic deeds moved us and led us to reaffirm the importance of education and action in building a democracy for the defense of human rights for all.

Finally, as a participant in the UNESCO chair program, I want to highlight the learning and teaching relationship established for many years with my colleague and friend Anaida Pascual. If writing is difficult and needs effort, it is more so when one wants to think, write, and "denounce, and announce" at the same time. Much of what I know about the theory of education for peace I have learned in thinking and working with Anaida. Her text *Acción civil noviolenta* (2003) was important for my understanding of non-violence in connection with education and the struggle for human rights and peace. After more than fifteen years working together, we have learned from each other as educators and lived together through (and even laughed at) our different styles of analyzing, presenting, and writing.

Act VII. Educating for Peace and Human Rights in Theory and Practice

My greatest challenge and achievement as an educator for human rights and peace comes from teaching a college course on education for peace. It is a great challenge to promote the contents of this introductory course taken by students from different departments of the University of Puerto Rico-Río Piedras. I aspire to create coherence among the content of the class, the educational lessons, and the practical possibilities that students can receive and develop. The diversity of students and topics are part of its richness and achievements of the last seven years.

From the moment I decided to teach the course, I thought it was important to highlight the relationship between educational theory and practice and between knowledge and action. Creating a praxis, "a liberating education" in the Freirian sense, has been my framework and aim. Adopting an education of "indignation and hope," as Freire (1996-2003) proposed, leads us to examine reality critically in order to understand it, and dream and think about alternatives to a culture of violence that surrounds us. I again acknowledge the work of Xesús Jares as essential to my thinking on the course and its content, including *Educar para la verdad y la esperanza* (Jares, 2005), which reflects Freirian principles. There are also works and ideas that travel through time, from the pioneer writings of María Montessori to committed contemporary theoreticians and educators like José Tuvilla Rayo, Alicia Cabezudo, Abraham Magendzo, John Lederach, Johan Galtung, Betty Reardon, Vincent Fisas, Federico Mayor, and Moacir Gadotti.

I employed diverse strategies in the course to enable understanding on these topics and their relationship with activities for human rights and peace. Although this is not the place to go deeper into this methodology, I wish to share some comments because they have influenced my learning as an educator. First, I emphasize the link between the contents of education for peace – that has human rights as its main axis– and the life and environment of the students. At the same time, I connect the contents of education for peace to local and global issues that either go against or make possible a world of positive peace. Second, I encourage the use of newspapers to promote student understanding and thinking. This is an important issue to consider and requires constant communication for the development of ideas and experience. Finally, I include educational and formative activities from different subject areas or professional backgrounds. Simply put, this course requires a constant search for materials and related topics about the development of a culture of peace from the students' different academic disciplines. It is also necessary to link these different disciplines in order to facilitate communication and resolution of conflicts in a country that keeps us constantly far away from this culture of peace. I also have to think and rethink my practice from a human rights perspective, with a critical and questioning approach to the process of education. So, as many of the authors collaborating in this book know by experience, it is not easy being an educator for human rights and peace, for it necessitates a political, ethical, and educational stand that we both formulate and put into practice.

Final Thought: The Defense of Human Rights is the Way to Develop Democracy and Peace

At the beginning of this account I noted that I would go back to the particular context of Puerto Rico, for I think it is important to mention the current situation of the country. For the last fifteen years, since we began working in the UNESCO Chair of Education for Peace, our conferences and writings have focused on many issues that require us to attend to the defense of and education for human rights and peace. One issue we have not gone into explicitly is the relationship between human rights, democracy, and peace. Not because we have a perfect democracy (if we understand by democracy only elections and representative democracy, then it is true that we could say we live in a democracy, even if under a colonial reality) but because until recently the absence of democracy was not one of our main concerns.

However, the economic and governmental policies of the last three years have changed the country. Influenced by the discourse and ideology of the North American extreme right, decisions have been made that have resulted in mass unemployment of thousands of persons and the deep erosion of many economic, social, and cultural rights that used to be acknowledged in Puerto Rico. In addition, the interdependence between party and government has been strengthened, fostering favoritism and fanaticism and making the "other," who does not share their view of the world, the object of ridicule and scorn. Meanwhile, state power has been strengthened by its control of all the branches of government, reducing opportunities for dissent and making the use of excessive force and police abuse accepted as the norm.

In a recent essay titled *"Como en el muro la hiedra,"* Efrén Rivera (2012, 69), former Dean of the Law School of the University of Puerto Rico, describes this process. Recalling the song by Violeta Parra (in the Tucuman voice of Mercedes Sosa) that describes how love slowly takes over us, Rivera warns, "There are more sinister events that operate gradually until they take over collective practices and consciousness with transformative results." He is referring to "authoritarianism as a political, social, and cultural attitude and practice," that becomes a regulating principle that is finally accepted as normal.

Now, more than ever, it is important to be an educator for human rights and peace. We have to educate to defend human rights from lies, manipulation, and Manichaeism. This inspires me to educate in and for democracy and peace at every educational opportunity because we have to recover and promote citizen participation beyond the traditional electoral processes. In view of the prevailing egoistic attitude of "every man for himself" unless a friend is involved, we must educate thinking individuals committed to the common good, the country, and its people. Of course, it is also necessary to train future educators who are capable of going beyond what is immediate and of understanding the interrelationships between the problems that we face today as a country and as humanity. I do not assert the potential of education naïvely but from the thoughtful and critical conviction that without education, submissiveness and despair will arise. On with education for hope and freedom!

BIBLIOGRAPHY

Bonner, Raymond (1984). *Weakness and Deceit: U.S. Policy and El Salvador.* New York: Times Books.

Céspedes Rossel, Nélida (1997). *La escuela y los derechos humanos de las niñas y los niños.* Lima, Perú: Editorial Tarea.

Coles, Robert (1997). *Children of Crisis* (Vol. 1-5). Boston, MA: The Atlantic Monthly Press.

Freire de Matos, Isabel (1997). *La escuela elemental puertorriqueña.* Periódico Claridad (17-23 de enero).

Freire, Paulo (1970). *Pedagogía del Oprimido.* México: Siglo XXI.

Freire, Paulo (1993). *Pedagogía de la esperanza. Un reencuentro con la pedagogía del oprimido.* Madrid: Siglo XXI.

Freire, Paulo (2006). *Pedagogía de la indignación.* Madrid, España: Ediciones Morata, S.L.

Jares, Xesús (1999). *Educación para la paz.* Madrid: Editorial Popular.

Jares, Xesús (2000). *Educación y derechos humanos.* Madrid: Editorial Popular.

Jares, Xesús (2005). *Educar para la verdad y la esperanza.* Madrid: Editorial Popular.

Magendzo, Abraham (1993). *Bases de una concepción pedagógica para educar en y para los derechos humanos. Guía para docentes.* San José, Costa Rica: Centro de Recursos Educativos, Instituto Interamericano de Derechos Humanos.

Magendzo, Abraham (2006). *Modelo problematizador para la educación en derechos humanos. Educación en derechos humanos: Un desafío para los docentes de hoy.* Santiago, Chile: Lom ediciones.

Pascual Morán, Anaida (2003). *Acción civil noviolenta: Fuerza de espíritu, fuerza de paz.* San Juan, Puerto Rico: Publicaciones Puertorriqueñas.

Polakow, Valerie (1985). *Whose Stories Should We Tell? A call to action.* Language Arts, 62 (December).

Rivera Ramos, Efrén (2012). *Como en el muro la hiedra.* El Nuevo Día (12 de August). http://www.elnuevodia.com/columna-comoenelmurolahiedra-1327616.html

Ross Epp, J. & Watkinson, A., eds (1997). *Systemic Violence in Education: Promise Broken.* Albany, NY: SUNY Press.

Seminario de Educación para la Paz (1994). *Educar para la paz: Una propuesta posible.* Madrid: Los libros de la catarata.

Yudkin, Anita (1993). *Protected victims: The schooling experience of displaced children in El Salvador.* Doctoral Dissertation, The University of Michigan. Dissertation Abstracts International. University Microfilms No. 9319669.

Yudkin Suliveres, Anita, Nellie Zambrana Ortiz & Anaida Pascual Morán (2002). *Derechos de la niñez y educación en derechos humanos: Herramientas en la construcción de una cultura de paz.* Pedagogía, 36 (Universidad de Puerto Rico, Facultad de Educación).

Subjectivity and Truth in Memory
Manuel Restrepo Yustin (Colombia)

> **Manuel Restrepo Yustin** majored in sociology and has a Ph.D. in Latin American History. He has been involved in human rights education for more than two decades. He is currently an advisor in Colombia for the UN Office of the High Commissioner for Human Rights.

[All notes by the Editor]

> "For the Athenians of twenty-five centuries ago, the antonym of memory was not oblivion, it was truth."
>
> Juan Gelman

I was born in Colombia in 1943, a few years before those fateful times known historically as "La violencia" ("The Violence").[1] The confrontation between liberals and conservatives, led by the economic and political elites, produced a blood bath in our nation. It was not an urban but principally a rural country, more patriarchal and religious than secular. The winds of modernity had not yet touched the imagination of the ruling class, who held tightly to a backward model of development based on the *latifundia*, a term borrowed from Latin for large private land holdings. I was aware of this because I spent the first years of my childhood in a rural setting.

My family was comprised of my father, a rich former seminarian of peasant origin who had received a privileged education in a European-influenced religious community; and my mother, a teacher who came from an immigrant family and spoke about her aristocratic background at every opportunity. Her education was a refuge that protected me from the violence of my surroundings. I was under the care of several nannies who made it possible for me to enter a world of mysteries, witches, ghosts, and spells, so that I inhabited the lands of *Pedro Páramo* even before the great Juan Rulfo, its author, wrote this novel where the dead could talk.[2]

---

[1] *La violencia* (The Violence) (1948–58) was a period of civil war in Colombia, between the Colombian Conservative Party and the Colombian Liberal Party, whose battles mainly took place in the countryside.
[2] Juan Rulfo (1917-1986) was a Mexican writer and photographer. His novel Pedro *Páramo (1955)* concerns a man who visits a literal ghost town, i.e., inhabited by ghosts.

Guided by my mother, I learned to read and write, and in conversations with my father I got to know that there were other ways of talking and dreaming which, in one way or another, served as an antidote to the esoteric stories and practices narrated by those marvelous nannies. I was entranced by the Latin, Greek, and few French phrases my father would recite, as well as by the fantastic stories that my mother used to read, taken from novels like *The Three Musketeers* by Alexander Dumas, or the fabulous story told by Victor Hugo in *Les Miserables*. It was also through my mother that I got to know Balzac.

Few of us can forget that significant instant when we showed our parents that we were able to read. The mystery of reading, of getting to know a language by other means, of communicating in a different way, is a marvelous act in itself. But, in my case, from the vantage point of my almost seventy years, that moment had a peculiarity that was not detached from my surroundings. My first reading exercises had to do with threatening, insulting posters that announced the disappearance of people close to us as, for example, the death of the great liberal leader Jorge Eliécer Gaitán.[3] His death made my mother cry and my father turn pale. It was through these readings that I began to understand that we were liberals and in danger of death in a predominantly conservative region. Looking back, I can say that I then began to feel, though not to understand, the meaning of a threatened identity.

I have another memory of my father as the local intellectual in a mostly illiterate region. He organized weekly literary gatherings in which he read to the peasants the latest news about the end of World War II. These peasants continued to read those reports years after the conflict ended. It was then that I got to know the evil and crimes of Nazism, but it was worse to discover that unlike my father, some of the people who surrounded me sympathized with the ideas of Nazism and Fascism, that disgraceful period in human history.

I believe that because of my father's Latin phrases and his references to the life of St. Augustine and because of my readings about the French court, the miserable sewers of Paris, and the peasant's daily life wonderfully narrated by Balzac that my mother read to me, I developed early on in my life a universal point of reference that opened my eyes and encouraged the desire to discover a diverse and changing world. My dream world enabled me to live in imaginary spaces that smoothed out the rough edges of a period when I began to perceive a contradictory and sometimes frustrating view of the world around me.

My memory retains an incident that describes this world I am writing about. I was traveling with my mother on a road that led to my grandparents' house. My mother, a teacher, had given me some simple reading exercises in order to check my development. The car in which we traveled stopped in front of an enormous tree on one side of the road, a luxuriant ceiba. There was a sign hanging

---

[3] Jorge Eliécer Gaitán (1903-1948) was a politician, leader of a populist movement in Columbia, and one of the most charismatic leaders of the Liberal Party. His assassination in 1948 set off the *Bogotazo*, massive riots that destroyed downtown Bogotá and lead to a violent period of political unrest in Colombian history known as *La Violencia*.

from the tree, which I endeavored with all my might to read so that I could show my mother what an expert reader I was. When my mother heard me, she immediately ordered me to keep silent. She was horrified at the indecent verse that to my meager if promising literary sense rhymed, but to my mother's sense of manners and upbringing was simply in bad taste. I still don't know if her censorship was the result of fear.

The verse read:

> They say birds
> Shit on trees.
> But this tree
> Shat on a bird.

Obviously I was able to read these words, but many years passed before I could understand the meaning of this verse. For those readers who are not aware of the context, I should explain that in those times perpetrators of violence and mercenaries were called "birds." A car crashed against the tree supplied the meaning of this literary device of popular culture. It served as statement of revenge against a member of the elite, who from his place of power had sponsored violence, someone whose name I still remember but which I will not mention here.

Violence, childhood, and reading are the three images I have used to illustrate the influential environment in which I began to form my first questions and practices, which were ultimately to affect my view of the world. Before attempting to explain their influence, I would like to say that these are all hypotheses that I have developed over a very long period.

The opportunity to compare and feel *difference* has been a vital idea for me and for the development of a sort of resistance to an environment that bombarded me with contradictory data, images, and feelings. My personal history is full of diverse landscapes: of a world with different customs; with different, unique, and irreplaceable human beings; with new tastes; with the sound of speech that names in different ways what the eyes see; with faraway places offered by my readings; and with my parents, who did not conform to traditional parental roles. The notion of accepting differences (with some exceptions that I will mention later on) is a quality that makes up a great part of who I am and have been. The process of becoming aware of this is something that I cannot measure.

This can all be summed up in those restless questions that drove those who lived with me mad: "Why don't the stars fall?" "Why don't I have black skin?" "Why is it bad to be a liberal or a conservative?" "Why did Hitler hate the Jews?" "Why are there poor people?" I believe that the ability to construct questions created in me a very particular sense of the relative concept of truth, of the imaginary constructions of local cultures, of the cosmos, but more than anything else, of the power of the imagination and the importance of a well-timed question.

Another treasure of my childhood was my moral education, understood in the broad and secular meaning of the word. The word *sin* was never heard in my house; I never suffered those nightmares that troubled my friends and made them think of religion as a terrifying court with judges sentencing sinners to eternal damnation. In my home the dominating logic was to analyze why things were done poorly or well. These two concepts were linked to the analysis of the consequences of any act. Later I realized that my parents managed to instill in me a vital ethic that has allowed me to make important decisions in my life.

I would like to take the opportunity to tell readers that I have sometimes felt lacking in all that is sacred. To fill this gap I tend to visit museums and churches since I have an intense taste for this type of art. I even cried when I visited Saint Peter's Church in Rome. I achieved previously unknown contemplative states when I visited the city of Jerusalem. I felt deeply moved by the Orthodox churches in Russia and Greece and by the Christian caves in the Turkish lands of Cappadocia. The ruins of Mayan and Aztec temples made me consider the profundity of spirituality. It also made me think that I should always be respectful towards what, in broad terms, we can call the sacred. I think this is the idea I wish to communicate, and in spite of my secular upbringing, I must confirm what I have said before: that in case of a fire, the only work of art I would try to save from the humble collection in my house would be a Christ from the Manuel Chili school, known as Caspicara, that I bought years ago from an antiquarian.[4]

Aesthetics was my mother's legacy. It has always followed me closely in everything I do. It influences what I like, my vision, and my way of relating to the world, so that I cannot but try to acknowledge this as homage to my mother, for aesthetics has allowed me to choose roads that have strengthened my humanity. The reader might ask me why. The answer took many years to emerge into a rule of conduct. In the beginning it was more like an intuition, almost a natural inclination, but with time it became a stand for life. I consider aesthetics to be a kind of ethic of my existence.

To a moral upbringing, a predisposition to accept all that is different, an appreciation for the aesthetic, and a vital ethic, I can add a passion for knowledge. These are evidently the basis of a heritage that, in spite of contradictions and tensions, I have managed to preserve and that partially explains who I am: an advocate and promoter of human rights. Nevertheless, I shall offer further evidence later on in this essay. This is a constant that runs throughout my biography.

It is interesting when reflecting on oneself to find the breaking points, those moments when everything seemed to fall apart, to recall what one learned from one's weaknesses, mistakes, fallacies, and critical situations. These insights bring us closer to realizing a more honest, imperfect being. They remind us that when these insights occur, we have to react in a spontaneous way. There have been a few of these special moments in my life.

---

[4] Manuel Chili (*c.* 1723-1796) was an Educadorian sculptor who exemplified the eighteenth century Quito School in the Andes region. His major religious works are polychromed wood sculptures in an elegant Spanish baroque style.

It might sound strange to hear me say that my first contact with the radio had to do with experiences that signal some contradictions with this universal vision I have mentioned. A rural radio program sponsored by the church revealed the immense popularity of mass media. I can't forget the excitement I felt at having a small radio my father would turn on at dusk, which broadcast national news and what was then a novelty: a soap opera called *Lejos del nido* (*Far From the Nest*). The main theme concerned a white rich girl who has been kidnapped by some Indigenous Peoples. There could be no better topic for spreading a discriminatory view about an ethnic or indigenous group. Its effects could be clearly seen in the threats of many parents when their children misbehaved: "I am going to tell the Indians to come and get you." My experience was not without a constant terror that this might happen. This is the origin of an attitude that for many years made me ignore the existence of more than one hundred indigenous groups who lived in my country at the time, and whose gradual disappearance I regret. Nevertheless, there was a contradiction and contrast present in this attitude. Once when I fell ill and a medicinal plant used by natives cured me, I asked a question that nobody answered, "Are natives also doctors?" It would take me a long time to understand their ancestral wisdom. I have mentioned this in order to settle a historic debt that made me incapable of understanding important aspect of my country, an issue that is still unresolved.

Finally the day came when my own life was touched by the diaspora generated by the violence that pitted brothers against brothers, friends against friends, neighbors against neighbors, lover against lover. Concealed as partisan disagreements, these hidden hatreds gave way to a blood bath and my final departure from the world in which I had grown up. At an early age I witnessed a murder that became a recurrent nightmare throughout all my childhood. This happened during one of my father's literary gatherings without his being able to do anything to stop it. As a result, my family had to abandon without warning the ancestral house where we had lived and move to a city, where I spent the second part of my childhood. An hour after we fled from our house, it was destroyed, as I was able to confirm years later when I returned in a painful visit. With that event we lost all the wealth that my father had managed to build for years.

Because we had to live in a humble neighborhood, our new life was made more difficult by weekend visits to my grandfather's elegant house, located in a grove that contrasted greatly with the dusty streets where we lived. These new circumstances were the cause of some adjustment issues, but also of some important lessons. They gave me the opportunity to imagine for myself a life project that would help me overcome the mediocrity and almost total marginality of a world that denied me the life my family education had shown me. At the same time they offered other opportunities, a sense of adventure and play and relationships with other children. My new environment seemed to belong to a Macondo-like world.[5] There were needs that could well be described in the manner of the novelist Alejo Carpentier[6] in his novel *El siglo de las luces* (*Explosion in a Cathedral*). It was a time of unforgettable moments in the present that became even more important in the future, for

---

[5] Macondo is a fictional town described in Gabriel Garcia Márquez's novel *One Hundred Years of Solitude*.

[6] Alejo Carpentier (1904-1980) was a Cuban novelist, essayist, and musicologist who greatly influenced Latin American literature during its famous "boom period" of the 1960s and 1970s. He is considered one of the first practitioners of magic realism, using the technique to explore the fantastic quality of Latin American history and culture. His

all I wanted was for my dreams to come true. For a long time I did not live in the present but rather in the dream world of the future.

This change offered me life lessons marked by the deep contrast between life in the country and in the city. In addition, it showed me the contrasts between a lost wealth that gave way to a life of poverty, the working class neighborhood that was the opposite of my grandfather's aristocratic mansion, the imaginings of pre-modernity and the slow but astonishing discoveries of a world on its way to a late modernity. In short, I urgently needed to find a way to oppose an environment that combined multiple deceptions and contradictions of which I had not been previously aware. It was a real lesson in class issues for a future sociologist, of the importance of informed dialogue for the future researcher, and of coexistence for a potential advocate of human rights.

My elementary school years were a long and painful period of my life. Before I go on, I would like to explain that my mother had previously homeschooled me, which had delayed my ability to socialize with other children. I then went to a humble school where my previous education appeared to have no place, nor did my fine readings, my style of dress copied from French magazines, my respect for difference, my constant questions, the way I related to others, nor my good table manners. From the moment I arrived, I felt I was not like the rest, and I started to hate all that my parents had taught me. I wanted to be more ignorant, rougher, and less aware of my personal appearance, more imperfect, more intolerant to others, and – why not confess it? – I even wanted to be violent.

The effect of this contradiction soon became obvious. I was the victim of terrible persecution. I made every effort brutally to defend myself, using a pencil as my weapon, the same pencil I had used for writing my dreams and outlining an imaginary future. On several opportunities I proved that my small instrument for writing verses, telling stories, or drawing landscapes could also be a weapon. From the victim I then turned into a perpetrator. After some time, however, I had to accept that I was not attracted to violence, and that my first attempts at hate, enmity, and vengeance were not the way to survive in that cruel world that a school or a classroom could be.

Those were hard years, but they were also filled with unseen creativity, in the sense that I practiced with other strategies that would allow me to create a survival strategy: resistance. I learned to resist violence and humiliations and to negotiate with the "enemy." I offered to do other students' homework in return for good treatment. I gave away or shared my allowance. I neutralized some aggressors and befriended others. Even now I believe that the best human beings I have ever met gained their knowledge in the process of resistance, both collectively and individually. I believe this was my case as a victim. It is what I would later get to know as the "pedagogy of fear." It is strange to recall that in a city where the population of African descent was significant, my best friends, those who never laid a hand on me, were my Black peers, who due to their race were also the object of violence. Their behavior expressed the solidarity of one discriminated being with another. This is

---

most famous novel is *El reino de este mundo* (*The Kingdom of This World*, 1949) about the Haitian revolution of the late eighteenth century.

why the end of the story for my parents, for me, and my Black friends was a ceremony of gratitude: an image that was a parody of that famous American film starring Sidney Poitier, *Guess Who's Coming to Dinner?*

These scenes from my school and city life put me in positions I had never experienced before. These situations involved a form of violence that goes not only against life, but also against dignity. They were situations of exclusion, of discrimination, of collective punishment, of restraints of freedom, of hindering the development of one's personality, and of impotence. But I believe that with some effort the solution to this dilemma is what can be called the choice between good and evil; it was a way out that found a fertile territory in symbolism, as many men and women have done by "raising up an altar from the filth."

In order to limit the effects of this violence, I channeled my emotions and anxieties into the future, into fantastic plans and the reading of any pamphlet, book, or newspaper that fell into my hands. I liked the circus, perhaps because I could visualize the metaphor of flying on the trapeze or the tragedy of imagining myself as a modern Icarus about to lose his wings. It was a whirlwind that forced me to seek new experiences. The time would come when a phrase from my literature teacher about what the Greeks called "aesthetic feeling" or from an occasional newspaper inspired in me a wish to visit a painting exhibition for the first time. From that moment on I have cherished art because it taught me to see in a different way, to contemplate other concepts of beauty, to value other means of communication, and in my case, to flee from a violence that produced a death wish in me. I managed to transform all this into truly emotional experiences in the same way that my wise teacher who dared to talk to us about beauty in Plato's terms had taught me. It was then that I discovered that I had received the most precious treasure of my life. It was the road to a symbolic world that saved me from sinking into a desperate state of victimization, for the truth is that I was a happy child and perhaps I was endowed with what modern psychologists call resilience.

The world of cinema deserves mention in my narrative, not just by way of anecdotes, but also because of the teachings and the awareness of social issues that I learn from films. I am a child of Mexican cinema, of Cantinflas, Tin-Tán, Pedro Infante, Jorge Negrete, Resortes, Sara García, and the bewitching beauty of María Félix and Dolores del Río. My first acts of independence were my escapades to the cinema, where I began to understand messages that in popular parlance are called *"cantinflesco."*[7] Cantinflas movies showed me a world of outsiders, indigenous cultures, scoundrels, and marginalized people who lived in a frenzied, creative, urban environment as dazzling as that of Mexico City. As noted by Carlos Monsiváis,[8] Mexican cinema, Cantinflas, and other film stars

---

[7] *Cantinfesco* is an adjective that comes from Cantiflas, an immensely popular comic Mexican film star. His manner of talking became so popular in the Spanish-speaking world that it became known as *Cantinflada*. It was common parlance to say *"¡estás cantinfleando!"* (You're pulling a "Cantinflas!" or "You're 'Cantinflassing!'") whenever someone became hard to understand in conversation.

[8] Carlos Monsiváis (1938-2010) was a Mexican writer, critic, political activist, and journalist. A critic of the long-ruling Partido Revolucionario Institucional (PRI), he was a left-leaning opinion leader whose views were disseminated on radio and television.

served as an "involuntary education"; in my case, it helped me overcome a prejudiced attitude considering popular speech to be clumsy, muddled, and lacking in delicacy. Maybe I had thought that way because I wanted to deny the fact that I lived in a low-income neighborhood. It was due to those films that I learned to appreciate the linguistic torrent in the popular speech of the inner city where illiteracy was the rule. I noted also an aspiration to modernity: men and women aspired to have what their parents couldn't have and what their grandparents couldn't even have dreamed of. It was the feeling expressed in the real, pained speech of those who were excluded, the speech of the peasant and of the laborer tired from working long hours, of indoctrinated Indigenous Peoples imploring *"tata dios"* (Father God) so that rain would fall on crops, desperate for the opportunity to drain the sap from the tired soil. It was the language of tricks and deceptions by the neighborhood thief or of the swaggering revolutionary who imitated the image of a libertarian Zapata, who loved the exploited hacienda workers and those without land. It was a comprehensive sociology lesson that I learned in those rundown neighborhood movie theaters and would never forget. The great realistic Italian cinema and the French New Wave were also a discovery that shaped my greatest passions and helped me to understand those languages. I will never forget *The Bicycle Thief* and *The 400 Blows*!

At the same time I continued to read, without any method to guide me, some classic works like Dostoevsky's *Crime and Punishment*, which questioned my conscience in a frightful manner. This particular book made me aware of the transcendental theme of guilt for a terrible crime, which my adolescent mind tended to justify. All this took place in a land so different from Russia. This allowed me to dream and suffer alone with other scenarios and atmospheres that included the czarist tyranny so faithfully described by the literary genius of Dostoyevsky. Some unsurpassable novels also left a deep mark on me: Thomas Mann's *Death in Venice*, with its thesis of aesthetic passion, and *The Magic Mountain*, as a portrait of a time of deep changes, especially in terms of a world view. These teachings anticipated my first sociology lessons. The same can be said of Albert Camus[9] in terms of the political and philosophical views I detected in his works, especially on the topics of education and culture for the future citizen.

It has not been easy to recall the most important moments of my adolescence, which runs parallel to my experience in high school, even though I could say that from the moment I began high school, I felt a deep emotion because I had begun to fulfill a life project that – as I already mentioned – I had planned for the long term. Nevertheless, I always remember a key thought from that time which had to do with my perception of my body. Understanding my body had to do with lessons and misconceptions crucial to my development. Though Spinoza, the philosopher, said that the "body is power," to me my body became a heavy burden to bear.

As I moved forward in this longed-for world of knowledge and as I discovered my new cognitive skills, physical education became a torture. I did not like soccer. I tried weight lifting, but it was too rough for me, and I gave it up. Finally, I found a way out of physical education and sports: I joined a

---

[9] Albert Camus (1913-1960) was a French Nobel Prize-winning author, journalist, and philosopher. His best-known novel is *The Stranger*. His views contributed to the rise of the philosophy known as absurdism.

marching band that at the time was known as *"de Guerra,"* a military band. It was the most famous band in town. The uniform, a copy of that worn by the Prussian army, was great bait for girls and for playing the role of a seducer. I convinced my father to pay for such an expensive treat, and he allowed me to enroll as a candidate. One had to pass an entrance test, but when my turn came the instructor, none other than our physical education teacher, told me, "You can't join the band. You are too thin and tall and do not fit in with the group. Your arms are too long for the drum and your lungs too weak for the trumpet." My body became a burden, something I could do without and which made me uncomfortable.

Unexpectedly, however, things began to happen outside my environment that turned out to be the antidote for that physical loathing and a mine of possibilities that my body created. With the help of a group of neighborhood friends, I turned into an excellent salsa dancer, that Caribbean and African music that is a fixture of the region where I was born, the *Valle del Cauca*. Suddenly word got out in the neighborhood about how special my dancing skills were, and I was able to witness, with a hint of social revenge, how some of the most outstanding athletes and members of the band could not equal my dance form or the skills and the movements I sketched in the floor with my long legs. I was encouraged by a furious but joyful energy that invaded me when I heard the sound of an orchestra, a musical group, or the radio shows that we were allowed to hear during our free time. The places where I practiced were somewhat dangerous, but dancing became a gateway to security.

What started as a rejection of my body turned into curiosity and into a feeling of pride that I still cherish for my dancing skills. Many lessons remain from that time, among them those that I received in my own street, the dancing lessons of my girlfriends, my neighbors' pranks, my attempts to avoid rules, my failed attempts at trying to imitate the worst rascals among my peers, and my constant, persistent quest for the limits of an imagination that made me dream of a new world in the future. The most important discoveries in love, sexuality, and desire permeated my high school years. Initiation rituals were not easy, but they turned into an opportunity to face issues like the relationship between genders and the human body. These lessons took place in a time of great changes: an important movement towards a secular society; the invention of the birth control pill; women's liberation; the bikini and the mini-skirt; the transformation from a rural to an urban country; an accelerated and disorganized process of urbanization; and the Beatles, who had great significance for me. There were new art projects by Fernando Botero, Enrique Grau, Bernardo Salcedo, Alejandro Obregón, Edgar Negret, and in literature, García Márquez. It was also the time of the Latin American Boom and Carpentier, Cortázar, Vargas Llosa, Carlos Fuentes, Octavio Paz, and Onetti were my faithful companions in a kind of vigil created by my deep yearning to grasp a reality distant from the blurry limits I could see in the old map hanging beside my desk. Jorge Luis Borges deserves a chapter on its own that I will mention later.

Following a suggestion made by my younger sister, a beautiful, impressively independent, and intelligent girl who did not have the time to develop politically because of her premature death, I decided to read about the Cuban Revolution. These readings planted the seed of uneasiness in my conscience, which was already interested in many features that would later become important questions in my professional future. All these experiences, from the saddest and most bitter of them to the extremely comforting and stimulating, served as small modules in a course of self-teaching that I followed closely and which did not lack in unexpected tutors.

Finishing high school meant going to college. Once again, I experienced one of those personal ruptures, discontinuities, and dark zones. It was the kind of disruption that makes us face limiting situations that I prefer not to dwell on, and of which I will only mention one important fact and that is the birth of my daughter. She is a beautiful creature who was deprived of the daily attentions of a loving, playful, and spoiling father because of my immaturity and other reasons I don't wish to recall. I have been lucky in that I was able to recover her love after some years because she waited patiently for my arms to open in a fatherly encounter that I celebrate in these pages. These ruptures and discontinuities, lessons in the meaning of life and also of grief, sometimes take too long to find expression in thought and feelings.

Up to now I have told about the elements that defined my development, my background, my personality, and my way of thinking and acting, but that also leave an open question that has never left me: Why didn't I become an artist or a writer? The answer is not at all clear, but I will offer some hypotheses. The first has to do with understanding art as a road to knowledge and as a way to approach the world, or maybe I should say, worlds. I always believed that formal education lacked something that art seemed to secure. Art was the threshold of my chosen profession: sociology. The second hypothesis is that there was a duality between choosing a career that would help me emerge from poverty and a career that had every possibility of being untenable in an environment hostile with regard to artistic and literary expressions. I had dreamt of being a dancer or a painter, but the implacable sword of prejudice cut off that dream with one stroke in the form of an outright "no" from my father. I also had to take into account the lack of available jobs and the near impossibility of getting an art scholarship. The only option was to submit to a kind of moral blackmail typical of people like me from families who have "come down in life," as it is commonly called. It involves complex elements like the wish to be what one once was, the possibility of a symbolic payment for our parent's sacrifices, and the pragmatic search for economic opportunities. I prefer the first hypothesis, although its efficacy is somewhat relative since I really wanted to go to college.

However, my college dreams were threatened by my father's low income. Getting into college meant sacrificing other persons that I have not mentioned until now: my two wonderful sisters. The fact that they were female left them with no better prospect than to be exemplary housewives. I always felt uncomfortable about this, and I am sure that for my father it was a painful decision, somehow justified by a patriarchal society. Years later, following my principles of equality and non-discrimination, I would have made the opposite choice.

There are a few gray zones in a not very chromatic line between black and white in this period of my life. Those gray zones are none other than my uncertainty on what subject to study and the acceptance of my father's sacrifice, something I am still grateful for and that reminds me of the meaning of poverty. As a coincidence, perhaps only by chance, my father at this time invented a process that saved the company where he worked a good deal of money. If correctly negotiated, this invention could have guaranteed him a prosperous and stable economic future. Nonetheless, the price of his clever discovery was a scholarship for his son. The company initially insisted I should study economics, but in an interview with the manager I was able to convince him to give me a scholarship to study sociology. It was a profession that had been stigmatized by the revolutionary positions that some of the Colombian founders of the field had taken during the sixties. The case was brought to the president of the company, whom I would manage to thank many years later; he was an illustrious leader who had some progressive tendencies, though I am not sure if they really contradicted his business interests or were just good business practices.

In a pamphlet I got from somewhere, I read that sociology had social change as a founding principle. It was with this idea in my mind that I started my studies, but when I got to college, I began to understand that social change was a category subject to many different interpretations. I have to confess that the theories on this topic by the North Americans Talcott Parsons[10] and Robert Merton[11] did not garner my attention, not did those of Herbert Spencer.[12] Marx's ideas seemed too radical and Max Weber's[13] too European to be of any use for understanding different explanations on the origins of capitalism. I am indebted to Emile Durkheim[14] for my first lessons on education. I was astonished by Georg Simmel's[15] intelligence, but few of his books were available, and I had to abandon him with only a few ideas learned about the processes of socialization and culture. I turned to Latin-American writers and discovered the first essays written by Fernando Cardoso[16], whose theories had to do with dependence. I was influenced by the much publicized exit of the Chilean Marta Harnecker[17] from Catholic groups in order to participate in the most dogmatic form of Marxism inspired by the Cuban Revolution, which would later be the basis for her famous book, a book I still keep as an icon of reductionism and oversimplification. I admired the solid and well informed historical work of Tulio Halperín Donghi,[18] who taught me that this American continent, so much ours and yet so foreign, suffers a constant strain between uniqueness and multiplicity, a fact that astonished the whole world.

---

[10] Talcott Parsons (1902-1979) was one of the most influential sociologists of the 1950s. He was particularly concerned with how structural elements were functional for a society.

[11] Robert K. Merton (1910-2003) was one of the founders of modern sociology. He developed notable concepts such as "unintended consequences," "role model," and "self-fulfilling prophecy."

[12] Herbert Spencer (1820-1903), a leading political theorist of the Victorian Era, is best known today for his application of Darwinian theory to human society as "the survival of the fittest."

[13] Max Weber (1864-1920) was a German sociologist and political economist best known for his ideas on bureaucracy and the thesis of the "Protestant ethic," relating Protestantism to capitalism.

[14] Emile Durkheim (1858-1917) was a French sociologist, social psychologist, and philosopher. With Karl Marx and Max Weber, he is commonly cited as the principal architect of modern social science and the father of sociology.

[15] Georg Simmel (1858-1918) was among the first generation of German sociologists. His neo-Kantian approach laid the foundations for sociological antipositivism.

[16] Fernando Cardoso (b. 1931) was the thirty-fourth President of Brazil, from January 1995 to January 2003. He is an accomplished sociologist, academic, and politician.

[17] Marta Harnecker (b. 1937) is a Chilean sociologist, political scientist, journalist, and activist. Her best-known book is *The Basic Concepts of Historical Materialism* (1976).

[18] Tulio Halperín Donghi (1926-2014) was an Argentine historian.

At this moment in my journey through the labyrinth of memory, the word *change* was often on my mind and the positions taken by different authors were almost impossible to reconcile. But I still had a long way to go and a lot to learn. An article by Rodolfo Stavenhagen[19] titled *"Siete tesis equivocadas sobre América Latina"* (*Seven Mistaken Theses on Latin America*) served as a type of agenda for my disorderly non-academic readings. Though I have now distanced myself from its arguments, I still acknowledge its importance. This essay presented an inventory of problems that served as reference for my studies, starting from his refutation of some mistaken ideas about Latin America like those of dualism; the idea of taking progress into what were then called "archaic zones"; the rural world as an obstacle to development; the existence, or lack thereof, of a national middle-class; or those social mobility theories that our parents liked so much that they said, "We have to go back to what we were"; the romantic view of *mestizaje* (the general process of mixing races); and the hope of a worker-peasant alliance that I could not understand.

As a student of sociology, I searched for a way to understand the complexity of our society, not only in Colombia but also in Latin America as a whole. For example, I remember that my thesis for the seminar on sociological theory was my argument that *Cien años de soledad* (*One Hundred Years of Solitude*) was in itself the best attempt to get near the mythic elements that gave rise to our culture. In order to explain how this came about, I could say it was a kind of ongoing struggle with my teachers and with Auguste Comte,[20] the founder of sociology (Of course, I almost flunked this seminar). Françoise Sagan's novel *Bonjour Tristesse* (*Hello, Sadness*) inspired me to work on a dissertation on social psychology in which I had to include some thoughts on the young. This essay was more like an outburst of my personal, political, and professional concerns. It only resulted in my teacher's giving me a very low grade and recommending that I should be given a Rorschach Test. Coming from a teacher, this was doubtlessly an insulting suggestion. These are the distances and repressions that academic power generates and against which I was to rebel so many times. But these events also opened the door to the appreciation of the concept of freedom of opinion, which would be an important benchmark during my life.

During a search, which was more like an initiation ritual into sociology, I found an interview with Che Guevara, a celebrity in those times, of which I only recall one question: Who is your favorite author and which one is your favorite book? His answer was Joseph Conrad, specifically his novel *Heart of Darkness*. My reading of this work lead me to an emotional state that made me experience a true sense of contempt for all the cruelty expressed by European colonialism. The phrase that Conrad uses to define Kurtz, the main character of this novel, would not leave my mind for years: "Kurtz was educated by Europe." On the other hand, it also brought me close to Che, the indirect cause of this literary adventure. I confess I went out in search of his famous diary, which I managed to acquire with all the sacrifices typical of a student of limited means. When I read it, I felt a new spirit in me that focused on the issue of commitment. Though I don't wish to make literary

---

[19] Rodolfo Stavenhagen (b. 1932) is a Mexican sociologist. He has served as United Nations Special Rapporteur on the situation of the human rights of Indigenous Peoples.

[20] Auguste Comte (1798-1857) was a French philosopher regarded as a founder of the discipline of sociology and the doctrine of positivism, which holds that the only valid knowledge is derived from empirical evidence.

comparisons, I want to say that my reading of Conrad and of the work of Che, who was assassinated in the Bolivian mountains, was preceded by four other works that made me aware of the great social divide that characterized this continent. I am referring to the novel *Huasipungo* by the Ecuadorean writer Jorge Icaza;[21] the epic poem *Los hombres del maíz* (*Men of Maize*) by Miguel Angel Asturias;[22] the work of the Colombian sociologist Orlando Fals Borda, *Campesinos de los Andes*, (*Farmers of the Andes*), and the urban ethnography of Mexico City by Oscar Lewis[23] in *Los hijos de Sánchez* (*The Children of Sanchez*). I was filled with a deep rage that I could not get rid of for the oppression suffered by our peoples, built on a foundation of sweat and blood and condemned to one hundred years of solitude.

With the exception of a small Jewish community that settled in the city where I lived and whose parents had been victims of Nazism, many of my friends probably felt the same fury. The more radical of the group were Christians who had just begun drinking from the first fountains of Liberation Theology. Others were reformists who espoused the *aggiornamento* (Bringing Up to Date), a term used by the Second Vatican Council to describe reform. My secular education kept me away from these groups. I could not solve the problem of my commitment, and I also felt an urgency to find a place where I could develop a working practice that would take me closer to people who lived in a more vulnerable position. I participated in several college camps that worked with peasants, but this only made me want to go further.

The private university I attended was Catholic, but it was the only one that taught sociology. It was an environment that allowed me to get to know young people from the local elite, who went around giving the impression they were rebels, as well as some middle-class students who were beginning to show some reformist and revolutionary interests. Time has allowed me to understand that some of the dissatisfaction felt by those young people had to do with a sense of rebellion against a traditional and patriarchal society founded on orthodox religious values, an exaggerated fixation on the value of money, and a cultural world that had no place for the novelties of a modern country. Added to this was an academic world that privileged applied science such as highway or mine engineering and that opposed new intellectual and scientific options.

A rebellious spirit was slowly taking hold of me, and without realizing it, I became part of clandestine groups who studied Marxism and who slowly made clear the possibility of something more than just theory: the possibility of creating a party that defended peasants and the proletariat. I confess, as a marginal note of great importance, that in my mind I included in the political proposal every

---

[21] Jorge Icaza (1906-1978) is best known for his novel of social protest *Huasipungo*, which brought attention to the exploitation of Ecuador's Indigenous Peoples by Ecuadorian Whites.

[22] Miguel Ángel Asturias (1899-1974) was a Nobel Prize-winning Guatemalan poet, diplomat, novelist, playwright, and journalist. *Hombres de maíz*, which is considered his masterpiece, is a defense of indigenous Mayan culture and customs that drew attention to the importance of indigenous cultures, especially those of Guatemala.

[23] Oscar Lewis (1914-1970) was an American anthropologist best known for his vivid depictions of the lives of slum dwellers and his argument that a cross-generational culture of poverty among poor people transcends national boundries. His well-known book *The Children of Sanchez, Autobiography of a Mexican Family* (1961) concerns a Mexican family living in the Mexico City slum of Tepit.

dispossessed and homeless being I had known in my literary readings: the natives of Icaza and Asturias, the peasants of Fals Borda, the inhabitants of post-revolutionary Mexico from the Mexican movies, the new inhabitants of the big Latin American cities, the *Hijos de Sánchez*, and those wretched beings on the other side of the world, the mother of all humanity, Conrad's Africa. Years later I regretfully realized that even though my characters were as real to me as *Remedios La Bella* ("Remedios the Beautiful" is a key character in *One Hundred Years of Solitude*), they had no place in the political agenda. Furthermore, we Colombians were lacking many elements of modernity: health, education, recent scientific and technological discoveries, communications, cultural projects, art, urbanization, sustainable development, the abolition of a patriarchal system, and many other issues. I will also add to this list the images of real people close to me – like my daughter, who wanted to paint and write novels, or like my girlfriend, who wanted to make music and sing. Others wished to cook, develop urban projects, research, or just use their imaginations, but there was no place for them. This could well be a lesson for the "end of night," to use another literary metaphor.

I also sometimes wondered – in an endless and anxious monologue – where one could find the characters of an author who deliriously seduced me, the great, unclassifiable Borges, so distant and yet so near, enigmatic and profound, just like his sublime blindness. Where could one put his labyrinths and memories? And what can I say about the heroes and tombs of writers like Ernesto Sábato,[24] or the unclassifiable stories of Filisberto Hernández,[25] the creator of the fantasy literary genre on our continent, or the ingenious modernist imagination and humor that Roberto Arlt[26] used to describe in indolent moods. But for me "the great march of the political party had to begin," and there would be no time for speculations and less for the sensibility spoken by the tempting and wise women of the novelist Jorge Amado[27] (Oh, my beautiful Gabriela!), or the literary metaphors of the vivid Caribbean language of the writer Cabrera Infante.[28] It fills me with sadness to acknowledge lastly that in that urgency of party politics there was no place for the baroque and cultured voices of those beings described by writer José Lezama Lima[29] in his novel *Paradiso,* that so scandalized the Cuban regime with stories of homosexuals and urban scenes from La Habana; these characters and stories did not fit either in the agenda of that recently created Maoist party to which I desired to belong.

---

[24] Ernesto Sábato (1911-2011) was an Argentine writer, painter, and physicist, called by one critic the "last classic writer in Argentine literature."
[25] Filisberto Hernández (1902-1964) was an Uruguayan writer known for his bizarre tales of quietly deranged individuals who inject their obsessions into everyday life.
[26] Roberto Arlt (1900-1942) was an influential Argentine novelist, dramatist, and journalist. He is considered to be one of the founders of the modern Argentine novel.
[27] Jorge Amado (1912-2001) was a Brazilian writer of the modernist school. He was the best known of modern Brazilian writers, his work having been translated into some forty-nine languages.
[28] Cabrera Infante (1929-2005) was a Cuban novelist, essayist, translator, screenwriter, and critic. *Tres Tristes Tigres* (*Three Sad Tigers*) is his best-known work.
[29] José Lezama Lima (1910-1976) was a Cuban writer and poet who is considered one of the most influential figures in Latin American literature.

These observations are important because much later they would leave their print on some essential decisions related to my worldview and to the possibilities of changing it. I must confess that being part of a Maoist party caused me to be in a state of constant alert and made me suffer many small annoyances. I will try to be brief in my review, but allow me to say that I found it difficult to overcome aspects of my life that in those times I began to call my "middle-class vices." My first annoyance had to do with a contradiction that can only be understood from an academic point of view. The party defined Colombian society as a capitalist society with feudal features. There was not much one could say against this oversimplification. The best I could do was to save my academic doubts for a better time. According to the party, reading literature was a middle-class vice. Even the genius of some Marxist authors was considered revisionist, treacherous, anarchist, and many other things. I really appreciated Trotsky's[30] genius, but the party considered him a traitor to the proletarian cause. Lastly, the issue of revolutionary violence bothered me deeply and set me in opposition to an ethical position I will detail later. Of course I ended up reading in secret and enjoying some fragments of the unfortunate Russian leader Trotsky, thinking that as a sociologist I could have some influence in changing the understanding of our society later on, and that the issue of violence would be discussed at a later time; all this was, of course, before war became a reality.

What about good food, luxuries, and trips? Forbidden. I consoled myself thinking that I would become an infinitely kind revolutionary who would sing during cold nights by a fire or praise the revolution at a humble table. My militancy put me in contact with many people, especially of urban origin: workers, middle-class intellectuals, and of course, the unemployed. I managed to develop fine-tuned organizational skills, which led me to important positions inside the party, even though I was accused of having a middle-class lifestyle. By then I had graduated and had gotten a position as a sociologist in an important textile company. This is why I witnessed a transformation in the rural class that nobody could stop and for which I felt totally guilty and used.

My position had to be confirmed by the University, but in order to obtain the President's approval, I had to swear in front of a religious figure that I was not a Communist. This was one of the most surreal events in my life. In the end, the best comment on the procedure was my own when I recklessly said to the President, "I have already sworn, but if you really don't want me to become a Communist, give me that job."

Other coincidences emerged: my post as sociologist had been originally proposed by the future – and sacrificed – icon of the Colombian revolutionary guerilla movement, the sociologist Camilo Torres (this was one of his last attempts at reform).[31] My first job was to research the possibility of

---

[30] Leon Trotsky (1879-1940) was a Marxist revolutionary and theorist, Soviet politician, and the founder and first leader of the Red Army. After leading a failed struggle against the rise of Joseph Stalin in the 1920s, Trotsky was removed from power, expelled from the Communist Party, and finally exiled from the Soviet Union in 1929. On Stalin's orders he was assassinated in Mexico in 1940. Trotsky's ideas formed the basis of Trotskyism, a major school of Marxist thought that opposes the theories of Stalinism.
[31] Camilo Torres (1929-1966) was a Colombian socialist, Roman Catholic priest, a predecessor of liberation theology, and a member of the National Liberation Army (ELN) guerrilla organisation. During his life, he tried to reconcile

establishing a factory in traditional agricultural areas and to develop a policy of industrial relations that would allow the transformation from agriculture to industry, from rural to urban, from pre-capitalism to capitalism. I had to use those theories that I had often rejected during my student years, from those of the North American Frederick Taylor, father of industrial sociology,[32] to the transition theories of Gino Germani,[33] so popular during the 70s due to his book *Política y sociedad en una época de transición* (*Politics and Society in an Age of Transition*). When I wanted to leave this job, the party resolved the contradiction between my status as a militant and my first executive wages: the party needed my wages to support financially other "professional" comrades.

There were more important issues in my new life that managed to balance some deficiencies imposed by the Central Committee of the party. The power I gained through the years allowed me some freedoms, such as choosing political tasks that would allow the construction of the social base required by the organization. One of these freedoms was establishing a union school, where we used both orthodox and unorthodox training methods and where we educated working leaders. We created the first groups who went out in the public arena and were widely acknowledged as magnificent orators and union leaders. As was the case in ballet and theatre schools, and in defiance of macho stereotypes, we practiced long hours in front of a mirror and used drama techniques in preparation for speeches. Being head of a popular drama movement with groups that totaled more than one hundred participants allowed me to exercise my literary tastes, but it also made me sacrifice quality for slogans. I coordinated this activity with a Chilean refugee persecuted by the dictatorship of his country. I was also in charge of a musical group conducted by my girlfriend, the prettiest girl in the university. It was flattering to be in charge of these three projects, but there was an important decision that had to be taken concerning the future of the party.

My work in the textile company would come to an end because the company looked with suspicion on my attempt to back a minority union that was openly leftist. My alleged support depended on an investigation headed by someone who until this day I consider one of my best friends, and it had to do with the brutal industrial engineering standards applied in the factory. The report was supposed to be secret, but some conclusions and recommendations were intentionally leaked for the purpose of securing an important negotiation between the union and company management. I was discreetly fired, and this event made me feel like a hero for sacrificing myself for the benefit of the working class; it also made me despise the executives who had been unable to understand that my research conclusions could not be the same as those of the company. That same day I obtained a post in the university and began my life as faculty member.

Before all this happened and while I was still an active party member and still researching industrial sociology, I gained teaching experience. It was at a recently created university that proclaimed itself

---

revolutionary Marxism and Catholicism.

[32] Frederick Taylor (1856-1915) was a leading proponent of scientific management, which aims to improve economic efficiency and labor productivity by use of scientific methods.

[33] Gino Germani (1911-1975) was an Italian-born sociologist who immigrated to Argentina in 1934 after imprisonment by Benito Mussolini.

to be revolutionary, going against the establishment, a place where the party and other leftist groups had great influence. This experience served as a training that later allowed me to enter the most important university of my region, where I would spend most of my working life. I am grateful for this stage in my life because I was part of unending discussions that repeatedly invoked outstanding voices of European theorists like Michel Foucault[34] with his important study on sexuality, Jacques Derrida[35] and his theories on writing and deconstruction, Georges Bataille's[36] viewpoints on the concept of utility, Gilles Deleuze's[37] statements on the "desiring machines" Simone de Beauvoir's[38] sociological view on the distinction between sex and gender (that makes me recall a phrase that took me years to understand: "One is not born a woman; one becomes a woman."), the provocative work of Jean Baudrillard[39] in *Fatale Strategies,* and the suggestive writings of Levi-Strauss[40] on the complexity of social structures. It now seems to me that those times were an authentic boiling pot for an astonished voyeur who was only beginning to get to know the labyrinth of politics. But what is really sad is that all this was happening outside a party that was still repeating the slogans of Mao Tse Tung. The aforementioned authors planted seeds of doubt in my militancy, which I tried to process during long wakeful nights.

Half way into my Maoist militancy and in moments of rest from my role as class warrior, I began to reflect on a profound dichotomy that affected me deeply: that of being an academic who wished to know more about those debates that interested me so much and that of a militant who had almost lost his voice from repeating parables like that of "the old fool that moved a mountain." That of being someone who loved his family but was slowly distancing himself from all that the institution of family represented, and that of a lonely warrior, a bird in flight who wanted to see new lands but realized he lived in a cage. That of someone who disobeyed his superiors to visit foreign lands under the pretext of work that needed to be done, but who was still considered an example of militancy. I visited Cuba in one of those trips, and it left me with a contradictory feeling. I admired the dignity of the Cuban people, a feeling I still have, but I disliked the prevailing censorship and

---

[34] Michel Foucault (1926-1984) was an influential French philosopher, historian of ideas, social theorist, philologist, and literary critic famous for a critical history of modernity.

[35] Jacques Derrida (1930-2004) was a French philosopher best known for developing a form of semiotic analysis known as deconstruction. He is associated with post-structuralism and postmodern philosophy.

[36] Georges Bataille (1897-1962) was a French intellectual and literary figure working in literature, anthropology, philosophy, economy, sociology, and history of art.

[37] Gilles Deleuze (1925-1995) was a French philosopher who wrote influentially on philosophy, literature, film, and fine art.

[38] Simone de Beauvoir (1908-1986) was a French writer, intellectual, existentialist philosopher, political activist, feminist, and social theorist. Though she did not consider herself a philosopher, she had a significant influence on both feminist existentialism and feminist theory. She is best known for *The Second Sex* (1949), a detailed analysis of women's oppression and a foundational tract of contemporary feminism.

[39] Jean Baudrillard (1929-2007) was a French sociologist, philosopher, cultural theorist, political commentator, and photographer. His work is frequently associated with postmodernism and specifically post-structuralism.

[40] Claude Levi-Strauss (1908-2009) was a French anthropologist and ethnologist whose work was key in the development of the theory of structuralism and structural anthropology. Considered one of the founders of modern anthropology, he argued that the "savage" mind had the same structures as the "civilized" mind and that human characteristics are the same everywhere.

restrictions of freedom. From that experience I concluded that the Caribbean sun and the music of the *son* (Cuban style of music) had abandoned Cuba. It was no longer the culture narrated by the great writer Guillermo Cabrera Infante in his novel *Tres tristes tigres*, (*Three Sad Tigers*), a culture that gave us a playful and rhythmic language and a rhythm of life that was slowly disappearing under the religiosity of the Revolution. This made me wonder if it was not possible as a revolutionary principle to defend the joy of a people as an untouchable and imperishable heritage. But the official channels in charge of my political project gave me a prompt answer: our revolution had nothing to do with Cuban revisionism.

I felt smothered by the monastic atmosphere that characterized the Maoist sects. This part of the Colombian left has always made me suffer, and it is something that I still criticize, a religiosity that does not permit daring activities where imagination and knowledge go hand in hand. Everything was a "sin," from reading certain authors to disagreeing with some intellectuals. Thinking was blasphemy; asking questions unthinkable. And not to dwell on this, I will say that the "critical and self-critical" meetings seemed more like confessions presided over by the Pope himself. Maybe an anecdote will serve as example of how absurd this practice was. Keeping to a style of dress that reflected my aesthetic education and my friendship with individuals who came from the middle-class although they worked for our "cause," created the nickname for me of "leftist Gatsby," as a parody of Scott Fitzgerald's great novel. There was also the French term "*la gauche caviar*" ("the Caviar Leftist"), which was a pejorative term for leftists who supposedly did not live according to leftist values. A funny experience, which included some of the sarcasm usually directed against certain political figures, led me to face one of the toughest decisions of my life. I took a position for which I endured a great deal because I was convinced that someday I would prove that my work was valuable and that my commitment to the cause would overcome this element of a class-based society. I must confess that this episode reminded me of the harassment I had experienced when I was young and the strategies I used to face it.

At this moment in my autobiography I feel the need to quote the German writer and Nobel Prize winner Gunter Grass from his work *Peeling the Onion*. This metaphoric title makes it easier for me to tell my own story as an exercise in the defense of my individuality, as something that happens to anyone who peels those layers of the onion: tears will not take long to come. But this quote also allows me to return to the thesis that asking no questions implies a type of commitment. And this is what happened to me. I did not raise questions about party violence or the party strategy that included the use of force, and specifically of war. I always thought that difficult decisions would have to be faced someday, and that by then I would be prepared or that a miracle would happen whereby those real structural changes would take place with the intensity like that in my own versions of the novels *Huasipungos* or *Hijos de Sánchez* or as might happen to the peasants of the Andes and thousands of revolutionary Che Guevaras. I confess, as Grass does, that I never threatened a human life, though I did contribute to the creation of a war project, a proposal that I, together with other dreamers who thought as I did, tried to eliminate. I am deeply grateful to them for helping me awaken from a long nightmare.

With the idea of blocking an issue as important as the approval of a violent act, I joined other comrades in proposing a policy that would vindicate the party in the political arena by means of a democratic participation strategy. This strategy would avoid a war in which civilians and civil society were sure to be the main victims, as shown by modern wars and conflict at both the national and international levels. But as experience should have taught me, this alternative proposal made no sense to the dogmatists. What followed were trials, expulsions, executions, threats, death sentences, and a reencounter with a deep solitude that tormented me. In psychoanalytic terms, my expulsion from that party that I had criticized so much was like the death of a father, like being left an orphan, the total collapse of a dream. I felt like vanquished warriors must have felt when they lost a battle, or like lost sailors when the winds of the ocean misdirect their boats.

I felt that the right to life was being threatened by internal division, the denial of the most basic freedoms, the impossibility of correcting mistakes, the refusal to build the country in any other manner, the madness of wanting to settle contradictions by intensifying the conflict and by annihilating the other, and the lack of respect for dissent and for the other. All these things created feelings that have never left me. I would have to reinvent myself like a human phoenix. And the first idea that came to my mind was to distance myself from that environment and search for a better harbor. In spite of myself, I had had several opportunities to attend graduate school in the United States. History widened my knowledge. It was like standing on a vantage point where I could see all, from Patagonia to the Pampas, the impregnable Andes, the contrast between the blue and calm Caribbean and the impetuous Pacific, the footsteps of the Aztecs and Mayans, and the wide North American plains that still recall the wise words of the native chief who predicted the destruction of his people when the modern horseman of the apocalypse arrived. On the other side of the sea were Europe, ancient Asia, and deep Africa.

The only geographic representation I had seen of the USA was an old map hanging behind a column in the university library. However, this trip allowed me to have a drawing of all this territory in front of me, near me, inhabited by me. I never imagined that in that place on the planet, barely intuited, stunned by a wave of anti-imperialist slogans from all over the world, I would have new experiences that would give new perspectives to my life.

A few months before leaving I had read some lectures by that wonderful woman who enriched contemporary philosophy, Hannah Arendt.[41] One phrase of hers, which generated a lot of polemic in its day, helped me face the grief I felt for leaving the country and the party:

> Never in my life have I 'loved' a people or group, neither the German, the French, the North American, the working class or anything else. I love only my friends, and

---

[41] Hannah Arendt (1906-1975) was a German-born political theorist whose work centers on the fact that "men, not Man, live on the earth and inhabit the world," the nature of power, and the subjects of politics, direct democracy, authority, and totalitarianism.

> I am incapable of any other love. I belong to them as a fact, above any conflict and
> any reasoning.

I thought a lot about this idea and it allowed me to have a more universal vision that included thinking of issues that affected this continent, and in more general terms, the contemporary world of the time. It was thus I inscribed in my heart a farewell to my party.

My studies in comparative Latin American history with special interest in Mexico, Argentina, and Brazil, helped me understand the complex process of development of those countries. There were two attempts at establishing positivism as a guiding social theory: *Porfirismo*[42] in Mexico and the court of Don Pedro II in Brazil[43] in Argentina. Faustino Sarmiento[44] applied the principle of "governing is populating," which went on until the twentieth century and which was made possible due to ships packed with *"golondrinas"* ("nightingales"), as Italian immigrants were then called, in order to make viable the industrialization process. The complexity of both histories went hand in hand with the perplexity I felt at my lack of knowledge of all development processes occurring in this region.

This relationship between past, present, and future made my head spin, but it also made me conscious of the need to overcome a reductionist view of the world that I had acquired during my Maoist militancy. It was at this time that I discovered three thinkers whose ideas allowed me to go through an internal renaissance that would modify my political views: Alfonso Reyes,[45] Mexican essayist, poet and narrator; Pedro Henríquez Ureña,[46] an intellectual from the Dominican Republic, and the Mexican historian Silvio Zabala.[47] Reading his thesis on Latin America, accompanied by literary, historic, philosophic, and poetic reflections, was a pleasure new to me. Though with different points of view, thoughts, and analysis, the debates I held with these authors had to do with an essential issue: our identity. The intentionally modern thesis held by Alfonso Reyes was the right to a universal citizenship, which interested me greatly and was my constant companion in long walks around Manhattan. With Henríquez Ureña I got to know Latin American literary circles and confirmed my notion of their importance when considering who we really were or what

---

[42] Porfirismo refers to economic policies named after Mexican President Porfirio Díaz (1830-1915) who opened Mexico to international investment, inaugurating decades of growing inequality between rapid economic growth and sudden, severe impoverishment of the rural masses by dispossessing hundreds of thousands of peasants and privatizing, subdividing, and selling communal indigenous landholdings, a situation that was to result in the Mexican revolution of 1910.

[43] Don Pedro II in Brazil (1825-1891) was the second and last ruler of the Empire of Brazil, reigning for over fifty-eight years during which he turned Brazil into an emerging power in the international arena. He was a vigorous sponsor of learning, culture, and the sciences.

[44] Domingo Faustino Sarmiento (1811-1888) was an Argentine activist, intellectual, writer, statesman, and the seventh President of Argentina. He was particularly concerned with educational issues including education for children and women and democracy for Latin America.

[45] Alfonso Reyes (1889-1959) was an influential Mexican writer, philosopher, and diplomat.

[46] Pedro Henríquez Ureña (1884-1946) was a Dominican essayist, philosopher, humanist, philologist, and literary critic.

[47] Silvio Zabala (1909-2014) was a Mexican historian, diplomat, and scholar.

we had deceived ourselves to be. From Silvio Zabala I received my first lessons in ethno-history and his notions on identity and *mestizaje*, so little broached during my education as a sociologist. It was at this time that I began reading the so-called theory of modernity, which was represented both in sociology and philosophy on this continent by Néstor García Canclini.[48] His book *Culturas híbridas* (*Hybrid Cultures*), a parody of the American philosopher Marshall Berman,[49] especially impressed me; it seemed as if all that had once seemed solid was melting into thin air.

But what I learned from my studies was not comparable to the feeling of standing one day in New York in the middle of Penn Station in New York City and wondering about the journey north by train alongside the Hudson. It was a feeling of freedom I had not felt in years, and I can only explain it in terms of the contrast with this feeling of calm and the random violence that permeated my country. I lived on Long Island and had forgotten the pleasure of walking in a park or down a street, snooping around corners, helping an old man cross the street, or stopping to read signs and drawings by anonymous authors and unknown street artists. I recalled with incredulity my country's traffic signs or the danger of travelling on highways, paying taxes, the distrust of civil servants, the misuse of the state treasury, the poor quality of education, and I can't remember what else. I just knew it was like a dream in the middle of a sleeping fever. Recovering, I felt that I was enjoying a state that was as close as possible to democracy and an unsurpassable academic environment. In the mist of these contemplations I received sad news: one of the most outstanding workers, whom I had trained in the small union school, had been brutally murdered by a group that called itself Muerte a Secuestradores (Death to Kidnappers, or MAS). I could not understand the new violent reality that awaited me in Colombia.

It is not my intention to praise the American system or see myself as bewitched by its way of life. I don't wish to make a comparative analysis. I just want to share a deep sensation that little by little came over me and that helps me explain how what began as exile turned into a vital turning point to a political position that validated a utopian concept, that of the "impossible" as mentioned by a character in *Alice in Wonderland* who says, "Why, sometimes I've believed as many as six impossible things before breakfast." From that afternoon in that legendary station in the Big Apple, I started dreaming of the past, but confident that the commitment that defined me was the dream of making true all those impossibilities I learned from traveling in this country of the North.

My experience in the USA could be compared to the opening of a door or window that leads to a big garden or an infinite landscape that showed me – notwithstanding all my lectures and academic history – that the world was "wider and more unknown" than I thought, and in this sense I had to use every opportunity to fill in the gaps that my astonished eyes discovered, thanks to the opportunity of working on a Ph.D. in the prestigious State University of New York at Stony Brook. Its international program was similar to that of the famous University of California at Berkeley.

---

[48] Néstor García Canclini (b. 1939) is an Argentine-born academic and anthropologist, known for developing his theory of "hybridity."
[49] Marshall Berman (1940-2013) was an American philosopher and Marxist Humanist writer. His best-known book is *All That Is Solid Melts Into Air: The Experience Of Modernity*.

Walking into that campus was like opening a door to surprise and astonishment. Indian turbans, Arab veils, Mongolian features, deep Oriental eyes, unconcerned Caribbean bodies, copper skins born from African rivers and springs, linguistic sounds that made me remember the Tower of Babel, and above all, a thousand smells that emerged from student kitchens as if I lived in a bazaar that blessed the sense of taste.

This environment helped me get close to a diverse world that was going through conflicts in several geographic locations. All this was reported from an office in the big building that housed student activities, the Human Rights Watch office, a name I would become familiar with. One day while looking at one of the posters, I met a man who greeted me in perfect English and who walked with uncommon majesty in a place so unceremonious. When he invited me for a coffee, I realized by the way he handled himself and by the impact of his physical features – of his height and a face that seemed to be carved in ebony – that he came from Ethiopia. I was more surprised to learn that he belonged to the royal house headed by Haile Selassie, which had been overthrown during the 1977 revolution. This dethroned king and now citizen of the world allowed me to meet a group of refugees and exiles who taught me geopolitical lessons I will never forget. I met Kurdish groups persecuted by the Greek dictatorship, black Africans who invited me to remembrance ceremonies in honor of the great Mandela, displaced persons from El Salvador and Guatemala, libertarian and independent minds from Puerto Rico, victims of torture from the dictatorships of Argentina, freedom fighters from Pakistan who were afraid when they found themselves near an Indian student, and what were then only critical voices from the Balkans. There was also a large colony from Iran, divided by different attitudes toward the Shah of Iran, the polemical tyrant, and his beautiful wife, Farah Diva, who by then was a member of New York's high society. Anxious Japanese students threatened to kill themselves when their academic achievement was not up to par. In this environment I managed to do something that gave me great experience and strengthened my passion for solidarity, respect for other cultures, and for service to humanity. I became secretary of the Graduate Students Association. From there, notwithstanding the pain that accompanies exercises in historical memory, we learned to write manifestos of thoughts, knowledge, and studies that would slowly be sent as letters to our family, friends, or lovers in our native countries. Without realizing it, I had started on a new road toward human rights.

Even before I returned to Colombia, I realized that I would find a new, divided, and weakened state, led by an elite incapable of considering itself a ruling class. It would be only a slight exaggeration to call it a *cipaya* class (middle class), a caricature of democracy; a constitution that though it invoked God did not believe in human dignity; a country consecrated to the Sacred Heart, to political parties incapable of thinking of programs that included a vision of society where everyone occupied a dignified position; a plural and multiethnic society that was invisible; a representative system that insisted on perpetuation so as not to yield its power to a participative society; political habits that had served to prolong imbalances and differences; and ignorance and lack of modern thought in the sense of placing capital, knowledge, and science in the service of development and culture. And there was one more issue: the appearance of drug trafficking and paramilitary groups that would signal another stage of violence, a stage that had begun a few years before my birth, thanks to the oldest guerrilla group in the world.

This time I couldn't make a mistake, but I still had to find a niche where I would fit in: with my own history as "victim" or as someone who with the backing of an ideology had tried to victimize others, with the ideals I pursued, with my illusions, with a new profession, with prudence made cautious by experience, with an impetuosity restrained by the knowledge of the long journey ahead, and above all with my eyes wide opened to the world.

When I returned to my country, I discovered a minority political phenomenon that was manifested through language. As if it had been absorbed, it appeared in the language of the many people I began to meet. There were two words that I had not heard before so frequently: *rights* and *humans.* It was the hurried and urgent late seventies and early eighties, and those terms were meaningful in a moment when the USA was modifying its politics toward this continent and had as candidate for President an unknown peanut farmer named Jimmy Carter. The Latin American bishops gathered in Puebla dared to speak to the faithful about their rights and about things that had occurred during the military dictatorships of Argentina, Brazil, and Uruguay. People wanted to recover the memory of the infamies committed; they loudly demanded the establishment of truth commissions on human rights violations. Echoes arrived from the May 1968 student movements in France with new and youthful ways of exercising politics, and the United Nations was strengthening its programs in several of these countries. One could not ignore that these were the fashionable words of the moment. I confess with shame that when I heard them, I felt again the fear of a new fundamentalism emerging.

My analysis and observations allowed me to classify the views on human rights that circulated in the academic and political corridors, including both right- and left-wing tendencies. My old party comrades declared that human rights were a middle-class invention; those on the right proclaimed the arrival of a threat to democracy. Only a small group of friends and peers from college saw them as a possible road that would lead to the strengthening of democracy and the creation of new political identities. I can remember the mocking comments about my friends who accepted this human rights cause. I even recall that these who accepted the cause of human rights were invited to an academic meeting with the sole objective of forcing them to defend their position in a hostile environment. There is nothing more insolent than ignorance or the lack of respect for the ideas of others, even if it is involuntary. Suddenly, my irony and skepticism faced fear. This paralyzing force began to cover the country, and as is always the case with societies that are on the threshold of obscurity and persecution, the first thing that is persecuted and eliminated is intelligence.

Between my doubts, fears, and a new search for political compromise, the unexpected happened: an attack on intelligence. Four of my peers were killed. One was a doctor, an old Maoist party militant and a partner in that painful rupture with the fundamentalist left. Another was a professor of anthropology whom I admired, an eminent humanist and doctor and the most noble, inoffensive Communist I have ever known. His death marked the beginning of a terrible political persecution at the university where I was a faculty member. This led me to a simple question: Why were they killed? The answer began to circulate in the hallways of public buildings, in newspapers, and on the radio: they were killed because they were human rights promoters.

In this state of things a new specialization with a strange name arrived in the academic media *"la violentología"* ("Violentology"). The university created the first group to study violence, of which I became a part, with an agenda that included the discussion of peace and human rights issues. We travelled through the country, wrote papers, and gave lectures, which were more narrative than analytical but which allowed the discussion of those issues. All this led me, by way of study and reflection, to a fundamental question: What is a subject of rights? Those experiences led me also to the issue of the right to justice, truth, and reparations. I realized that I wanted to have all the features of an individual who has identity, autonomy, and individual thoughts and who practices respect for others; someone who can put himself in the place of somebody else; but above all, someone who rebels against the abuse of power. As if destiny had intervened, an important national process marked my not-very-clearly defined political identity: the proclamation of the 1991 Constitution. Up to this point the state agenda had been to keep Colombians ignorant about their fundamental rights. I now felt I had the mandate to address this historic ignorance. From that moment I had several opportunities to hold posts of great responsibility related to the world outlined in the Universal Declaration of Human Rights, which, I am embarrassed to say, I had not yet read.

I owe my first specialized lessons on the subject of human rights to the philosopher and educator Estanislao Zuleta, the historian Álvaro Tirado Mejía, the jurist Carlos Gaviria, the sacrificed Héctor Abad Gómez, Leonardo Betancur, and Luis Fernando Vélez, the researcher and educator Abraham Magendzo, the Instituto Interamericano de Derechos Humanos (The Inter-American Institute of Human Rights), and the thousands of people who are dedicated to human rights issues that, as members of civil society, have taught others about this subject. My activity as an educator has given me the opportunity to work for the Colombian Office of the High Commissioner for Human Rights of the United Nations.

The recovery of important events in my life, brought back from memory, has allowed me to hold on to milestones that led me to establish my commitment to human rights. I can tell my readers that all these events form an indissoluble unit that – like the poem I used to begin my lectures – makes me repeat this phrase: "Multiple souls abide in me." These souls were molded through the perception of my autobiography, an appreciation of historic memory, the inexhaustible search for truth, my work as an educator, and the certainty of being part of a common history. I have participated in processes that have strengthened my individuality, the conscience of a legitimacy crisis of the State, and the documentation of human rights abuses in our society. I have taken a stand that values peace and says no to violence. I have worked for projects that mean a true entrance into modernity and seek to break the circle of fear. The need for words to assert this unflinching search leads me to say, as the great poet Pablo Neruda once stated, *"Confieso que he vivido"* ("I confess I have lived").

Publication Partners

THE UNIVERSITY OF MINNESOTA HUMAN RIGHTS RESOURCE CENTER
N120 Mondale Hall
229 19th Ave S.
Minneapolis, MN 55455
USA
www.hrusa.org
www.law.umn.edu/humanrightscenter/index.html
www.thisismyhome.org
www.humanrightsandpeacestore.org

UNIVERSIDAD ACADEMIA DE HUMANISMO CRISTIANO
(ACADEMY OF CHRISTIAN HUMANISM UNIVERSITY)
Avda Condell 343, Providencia,
Santiago, Región Metropolitana,
Chile
www.academia.cl

CENTER FOR THE STUDY OF GENOCIDE AND HUMAN RIGHTS - RUTGERS UNIVERSITY
UNESCO CHAIR FOR GENOCIDE PREVENTION
Rutgers, The State University of New Jersey
Hill Hall 703
360 Martin Luther King Blvd. / Hill Hall 703
Newark, NJ 07102
USA
64 College Ave
New Brunswick NJ 08901-1183
USA
www.ncas.rutgers.edu/cghr

RUTGERS GRADUATE SCHOOL OF EDUCATION
Graduate School of Education
Rutgers, The State University of New Jersey
10 Seminary Place
New Brunswick, NJ 08901-1183
USA
www.gse.rutgers.edu
www.gse.rutgers.edu/content/local-and-global-partnerships

List of Organization Websites

Human Rights Education Networks

Creando Redes Ciudadanas, Educativas y Responsables (CReCER)
crecer-ddhh.blogspot.com

Democracy and Human Rights Education in Europe (DARE)
http://www.dare-network.eu

Human Rights Educators USA
www.hreusa.net

Red Interamericana de Intercambio de Experiencias Educativas para Promover la Educación en Derechos Humanos (RIIEEEPEDH)
(Interamerican Network for the Exchange of Educational Experiences to Promote Human Rights Education
redlatinadeedh.com.ar

U.S. Human Rights Network
www.ushrnetwork.org

Human Rights Resource Centers and Non-Governmental Organizations

Amnesty International (International Secretariat)
www.amnesty.org/en/

Consejo de educación popular de América Latina y el Caríbe (CEAAL)
(Council for Popular Education in Latin American and the Carribean)
www.ceaal.org/v2/index.php

Amnesty International - USA
www.amnestyusa.org

Center for the Study of Genocide and Human Rights- Rutgers University
UNESCO Chair for Genocide Prevention
www.ncas.rutgers.edu/cghr

Equitas – International Centre for Human Rights Education
www.equitas.org

Human Rights Education Associates
www.hrea.org

Human Rights Educators USA
www.hreusa.net

Human Rights Watch
www.hrw.org

International Training Centre for Human Rights and Peace Teaching (CIFEDHOP)
www.cifedhop.org

University of Minnesota Human Rights Resource Center
www.hrusa.org

UNESCO Chair for Genocide Prevention
www.ncas.rutgers.edu/cghr

University of Connecticut Human Rights Institute
humanrights.uconn.edu

The United Nations

UNESCO United Nations Educational, Scientific and Cultural Organization
en.unesco.org

UNICEF: United Nations Children's Fund
www.unicef.org

United Nations High Commissioner for Human Rights
www.ohchr.org/EN/Pages/WelcomePage.aspx
www.unhcr.org/cgi-bin/texis/vtx/home

United Nations: International Human Rights Law
www.ohchr.org/EN/ProfessionalInterest/Pages/InternationalLaw.aspx

US Fund for UNICEF
http://www.unicefusa.org

Intergovernmental Organizations

Council of Europe: Human Rights
www.coe.int/en/

Instituto Interamericano de Derechos Humanos
Inter-American Institute for Human Rights
www.iidh.ed.cr

Organization of American States: Inter-American Commission on Human Rights
www.oas.org/en/iachr/

Selected Websites Referenced By Chapter Authors

Rosa Barreda
Instituto Peruano en Educacion en Derechos Humanos y La Paz (IPEDEHP)
(Peruvian Institute of Education on Human Rights and Peace)
www.ipedehp.org.pe

Vera Candau
Novamerica
www.novamerica.org.br/home.asp

Nélida Céspedes
Consejo de educación popular de América Latina y el Caríbe
www.ceaal.org/v2/index.php

Silvia Conde
Albanta; Colectivo para El Desarrolo Educativo
www.albanta.org.mx

Enver Djuliman
Norwegian Helsinki Committee
nhc.no/en/

Mónica Fernández
Red Interamericana de Intercambio de Experiencias Educativas para Promover la Educación en Derechos Humanos
redlatinadeedh.com.ar

William R. Fernekes
Human Rights Educators USA
www.hreusa.net

Nancy Flowers
Human Rights Educators USA
www.hreusa.net

National Seed Project on Inclusive Curriculum
www.nationalseedproject.org

Judy Gummich
Generation ADEFRA
www.adefra.de

Shulamith Koenig
The Peoples Movement for Human Rights Learning (formerly the People's Decade for Human Rights Education)
www.pdhre.org/about.html

Elena Ippoliti
United Nations Office of the High Commissioner for Human Rights
www.ohchr.org/EN/Pages/WelcomePage.aspx

Claudia Lohrenscheit
International Social Work and Human Rights Department, University of Applied Sciences, Coburg, Germany
www.hs-coburg.de/ueber-uns/fakultaeten/soziale-arbeit-und-gesundheit/personen/prof-dr-claudia-lohrenscheit.html

Abraham Magendzo K.
UNESCO Chair in Education and Human Rights, Academia de Humanismo Cristiano University, Chile
www.unesco.org/en/university-twinning-and-networking/access-by-region/latin-america-and-the-caribbean/chile/unesco-chair-in-human-rights-602/

Ed O'Brien
Street Law, Inc.
www.streetlaw.org/en/home

Greta Papadimitriou
Comisión de Derechos Humanos del Distrito Federal de Mexico
http://cdhdfbeta.cdhdf.org.mx/

Jefferson R. Plantilla
Asia-Pacific Human Rights Center
www.hurights.or.jp/english/

José Tuvilla
Cultura de Paz y Educacion
tuvilla.blogspot.com

Kristi Rudelius-Palmer
This is My Home: A Minnesota Human Rights Education Experience
www.thisismyhome.org

Susana Sacavino
Observatorio ed educacao em dreitos humanos em foco
www.observatorioedhemfoco.com.br

Cosette Thompson
Amnesty International USA
www.amnestyusa.org

Felisa Tibbitts
Human Rights Education Associates
www.hrea.org

José Tuvilla-Rayo
International Training Centre for Human Rights and Peace Teaching (CIFEDHOP)
www.cifedhop.org

Felice I. Yeban
Amnesty International Philippines
www.amnesty.org.ph

Anita Yudkin
UNESCO Chair for Peace Education, University of Puerto
unescopaz.uprrp.edu/act/Foros/towardsculturepeace.htm

Manuel Restrepo Yustin
Universidad Pedagogica y Tecnologica de Colombia Derechos Humanos Maestria UPTC
www.uptc.edu.co/facultades/casa_bogota/derechos_humanos/inf_general/index.html

Index

A

Academy of Christian Humanism University (Universidad Academia de Humanismo Cristiano) Santiago, Chile i, 99, 107
Adult Education 8, 177
Afro- Deutsche Frauren (Black German Women, ADEFRA 93, 95–98
Allende, Salvador 56, 114
Amnesty International (AI) 7, 50, 57–58, 72, 81–82, 96, 148, 159, 161, 165, 176, 182, 197, 199–200
Argentina 45–49, 54, 68, 74, 153–155, 226, 228–229
Asia-Pacific Human Rights Information Center 127
Asociación Pro Derechos Humanos de España (The Human Rights Association of Spain, APDHE) 167, 176
Atención global al rezago escolar en escuelas rurales de Chihuahua, Coahuila y Durango (Focused Attention on Students Who Fall Behind in Rural Schools of the States of Chihuahua, Coahuila and Durango) 28
Autonomous University of Aguascalintes (UAA) 114, 119

B

Balkans 38, 42–43, 228
Barreda, Rosa 3
Bosnia-Herzegovina 163
Brazil 13–14, 16–17, 133, 136, 153, 155–158, 226, 229
Brazilian Constitution of 1988 17
Bullying 81, 106, 108, 151
Buskerud Univeristy College, Norway 42

C

Candau, Vera 13–14, 140–141
Céspedes, Nélida 20, 200
Children's Rights 22, 24, 33, 36, 59, 176, 200–201
Chile 31, 56, 99–101, 103, 107–108, 114, 157
Ciudad Jiménez 29
Civic Education 159, 163, 173

Civil Rights Movement 62
Colombia 207, 217–221, 224, 227–228, 230
Comisión de la Verdad y Reconciliación (The Truth and Reconciliation Committee, CVR) 24
Comisión Nacional de Derechos Humanos (National Commission on Human Rights, CNDH), Mexico 32–33
Communism 38, 100, 135, 139, 148, 154, 221, 229
Conde, Silvia 27, 117
Corporate Social Responsibility 181
Cuba 16, 199, 215, 217, 220, 223–224

D

Disability 93–94, 98
Displaced persons 23–24, 169, 198–199, 228
Djuliman, Enver 38

E

Economic Rights 7, 21–22, 24, 26, 29, 47, 66–67, 70, 72, 75, 78, 100, 116, 125, 137, 156, 174, 185–186, 188, 194–196, 204, 207, 216–217
Educar para reconstruir la vida (Educating to Reconstruct Life) 23
Education for Freedom (EFF) program 182, 200
Education for Peace Collective , A.C. (CEPAZ) 118–119
Edupaz 31
El Salvador 4, 20, 95, 198–199, 228
Equitas, the Canadian Center for Human Rights Education 181

F

Fernández, Monica 45, 51
Fernekes, William i, 55, 112
Flowers, Nancy i, 58, 60–61, 112
France 148, 159–163, 229
Franco, Francisco 16, 168, 170–171
Freire, Paolo 17, 56, 102, 114, 116, 124, 134, 141, 168, 182–184, 186, 197

G

Gender 30, 70, 75, 91–95, 107, 117–119, 145, 151, 215, 223
Germany 83–84, 91–92, 96–97, 169
Girls education 4, 6, 11, 27, 36, 47–48, 61, 63, 70, 76, 88–89, 92, 215
Giroux, Henry 56, 198
Gramsci, Antonio 182–183
Guevara, Che 218, 224
Gummich, Judy 83

H

Helsinki Committee 40, 42, 44
Holocaust 57, 59–60, 70, 89, 100–101, 109–110, 165
Human Rights Cities 74
Human Rights Commission, Mexico 118
Human Rights Education Associates (HREA) 44, 60, 74, 104, 165
Human Rights Educators USA (HRE USA) 60

I

Indigenous Peoples 67, 101, 123, 125, 144, 211, 214
Instituto Federal Electoral (Federal Electoral Institute, IFE) 34
Instituto Interamericano de Derechos Humanos (The Inter-American Institute of Human Rights) 20, 230
Instituto Peruano de Educación en Derechos Humanos y la Paz (The Peruvian Institute of Education for Human Rights and Peace IPEDEHP) 7
Ippoliti, Elena 80
Israel 65, 70–71, 73, 101, 183
Italy 80–82

K

Koenig, Shulamith 65

L

La Red de Maestros Promotores (The Network of Teacher Advocates) 8
La Red Peruana de Educación en Derechos Humanos y la Paz (The Peruvian Network for Education on Human Rights and Peace) 8
La violencia 207
Levinas, Emmanuel 68, 109
LGBT 19
Liberation Theology 5, 21, 219
Lohrenscheit, Claudia 83

M

Magendzo, Abraham 20, 31, 45, 83, 85–86, 115, 117, 133–134, 200, 230
Mandela, Nelson 65–66, 75, 77, 96, 228
Maoist 220–221, 223–224, 226, 229
Marcos, Ferdinand 122, 182–183
Martin Luther King 89
Marxism 101, 154, 183, 187, 217, 219, 221
Marx, Karl 141, 217
Mexico 27, 31–32, 34, 36, 108, 113–116, 118, 120, 213, 219–220, 226
Movimiento Socioeducativo Educar en Tiempos Difíciles (Socio-educational Movement for Educating in Challenging Times) 158

N

National Council on Human Rights 19
National Human Rights Coordinating Committee 9
National Liberation Zapatista Front 117
Norway 38, 41–42, 44, 127
Novamerica 18–19, 156–157

O

O'Brien, Edward 111
Organización de Estados Iberoamericanos para la Educación, la Ciencia y la Cultura 34
Organización de Estados Iberoamericanos para la Educación, la Ciencia y la Cultura (Ibero-American Organization for Education, Science and Culture, OEI) 34

P

Papadimitriou 113, 120
Peace education 114–116, 118
People Power Revolution 128, 182
Peoples Movement for Human Rights Learning 72–73
Peru 3, 5–9, 11, 20–23
Philippines 121, 181–184, 186–187, 189
Pinochet, Augusto 56, 103, 162
Police training 183–185
Pontifical Catholic University in Peru 5
Pontifical Catholic University of Río de Janeiro 157
Popular Education 5, 16, 20, 31, 102, 105
Praxis 31, 186
Programa de Derechos Humanos, Educación y Ciudadanía (Program on Human Rights, Education, and Citizenship) 156

Programa Interdisciplinario de Investigaciones en Educación (Interdisciplinary Program in Educational Research, or PIIE) 106, 115
Puerto Rico 34, 194–196, 200–204, 228

R

Racism iii, 9, 22, 42, 62, 67, 84, 93–95, 101, 146, 148
Ramos, Aura 133
Rayo Tuvilla, José 167, 169, 175, 203
Reconciliation 24–25, 40, 42–43, 62, 106, 151, 163, 183
Refugee 38–39, 70, 159, 181, 183, 199, 222, 228
Right to Education 20, 116
Rodino, Ana María 200
Romania 161–162
Roosevelt, Eleanor 64–66, 69–70, 73, 168
Roosevelt, Franklin 66
Rorty, Richard 109, 198
Rudelius-Palmer, Kristi ii, 60, 112, 142
Rural Education 6, 11, 15, 25, 29, 123
Rutgers University 55–56, 60

S

Sacavino, Susana 153
Save the Children 23
Seminar for Education for Peace of Madrid 201
Sendero Luminoso (Shining Path) 9, 23
South Africa 95–96, 112, 148, 198
Spain 16, 31, 117, 159, 167–171, 173, 176–178, 186, 194, 201
Street Law, Inc 111–112

T

Tarea 20, 23
Thompson, Cosette 58, 159
Tibbitts, Felisa 44, 60, 165

U

UN Convention on the Elimination of All Forms of Discrimination Against Women (CEDAW) 67
UN Convention on the Rights of the Child 22, 59, 200
UN Decade for Human Rights Education 73, 183
UN Declaration on Human Rights Education and Training iv, 73
UNESCO 19, 50, 52, 69, 73, 107–108, 115, 165, 167, 176, 178, 201–204
UN High Commissioner for Human Rights 50, 69, 165, 207, 230
UNICEF 23, 165, 199
United Nations Declaration on the Right to Development 125
Universal Declaration of Human Rights (UDHR) 66, 69–70, 74–75, 77–78, 80, 82, 112, 124–125, 163, 177, 230
Universidad Complutense 16
University of Leuven, Belgium 14
University of Minnesota Human Rights Resource Center ii, 112, 144
University of Puerto Rico-Río Piedras 200–204

V

Vienna Conference on Human Rights 19
Vienna Declaration on Human Rights 73
Vieques Island 202
Vietnam War 111, 148

W

Women's Rights 6, 30, 51, 63, 67, 69, 71–77, 91, 101, 183, 215
World Association for School as an Instrument of Peace (EIP) 172

Y

Yeban, Feliece 181
Yudkin, Anita 194
Yugoslavia 38–40, 42, 44

About the Book

In TOWARDS A JUST SOCIETY twenty-five educators from around the world respond to the question: How and why did you commit yourself to human rights education? Their highly personal narratives recount the diverse ideological perspectives and life experiences that have shaped their work in this growing field. They also reflect the authors' individual engagement with significant events of the twentieth century critical to the construction and attainment of human rights: the horror of the Shoah, racial segregation in the United States, the revolutionary dreams of the 1960s, the separatist movement in Puerto Rico, dictatorships and human rights violations in Latin America, the "People Power" Revolution in the Philippines, the rebuilding of democracy in Spain, political violence in Colombia and Peru, the war in the Balkans, the drug violence that permeates schools in Mexico, and the challenges of inclusion and the recognition of emerging identities in Europe.

www.ingramcontent.com/pod-product-compliance
Lightning Source LLC
Chambersburg PA
CBHW080241170426
43192CB00014BA/2527